Dear

No one knows new fathers better than Boot Camp For New Dads. This comprehensive guide offers the collective wisdom and real life advice of over 100,000 men from across the nation who have worked together in Boot Camp workshops preparing to be fathers. Like our workshops, it provides the orientation a new father needs to support his wife, get confidently connected with his new child and personally navigate the initial year of fatherhood.

We come in all types, respect each other's ability to make his own choices, and our only agenda is to learn how to do our best for our new families. A must for any man wanting a solid start on becoming a good dad, *Hit The Ground Crawling* brings these lessons down to a very practical level for you.

As your child and family grows, you will want to know you did your best as well, right from the beginning. The objectives of this book are to assure that you understand what you need to do, and help you to get the job done no matter what it takes.

Happy Parenting

Patty 712-5800

7, 2 243

HIT THE GROUND CRAWLING

Published by

Dads Adventure
230 Commerce Ste. 210
Irvine, CA   92602

First Edition

ISBN -   0-9727829-0-7

Library of Congress Control Number: 2005901596

Information and advice in this book have been carefully researched, and every effort has been made to ensure accuracy. Although health care professionals have reviewed pertinent chapters, the book should never substitute for the advice of your personal physician. Dads Adventure assumes no responsibility for any damages or losses incurred as a result of following the information contained herein.

Visit us on the web at newdads.com

The Essential Guide for New Fathers

HIT THE GROUND CRAWLING

**What You Need to Know From Over 100,000
Men Who Have Been There**

Greg Bishop

TABLE OF CONTENTS

PART ONE: LAY OF THE LAND

Welcome
Our Unique Perspective
Preparing You for the Worst and the Best
Boot Camp For New Dads
Initial Words of Wisdom
Advice On Advice
Finding Solutions
Join Us

A Century of Decline
Crisis in Fatherhood
The Risks Facing New Fathers
Good Dads are Priceless
What Men Bring to Caring for Children ⎤
What Caring for Children Brings to Men ⎥ INTRO
Potential of New Fathers ⎦

First Wonder of the World
Amazing Transformation Within Mom
Connecting With Your Child Before Birth
Things To Know About Babies
Cool Things Babies Can Do
More Things To Know About Babies
The Best That Life Has To Offer

Family Planning
Tough Transformation
Babies Can Push Us Together or Apart
First Babies Are Tough On New Moms ⎤
New Moms Can Be Tough On New Dads ⎦ INTRO
What We Have Here is a Failure to Communicate

PART TWO: RUBBER HITS THE ROAD

PART THREE: HITTING YOUR STRIDE

PART 4: APPENDIX

About Boot Camp For New Dads

Boot Camp For New Dads started on Father's Day 1990 when four fathers, with their babies on their laps, sat down with a dozen men who had their first baby on the way. The veteran dads' objective was to orient the men on the realities of fatherhood.

For three hours, veterans talked about their experiences and offered advice while caring for their babies. When several "rookies" said they had never held a baby before, the veterans carefully handed them their own. It was like a nursery in a locker room, and any nervousness evaporated as the guys started kidding each other about technique, etc.

The babies' crying and smiling made the hands-on training all the more real. The men got to know and trust each other, and a very frank exchange occurred. With everything said staying in the room, nothing was left off the table.

After watching the veterans care for their babies, the rookies went home feeling "I can do this too." They did, and returned as veterans themselves with their own babies to orient the next group of men.

This man-to-man approach to preparing men to be fathers has proven very effective, and today Boot Camp operates in 250 communities across 40 states and in the U.S. Navy, Army and Air Force. There are 400 coaches and over 100,000 veterans; just regular guys from all walks of life.

About The Author

Greg Bishop, a brother of twelve and father of four, had changed lots of diapers by the time he started Boot Camp For New Dads in 1990 with some friends. He conducted the workshops monthly on Saturday mornings for six years when he wasn't coaching his Pee Wee soccer teams.

After a deluge of interest from other communities, Greg founded the non-profit New Fathers Foundation to expand Boot Camp throughout the nation. When the funding failed to materialize, he formed Dads Adventure, Inc. to sponsor Boot Camp.

His day job is CEO of Trauma Care of America. He remains Head Coach of Boot Camp For New Dads, and he and his wife Alison have raised Jonathan, Jennifer, Katherine and Peter.

Acknowledgements

Hit The Ground Crawling would not have happened without the contributions of many. The veterans of Boot Camp For New Dads, who taught us everything we know, and the 400 Coaches who conduct Boot Camp workshops, whose passion and commitment have fueled our success. This goes especially for Chuck Ault, always ready with insightful comments and his seal of approval for anything that I might catch heat over in the "boys will be boys" department, as well as Barry Fitzgerald, Billy Kaplan, Will Housley, Chet Adessa, Bill Horan and Gary Radvansky.

The many Childbirth Educators who partnered with us as professionals, and supported us as mothers. Particularly Ann Corwin, Sue Englund, Dawn Horan, Linda Todd, Laura Carroll, Beth Mednick, Barb McElveen, Candy Mueller and Marcia Westmoreland, who lent their time and expertise to help make this book better. And of course Mary Bowman of Saddleback Memorial Medical Center, who was always willing to come through for Boot Camp and help arrange TV interviews, focus groups, etc. Our medical reviewers, Peter Anzaldo, MD, who delivered three of my children, and Clyde Wesp. Jr., MD.

Racquel Palmese, a terrific editor, mother and grandmother, who shares our belief that every baby deserves a dad who loves and cares for them, for this book would not have happened without her. Debbie Sykes, our Executive Director, who helped me build Boot Camp for over a decade, Susan Worsham, who supports Debbie, formatted the book and developed www.newdads.com, and Steve Dubin, Boot Camp Coach and PR professional who has guided us through the maze of media opportunities and pitfalls.

Alison Bishop, my wife and partner in life whose decades of support includes developing Dads Adventure, Inc., our son Jon Bishop, who proved to be a fine editor and who came through when I needed him most, and our daughters Jennifer, Katherine and son Peter, whose love and support makes my working together with other fathers to do our best worthwhile beyond words.

*This book is dedicated to all the men who are doing
the job for their kids, no matter what it takes*

PART ONE: LAY OF THE LAND

1

A Big Job Ahead
We'll Lend a Hand

Welcome

We are truck drivers, architects, students, engineers, soldiers, salesmen, managers, cooks, sailors, firemen, lawyers, full-time dads, laborers, business owners, and more.

We used to play golf, shoot hoops, go fishing, drink beer, play cards, make love, sleep through the night, talk sports, and much more. We are short, tall, young and older, and come in all colors and from all cultures. Nothing special about us; just guys who want to be good dads to our kids.

Remember those days when all you were good for was opening jars and killing bugs? Well those days are over.
   BC Veteran to Rookies

We are fathers and we have been there, and are going to give you a hand because other guys who went before did the same for us. It is going to be the adventure of your lifetime, and we are going to help you make the most of it. In turn, you can return the favor to a friend, co-worker or younger brother who comes next.

As fathers, we share an extraordinary challenge. We encounter many new issues presented by our babies, new moms, finances, jobs, in-laws, and our own personal feelings as we work through perhaps the most fundamental transition in our lives. Like climbing a big mountain, there are times it will take everything we have.

Becoming a father presents each of us men a unique opportunity to show what we are made of. Fatherhood is an awesome responsibility, and we are going to help you get a good start.

We wish you strength and fortune in meeting the challenges ahead, and experiencing the best that life has to offer.

Veterans of Boot Camp For New Dads

Our Unique Perspective

Three percent of the nation's new fathers participate in our workshops. While still few in numbers, we have carved out a beachhead for men in the world of babies, which has been turf owned by women since the beginning of the human race.

We basically set up a clubhouse and posted a "no girls over 2 feet tall allowed" sign, which enabled us to relax and be comfortable in this peculiar world of pastel colors where women talk openly of sore nipples and haze us with graphic movies of births.

Our new vantage point has given us a unique perspective on the issues surrounding fatherhood. Instead of being told what we think and what we should do as fathers, we are comparing experiences and finding out for ourselves. We are also coming up with strategies on how we can do better.

We also have a fresh perspective on new mothers. Giving birth is awesome, of course, but our mates' overall transformation into moms over the course of pregnancy and the first year is even more incredible. Perhaps the most important issue of all is how a baby impacts our relationships with our wives, since working together is critical to building a family.

Seeing a baby through the eyes of a father provides a whole new outlook as well. New issues arise regularly in our workshops, such as whether babies can suck so strongly that you could stick them on glass like a suction cup (use your finger as a pacifier and you will see what we mean). Another milestone in fatherhood: a discussion on football led to ground breaking research on how football and big screen TVs can benefit babies.

Rule #1: Change the First Diaper
Really. Diapers symbolize the classic resistance of men to caring for babies, and there will be the expectation that you will resist, particularly from the women around you. Set the tone that you are here to play. Ask the nurse in the hospital to walk you through changing your baby's first diaper. When you get home, show mom how.

You may never have to change a diaper again. Just kidding, babies can go through 6,000 diapers by the time they are three, and chances are you will get stuck with a few more.

To our great advantage, the women around us have welcomed and supported us. Bottom line, moms want their babies to have good dads, which is what we want to be. Some are skeptical about our research, however.

What We Cover

Our focus is on real issues that prove important to real dads, and our emphasis is on what works. We cover strategies for working together with new moms, caring for crying babies, balancing your responsibilities at work and home, dealing with relatives, keeping your family safe, and much more. You will also find important guidance on standing your ground as a father, serving as a protector for your new family, and understanding the changes that fatherhood will bring you personally.

You guys talked about...."What does my future hold for me?. Forget (worrying about) your future. Your future is in your arms. When you hold your baby, you'll know what I'm talking about.

Veteran Dad

Four Sections
Hit The Ground Crawling is divided into four sections designed to get you prepared for and successfully through the first six months when new babies and your transformation into a father are most demanding:

Part 1 - Lay of the Land - When encountering a new challenge – particularly a demanding, life long adventure – you need to know what you are getting into, what will be expected of you, and what risks and opportunities you will encounter. This section provides answers and helps you get ready to be a father.

Part 2 - The Rubber Hits the Road - Your child's birth is when fatherhood gets serious. You will find practical information from a father's standpoint on all the basics: getting ready, the birth itself, taking your baby home, caring for your baby, supporting your mate, and comforting your crying baby.

Part 3 - Hitting Your Stride - After a month or two you will have the basics down and be ready to focus on raising your baby, especially your important role in playing. This is also the time to do a status check on your own feelings and progress as a father, and work on reconnecting with the new mom in your life.

Part 4 - Resources - Includes resources on where to find information and help with special sections on family safety, finance, babies with special needs, chronicling your family with pictures and video, and our plans to change the world by helping men do their best for their kids.

Preparing You for the Worst and the Best

Becoming a father can be very tough. We don't sugar coat it; we tell it like it is for a lot of men, which is how it might be for you. Or it might not. If you assume that all the hard stuff you read about will happen to you, you are getting it wrong. Nobody gets hit with all of it; we just want you to be prepared for whatever might happen.

The dire warnings of colicky babies and cranky wives may barely do justice to what you experience, or your easy time may leave you wondering how you got so lucky.

We remind you that whatever problem you encounter, you have lots of company. But probably not as often as we should. One of the most prevalent comments at Boot Camp: "I didn't realize that you guys were going through the same thing". It makes it much easier to constructively deal with the problem and get beyond it, knowing that many others are in the same boat.

Becoming a father is also wonderful. We point out the highlights, because you want to be prepared for those as well. You won't find a lot of talk about the joys of fatherhood, however, as they are almost impossible to put in writing. You will know it when you feel it.

Just be ready for whatever comes your way, good or bad, because either way, you will want to make the best of it.

If You Have Another Perspective, Tell Us

Every father's circumstances are unique, and it is a huge challenge to accurately represent the universal new father's experience in one book. Many issues surrounding babies are highly charged, eliciting strong feeling on all sides.

If you have a different perspective, or flat out disagree with something we say, let us know through www.newdads.com. If you have an idea how we can do better, let us know and we will pass it on to thousands of other fathers.

It is almost a sacred duty to get it right, so we will be revising this book regularly, based upon comments from men like you.

[Handwritten margin notes:]
discussion Topic

Pitfalls

worry   inlaws

sleep   marital conflict

colic

cranky wife

free time

expensive

sex

divorce

good enough dad

temper

Boot Camp For New Dads

Boot Camp's success is based upon our respect for the "veteran" new fathers who participate. It is their experience that counts; what they deem important drives the discussion. Their insights collected over the years provide the program content.

The veteran dads' expectations that each man will do their best for his child are implicit in everything they say and do. Their frank explanations of the realities they faced, and their encouragement, create a trusting and motivating environment. The veterans also enjoy a sense of pride and confidence when they can say, "Hey, I've been through this, and you'll make it too."

You Will Find Yourself Here

In Boot Camp, as a young truck driver orients a corporate lawyer on the fine points of burping, a veteran guides a rookie through his first diaper change. Men of different cultures, ages, incomes and ethnic backgrounds quickly find common ground and mutual respect when they work together to learn how to take care of their new families. Those facing more challenging circumstances provide an added source of inspiration. A sense of brotherhood, a feeling that we are in this together, is felt by all.

Why We Call It Boot Camp

We originally called it Bootee Camp. Women thought it was cute; the guys didn't and so we decided to change it.

Military boot camps are designed to orient and prepare men for a new, challenging, life changing role that requires them to do their very best, and sometimes more. Like the first months of fatherhood, you don't get much sleep, and may at times think you will not make it. The process breaks you down and then builds you up, imparting a strong sense of pride. Where previously you looked out for yourself, now you have others depending on you. Life as you know it has changed.

Participants from a local U.S. Marine base noted the parallels. In 1991, we became Boot Camp For New Dads and the name stuck. Probably a good thing, because BooteeCamp.com is not about babies.

After listening to all the rookie and veteran dads, I've realized that everyone else…has the same concerns about being a father I have. I feel so relieved now, knowing that I'm not alone.

Rookie Dad

I enjoyed Boot Camp on both occasions that I attended. I felt the sessions were too short, or maybe that it should have been a two-day meeting. After our baby arrived, I discovered the true value of the course. It frightens me to think of how I might have handled the experience had I not attended Boot Camp.

Veteran Dad

Initial Words of Wisdom

The challenges that experienced fathers say are most important, and some of their best advice is as follows:

I was a bachelor for 12 years before I got married. So being a husband for the first time was quite a shock. Then, before I even had time to enjoy being married and adjust to my new role as a husband, my wife got pregnant. All of the sudden, I'm a father. It happened so fast.

Veteran Dad

① **The basic challenge you face is not changing diapers or comforting a crying baby, but working with your wife to form a new family.** The pressures and demands that new babies bring often place a serious drag on your relationship just when you need to be working together. It is essential that you take the long view and form a team approach that benefits the baby, strengthens your relationship and provides long term stability for your family.

② **The tremendous changes experienced by new moms can be very tough and confusing, and they in turn can be tough on new dads.** If this is happening to you, keep in mind you have lots of company. In fact, part of the basic job description for new fathers is to serve as mom's punching bag. As men, we are built tough, and if we understand what's happening, we can take the hits. It will pass, and we get a baby out of the deal.

③ **Fatherhood is about growing up and accepting responsibility.** For most men, this takes time, so cut yourself some slack, but keep moving forward. We all have an instinctual desire in our hearts to do right by our children, but things get in the way. Those who do the job learn that the rewards are well worth the sacrifices; those who don't will never know what they are missing.

④ **There is no one right way to be a dad.** Every baby, mom and dad is unique, and there are different approaches to each issue. Lots of choices need to be made and you – along with mom – are the one to decide what works for your new family. You also need to learn to trust your instincts; most of what you need to know comes naturally.

⑤ **Men bring their own unique strengths to parenting, and you should be confident that you are fully capable of caring for your baby.** Men have been told that we are inherently incompetent in caring for babies. This becomes a self fulfilling prophecy if we believe it ourselves. Develop your understanding and capabilities as a father, and make the most of the practicality, creativity and stamina men bring to parenting.

We learn best from men who are doing the job. Talk to your brothers, friends and other dads around you. You can blow off steam, gain perspective, and get some new ideas. If you connect and share experiences with other fathers, you will be surrounded by men who will help you do your best.

If you don't take care of yourself, you won't be in a position to take care of your new family. Keep in mind that your good health and mental well being are essential to all of you.

While fatherhood is forever, it occurs one day at a time, and some days will be better than others. You are going to make mistakes, and each new day presents an opportunity to take another shot. It is a tough transition, and we must be patient with our babies, our mates, and ourselves.

Advice On Advice

If you listen to the "experts," you'll think you need a Ph.D. in infant development to take your baby home. There are many self-appointed experts who are full of advice on exactly how you should care for your family, many conflicting with one another. And then, of course, there are the multitudes, ranging from your mother-in-law to strangers on the streets, who want to tell you whether you will be having a boy or girl, or the kinds of foods mom should be eating, or how you should be playing classical music at home so your baby is born a genius.

Many of these people probably never had children, because if they had, they would understand that the last thing a new parent needs is some dogmatic, self appointed expert going off and giving him something else to worry about.

Take all advice, including what you read here, with a grain of salt. Keep in mind that ultimately, you and your mate will decide what is best for your new family.

There's so much information out there and everyone is going to give you advice. Some of it is appropriate, some just doesn't fit, and some is just so crazy you wonder what planet these people came from. I've learned to be very diplomatic about responding to the advice I get from other people.
Veteran Dad

Finding Solutions

Hit The Ground Crawling is designed to serve as a comprehensive resource of information specific to new fathers. It generally excludes information available from other sources, such as physicians, nurses, childbirth educators, and books, web sites and magazines on pregnancy and babies.

Visit www.newdads.com to add your comments.

www.newdads.com serves as a supplement to this book, offering additional information and the opportunity to get answers to your questions and even contribute your own insights.

As the father of a new family, you will want to know how to find information and help for the many issues that can arise as your family develops. An extensive Resource Guide for new fathers is located in the appendix.

Join Us

Boot Camp For New Dads is acclaimed by virtually all who participate, and if one is located in your community, you will find it enlightening, unique and very worthwhile. To find the workshop location closest to you, visit www.bcnd.org.

Your experience will be valuable to those who follow you, and you can also participate in this exchange by contributing your own insights and asking questions at www.newdads.com.

You can also join us by simply doing your best and setting an example for the men who follow.

2

A Great Time to Become a Dad

You could not have picked a more challenging time or better decade to become a dad.

Fatherhood is tough, and despite their best intentions, many fathers fail their children. While most men are doing the job, 24 million kids will go to bed tonight in a home without their father. Millions more living with their fathers are being neglected or just ignored. This is a root cause of child abuse, teen pregnancy, drug and alcohol abuse and legions of aimless young people without dreams for their future.

My dad really never did anything except work all the time, so I want to be the opposite of that with my boy.

Rookie Dad

There are reasons why failure is an option for so many fathers. In many cases, their own fathers failed and no one is surprised when they do as well. Many do not know how to be fathers, others are pushed out by family breakups, and some simply do not have what it takes. Despite a societal stake in their success, there is little support to help them succeed. Most of these men assumed it would be different; that they would be good dads, but they were not prepared.

As a result, far too many children do not have a capable father who loves and cares for them, and far too many men are without the love and respect of their children. Compared to the high standard set by motherhood, fatherhood in America has become a national disgrace.

The Bar is Rising
The good news is that the nation's fathers are turning the corner on this enormous problem. Fatherhood is coming out of a century long slump, and the driving force is dads like you who want to do their best as fathers. Especially those who want to provide their children the strong connection they missed from their own fathers. The downside of fathers who were not there is very clear to all of us, and we are not going to let it happen to our kids. Or ourselves.

My dad was great, and I hope to be like him. He was my little league coach and (he was) always there for me, and still is.

Rookie Dad

This decade the bar is rising. Fathers are bringing a renewed and intense commitment to their children, and this in turn is creating new respect for the importance of all fathers. It is opening doors and creating opportunities for you, as well as producing new expectations and challenges. While your job as a father is tougher today, you will find that the dedication and encouragement of your fellow fathers will put wind in your sails to help you get the job done.

A Century of Decline

It wasn't always this way. In early America, most fathers spent the bulk of their waking hours with their children on their farms or in their shops, with their homes close by. The role of fathers with respect to their children involved education, teaching skills such as hunting and a trade, spiritual guidance, discipline, and of course, playing.

The institution of fatherhood in America began its decline with the Industrial Revolution, which sent men away from their farms to factories in the cities, and away from their shops to corporations. More and more fathers began spending their waking hours at work away from their families.

By the mid-1900's, men increasingly identified with their firms and employers, which competed with their families for their time, attention and loyalty. Larger paychecks provided new cars, bigger houses, and automatic washing machines that seemed to make this trade-off worthwhile. But the intangible costs in terms of fathers' relationships with their children occurred incrementally and unnoticed, like the erosion that levels a hill over time.

Unimaginable Failure

A father was sentenced in Fort Lauderdale to 20 years in prison for the death of his 9-month-old daughter, whom he left in a sweltering car at the racetrack while he bet on horses.

Antonio Balta, 28, pleaded guilty to aggravated manslaughter for the 2004 death of his daughter, Veronika, at Gulfstream Park in Hallandale Beach.

Balta told police he left the girl strapped in her car seat most of the day. He said he left a car window cracked less than a half-inch.

LA Times, 3/21/05

Caring for children became "women's work," and fathers willingly gave up the dirty work of changing diapers without understanding they were also giving up a close relationship with their babies. Fathers were relegated to the role of breadwinners away from the home, and disciplinarians ("wait until your father gets home!") when around. For many, these thankless tasks were a recipe for distant relationships and, ultimately, disengagement from their children.

Fathers who were poor, particularly those who grew up without an involved father, were subject to a more damaging set of social dynamics, and they, their mates and children bore the worst of this crisis. Many such fathers actually came to believe their children would be better off without them.

Over the past decade even the value of fathering was questioned and it became acceptable for women to have children with a father's involvement limited to that of a sperm donor.

Crisis in Fatherhood

The sheer number of absent, disconnected or even abusive fathers has become a national crisis. The stats are staggering:

- Of the 24 million children in America who live in a home without their father, 50% have not seen their fathers in the past year, and 40% have never been to their fathers' homes.

- The rate of child abuse and neglect is double for children living in a home without their fathers.

- Violent criminals are overwhelmingly males who grew up without fathers: 60% of America's rapists, 72% of adolescent murderers, and 70% of long-term prison inmates.

- Children living without fathers are more likely to live in poverty, drop out of high school, be treated for emotional or behavioral problems, or commit suicide as adolescents.

- Even children living with their father and mother are about 70% more likely to smoke, drink, and use drugs if their relationship with their father is fair or poor.

Children suffer when raised without a caring father and America is the world's leader in fatherless families. As a nation, we have our work cut out for us.

The Risks Facing New Fathers

About 1.5 million men become fathers for the first time each year in America. Ninety percent attend their baby's birth and watch their first child come into the world. No matter their circumstances, these are motivated men, and they want to do right by their children.

Once their baby comes home, however, a father's pattern of involvement, for better or worse, quickly becomes entrenched. For many, a window of opportunity begins to close. Their babys' and mates' needs are the focus of attention, and their attempts to step up to considerable new challenges are often not supported or even noticed. Fathers become isolated, even from their former friends and each other. They do not form natural support groups, like moms, and rarely talk about their children or their concerns as fathers, often because no one asks.

I never knew my father. He left when I was one. I really missed having a dad like the other kids, and want to be there for my child.

Rookie Dad

My father owned a hardware store and worked long hours. He spent his time off with his friends or watching TV. He rarely even talked to me, except when I did something wrong. He came to my baseball game once, but left early because I wasn't playing.

Rookie Dad

For new fathers in these circumstances, enthusiasm for their new role wanes. Those who are not involved experience the burden of a baby's cry, their overwhelming new responsibilities and the loss of their mate's attention without any of the rewards. At this point, the risk of failing to step up to the challenges a child presents becomes high.

If he does not establish a strong connection with his child, a father will lack the strength and motivation to step up to his new responsibilities. An innate sense of failure forms, which he rationalizes away. ("It's women's work, diapers smell, my own father didn't, what do I know about babies?").

To become involved at a later date, he must first accept his failure to meet the needs of his own child. Overcoming this new hurdle, without a sense of what his child can mean to him, becomes less likely over time. Men who do not do the job for their children largely do not know what they are missing.

Honoring Our Fathers Who Did Their Best
Many of our fathers stood their ground and became real dads, making their children the priority of their lives. They tell us it was the most demanding and rewarding part of their lives, and their sons will say they aspire to be as good to their children. These men have set a high standard and made us aware of the possibilities; today they serve as role models for generations.

Good Dads Are Priceless

I was very fortunate to have a good relationship with my father. His father was not around from time to time, so he gave it to us in spades. He spent a lot of time with all the kids. I'm looking forward to doing the same thing with our child.

Rookie Dad

The return on investment for good fathers is huge. Research indicates that children whose fathers are a consistent, positive force in their lives do better socially, intellectually, and on a broad range of other factors ranging from economic status in childhood to peer relationships in adolescence, to productivity as adults. These children are also less likely to witness the breakup of their family, or be subject to poverty, teen pregnancy, violence or abuse.

An infant who spends time alone with dad smiles more often, and is more likely to offer toys to him. They look at and manipulate objects more enthusiastically, indicating an enhanced desire to explore and understand their world. Babies of engaged fathers experience more diverse social interactions and become more intellectually advanced.

According to the National Fatherhood Initiative's *Father Facts:*

- Children whose fathers were involved with their care manage stress better during their school years.

- Engaged fathers promote a child's physical well being, perceptual abilities, and positive relationships.

- Boys and girls reared with engaged fathers demonstrate more self-control and greater ability to take the initiative.

I don't know why I am here. I didn't even want a baby.
Tim 19, at Boot Camp

Children are not the only beneficiaries of this strong father/child bond. Research indicates that men who assign a high priority to raising their children are more likely to be successful in their careers at midlife, to have happier marriages, and be more involved in their communities. Children of involved fathers are much more likely to be responsible fathers themselves. Even poor, unwed fathers, when asked what their lives would be like without their children, often said, "I'd be dead or in jail."

Raising children brings out the best in men, to the benefit of their children, mates, communities, and themselves.

What Men Bring to Caring for Children

Moms are innately warm, comforting, nurturing, and even nourishing to their babies. Babies come from mothers.

He turned my life around. He actually gave me a life.
Tim 20, back at Boot Camp as a Veteran

So what are dads good for? A lot, it turns out, and it goes way beyond just assisting mom. First, we introduce our babies to new and interesting things, starting with ourselves. You will find your baby looking intently at you, checking you out. She is essentially fascinated. And very soon, dad's presence or even your smell means it's time to play, which according to recent research, is critical to baby brain development. Apparently when we play and roughhouse, that beautiful little mind goes into full gear.

Research has identified lots of ways our involvement pays off for our children. Greater self control and the ability to take the initiative are the payoff for boys and girls raised with an involved father. A close, warm relationship with our daughters will strengthen their feelings of competence and a sense of femininity. (Ultimately, it is up to us to show them what a good guy is all about.)

A father's care and love contributes as much to a child's intellectual and emotional development as mom's love does. The love and care of mom and dad have an equal impact on their children's well-being, happiness, and academic success. In some areas, a father's impact is greater. A father's love is the major factor in combating a child's problems with conduct, delinquency or substance abuse.

Mostly, though, we dads have an innate desire to protect our children, and care and provide for them in any way we can, no one else can do what we can. We look out for our kids, and often are simply there for them when they need us.

The bottom line is that we offer our children a great deal.

What Caring for Children Brings to Men

Little can compare to a child's love, to your baby falling asleep in your arms, comforting a daughter scared by a nightmare, or a son's delight over knocking down the block tower you built. No matter what happens in the rest of one's life, a dad can always be special to his children.

But for men, trying to explain the full impact and joy a child can bring, before he arrives, and before that first smile, is a little like someone telling us when we were ten how we would feel about girls at 16. A few of us had figured it out, but most of us required a lot more evidence, which ultimately came from our hearts.

We would like to tell you all that we have discovered as fathers, but words simply cannot do justice to what our children mean to us. You will have to trust us on this until the time your baby looks right at you and smiles and you begin to experience it for yourself and understand.

On what has been most surprising and rewarding…The pride I feel when I am with my family. How when I come home after a bad day at work and my daughter's smile makes me feel better.

Veteran Dad

We can tell you that as a deep and rich relationship with your child develops, you will experience an unparalleled sense of purpose and manhood that fills your heart and soul and fulfills the core of your being. It will have a broad, pervasive impact upon you that gives real and deep meaning to your life. Your baby will also provide you a new and powerful source of strength, as we fathers are capable of amazing feats when our children are in need.

Fatherhood is a noble endeavor; fathers provide for and protect their children, teach them by both word and deed. It is truly wonderful to hold a smiling, talking baby who thinks you are the greatest. It is fun to be the one whose main role is often to play.

We become men in the finest sense of the term. Our babies encourage us to grow up, become better people. Over time, as good as we can be.

It is great to feel like a man, and for our new families, we are most definitely the man. It is amazing how this works; men with incredible accomplishments will tell you all they have done doesn't hold a candle to the importance of their children.

Changes are gradual; you learn and grow together.
Veteran Dad

The Potential of New Fathers

The great news now is that the tragic disconnection of American fathers and their children over the past century has run its course, opening unprecedented opportunities for today's new fathers. You may not appreciate this yet, but you and many other fathers who are committed to doing your best are on the front lines of a renaissance in fatherhood in America. You are helping change the world that your child will grow up in by redefining and strengthening the role of fathers in the lives of all children.

Throughout history men have always responded to the challenges presented by society. Today America's fathers are being challenged to build something new, to take another hill. This time it is in our own backyards, where our children are asking us to be dads. A door has opened and men across the nation are going through it. It is good to have you among us.

3

A Man's Intro to Babies

After a century or so of baby care being considered women's work, men collectively don't have a lot of experience with infants. Few of us played with dolls or fantasized about having babies while we were growing up. Most first time fathers have never even held a baby, and for most guys, puppies are more interesting.

For those who have endured a relative or friend treating their baby like a cross between an Olympic gold medal winner and a movie star, well, the whole baby thing can obviously get way out of hand. (One visit to a baby store will confirm this).

Many of our own fathers didn't witness our births or change many diapers, and even today, some are not comfortable with the hands-on approach we are taking with our own babies. As a result, babies are somewhat of a mystery to men and some are not sure whether they are supposed to even like them, much less know how to take care of them.

People expect new fathers to be clumsy and confused about babies. You may find that when your infant starts crying in your arms, female friends and relatives will instinctively offer to take him, as if you are incapable of caring for your own baby.

When I see them (twins) in the morning, they are so happy and excited to see me.
Veteran Dad

Therefore it is a very pleasant surprise to find out that not only are our babies fascinating, they are incredibly lovable. The notion that men are inherently ignorant and incapable when it comes to babies evaporates the first time you rock your baby to sleep in your arms.

Bottom line: it will be up to you to cut through all the noise around you to get to know your own baby and chart your own course regarding her care. This chapter provides basic background information on babies to help get you get started early.

First Wonder of the World

Billions of babies born over millennia would seem to preclude any one being special. But yours will be, and once you discover how incredibly smart, alert and cute your own baby is, you might find it hard to avoid replicating that Olympic gold medal/movie star scene.

Try to really fathom the notion of a baby: Making love, your sperm wins the race (you had a half billion entries) and joins the other half of that incredible DNA puzzle in her egg. Then that egg grows into a little tadpole, and transforms in your mate's belly into a tiny little baby that gets a heart beat, grows and then starts to kick. And then that baby is born, and you look down at this little person, part you and part mom, with arms and legs and fingers and toes and a great set of lungs.

You put your finger in her hand and she grabs it. The doctors describe it as a reflex action – but all you know is your baby has a grip, and her tiny hand, with its delicate, intricate, exquisite little fingers, is wrapped tightly around your finger, as well as your heart.

Try to picture your baby right after she is born. Even though she cannot focus clearly, her eyes are full of curiosity, absorbing this new world that she sees for the first time, perhaps with a touch of fear … And then she blinks her eyes, gazes up at you, and sees a father who will always protect and take care of her.

Your baby represents the future of mankind, the meaning of life and your own immortality all at once – not to mention her unique and incredible potential as a human being. Accepting the enormity presented by your child will take you years.

There are many wonders in this world, and may you be fortunate to show some of them to your child. But your child herself will be the most amazing wonder, and the one you helped make.

She lives on Mongolian time, demands that I walk her when rocking should do, eats and poops, sometimes simultaneously, cries like a banshee, and at times nothing I do will console her. My wife would trade me for hired help in a nannysecond, my boss thinks I lost my edge, and thoughts of golf with the guys trigger hysterical laughing. Just when I am at the end of my rope, she looks right at me and smiles. It probably is just gas but I think she likes me. I can't believe it myself sometimes, but I wouldn't trade her for the world. I am going to have to get her some golf clubs.

Veteran Dad

Amazing Transformation Within Mom

While the rubber hits the road at birth, your baby is being built as we speak. A look inside will reveal that the happenings in Monster Garage are nothing compared to what's going on in mom's belly.

A basic rundown with some of the highlights, presented for the average baby, in the month-by-month schedule which will govern your life for the next year or so, are as follows:

Triathlon with 500 Million Entries at the Start

Women produce one egg every month, which lives for roughly a day or two. If you time it right, one roll in the hay will send about 500,000,000 sperm in a mad dash to capture the flag in a 48 hour window of opportunity. It's a very tough obstacle course; 90% die crawling to the cervix. And after an hour, only about 2,000 of the sperm make it through the uterus to the second round: the swim up the fallopian tubes.

The egg is in one of the tubes, and only 100-200 sperm get a shot at going for the glory. They basically try to head butt their way through the egg's outer membrane, and after the first one does so, the membrane becomes an impenetrable wall and the rest all die. The winner becomes one with the egg, determines sex, hair and eye color, NFL/NBA potential, and then starts to grow into a full on baby. Talk about king of the hill!

Month One: Microscopic Tube

Mom's fertilized egg divides into two, then four, eight, sixteen cells and so on, multiplying at an ever increasing rate into billions and billions. Due to an incredibly awesome design, that egg contains specific blueprints and instructions for every one of those cells.

Month Two: One Inch Tadpole

With a big head and tail, and with arms, legs, fingers and toes that are beginning to form, Junior looks like a tadpole transforming into a frog. His nervous system is developing along with eyes, ears and internal organs, and his tiny heart begins to beat.

Month Three: All Internal Parts Present

He is starting to look like a baby, with eyes, a nose and lips, elbows and knees. While his evolutionary tail disappears, his arms are longer than his legs in tribute to the primate past in his ancestry. He triples in length to three inches, and weighs in at one ounce.

Month Four: Sucking His Thumb

His legs have lengthened, bones and muscles are growing, and teeth, soft fingernails, eyebrows and eyelashes are forming. It is now clear that he is a he, or she is a she; growing rapidly to 5 inches and 3-4 ounces, you could cradle him in your hand.

Month Five: On The Move

Your baby is getting bigger and stronger and his movements might now be felt by mom. His brain is developing rapidly, particularly the front where thinking occurs. He can now hear, his hair is growing and he may suck his thumb. He is 7 inches, 10-12 ounces.

A Navy Tradition
When the U.S. Navy ship returns to port, sailors who became fathers while on deployment are the first to get off. It is quite a scene as their wife hands them their baby dockside and those new fathers meet their child for the first time.

Month Six: Little Person
He looks like he will at birth; just much smaller and skinnier. He is getting stronger rapidly and mom may soon be able to tell if he is punching, kicking or head butting as he trains for his big entrance into the world. His lungs prepare to breath, and he is about 9 inches long and weighs about a pound and a half.

Month Seven: Lights Coming On
The little guy is starting to fatten up, and his brain is enlarging rapidly, with its lifelong functions coming online. His eyes open and he starts to distinguish between light and dark, as his hearing continues to develop. He weighs in at about 3 pounds and is 11 inches long.

Month Eight: Getting Strong
His brain and nerves are now in charge and mom's antibodies are passing through the placenta to give him several months of immunity against infections. He may hiccup, and hair may cover his head. At around 5 pounds and 17 inches, this boy is getting ready for game day.

Month Nine: Raring to Go
He is so tight in there that all his stretching and squirming works like resistance training in building his strength. He typically gets into launch position: head down in mom's pelvis, facing her back. A full term baby is typically 6-10 pounds, and 17 to 22 inches long. They can get big – a Brazilian baby recently weighed in at 16.5 pounds!

Can you possibly imagine the feeling mom has when she feels her baby move for the first time? This is the month it happens; in another month or so, you'll be able to feel him kick.
Head Coach

Connecting With Your Child Before Birth

Remember, mom's connection is hard wired; fathers have to build theirs. A good time to start is now while your little one is in the oven. It may seem surreal at first, but as you track your tiny progeny's growth and development, he becomes real enough to talk to, and if you do, he will recognize your voice after birth.

Recommended steps in building your connection are as follows:

Get The Picture
The much more detailed version of the amazing story of a baby's development, complete with incredible "in utero" pictures, can be found in books like *A Child Is Born* by Lennart Nilsson. Get a hold of one and go through it with mom, and you will have taken a big step in tuning into your baby yourself and letting mom know you will be there with her every step of the way.

Listen to Her Heartbeat

Go with mom to her doctor visits and you will be able to hear your baby's heartbeat at 3-4 months with a stethoscope, and perhaps earlier with an ultrasound device. Try a stethoscope on your own heart and you will find it louder but with the same beat as your baby's heart.

The Impact of a Father On His Child

After the birth, a baby is usually scared, screaming, flailing around, and quite frankly, just pissed off that he's been born. I would carry the baby into the newborn nursery, start checking his vital signs, etc., and the monitor would show a high heart rate, elevated blood pressure, rapid respirations, all of which reflect how stressed he is.

Then I'd see the baby's father hanging around, often not sure what to do, also looking a little stressed and unsure of his surroundings. So I would say, "Come over here, stand right here next to your baby, and just start talking to your son." I would encourage the father to lean down close to his baby, and speak some quiet words of comfort. I would say, "It's, okay. . . he knows your voice.. . . go ahead and talk to your baby."

The father would start to talk to his child, sometimes using his child's chosen name, and say things like, "I love you. It's okay. I'm here. You're going to be okay. You're safe. You're my son. I love you. Everything's going to be alright. I'm here now, I'm here."

Remarkably, once the baby heard his father's gentle voice, he would calm down, his body would relax and find rest, he'd become very quiet. The baby's heart would stop racing, his respirations would calm down. This little newborn child would often strain to turn his head towards '*that voice*', blinking through the bright lights, instinctively trying to '*see*' the voice that he knew so well.

In this very scary new world outside of his mother's warm and safe womb, this little child had found peace, he knew he was safe, he knew he was not alone, he knew everything was going to be alright, he knew he was where he was supposed to be. . . .within the sound of his father's voice.

My sisters and I had that our whole lives with our father. Whenever we heard our father's voice, we knew everything was going to be okay, we knew we were safe, we were loved. Just the sound of Dad's voice seemed to make everything okay.
Julie, a former nurse in the newborn nursery, in a eulogy to her father

Hit The Ground Crawling

See Him Move in a Sonogram

You and mom get to see him for the first time when the doctor checks him out on a sonogram, and he might even move while you're watching. Ask the doctor to describe him, particularly any special features; now is also when his boyhood is visible. He is all there, gaining strength, and this picture is worth a lot more than words.

Feel Him Kick

After six months and a few attempts when mom invited you to put your hand on her tummy, you will feel your baby move for the first time. Whoa, he is really in there! You have heard him, seen him and now can feel him move. Later on you'll find it amazing how hard your baby can kick. Spoon with mom to feel him move while lying in bed.

Talk to Her

The combination of mom's heart beat, blood flow and gastric processes is going to muffle anything you say to her (perhaps a good thing if you decide to sing). It really doesn't matter as she will recognize your voice after she is born, giving her comfort in her new world.

Talking is mostly for you, though. There are lots of things to say to your baby and she has lots of time. So tell her, and discover another of the unexplained mysteries about babies - somehow they seem to understand what we say to them.

Think About What He Will Be Like

Men initially connect with their babies by fantasizing what they will be when they grow up. In our dreams, our babies generally do the things we like to do, or would want to, sometimes together with us. So whether it is joining you in your business, or playing professional golf, your baby can be whatever you want her to be. When she decides herself in a couple of decades what she wants to do, you'll probably think that it is an even better idea.

Things to Know About Babies

Basic facts that are good to know about babies include:

Five Minutes to Get Comfortable

Most fathers-to-be are unsure of their ability to care for their baby. In Boot Camp workshops, with even the most nervous guys, it takes all

Don't believe the doctor when they do the ultrasound about the sex of the baby. We actually didn't want to know what it was going to be, but the doctor...said it would be a girl. So we were prepared and had about three names for a girl. And then he popped out and then we go "what's his name?" and then thought "Wait a minute..."

Veteran Dad

of about five minutes to get them comfortable holding a baby. The first minute they are awkward and stiff, but soon they relax and that baby just melts into their arms. Babies are built to do that; they are very flexible and they totally relax when they are calm and quiet. Of course, it takes longer if the baby is crying, or if there are women around saying "how cute" or telling you how to do it their way.

Babies Don't Break

They seem so fragile and delicate, they could break if you hold them wrong. Actually, it is their surprising strength that can get them into trouble, when they suddenly roll over near the edge of a bed or push off the changing table with their legs. You want to be gentle, but babies are also built to be handled, they are very flexible and don't easily break. Just be careful they don't fall.

Don't Expect Love at First Sight

The little guy growing inside mom is the focus of her dreams for nine months, so most moms are head-over-heels thrilled at seeing their babies for the first time. Connecting with a baby generally comes naturally for moms; dads have to work at it. In a recent study, 70% of new fathers reported it took them weeks and months, not hours, to bond or form a strong attachment to their babies. This is especially the case if you expect yours to look like a Gerber baby right out of the chute; newborns tend to have skinny legs, cone-shaped heads, blotchy skin, and flat noses.

All Babies are Unique

A baby can actually have "your" ears or nose at birth. And with luck, mom's disposition. Or not. A few sleep through the night within the first week, and some scream with colic for three months. Which means that much of the standard advice you hear will not apply to yours. It also means that after a couple of weeks at most, the world's expert on caring for your baby will be you.

Your Baby Will Rule Your World

Babies command a great deal of power. They wake you up and demand room service every couple of hours throughout the night for months on end. And you do it. These days, parents are bombarded with "should do's" regarding their babies. Be careful, or you might find yourself taking up the violin so you can play Bach to boost your baby's brain while in the womb.

Cool Things Babies Can Do

Babies are underrated from a guy's perspective, because moms, who have been in charge for a century, simply don't appreciate certain things that babies do. Examples of cool baby capabilities that have been largely ignored due to this perspective problem are as follows:

Develop Amazing Upper Body Strength
If us guys were in charge, baby wrestling could be the next hot sport. At one day old, a baby can almost do a pull up when he grabs onto your pinkies. At several weeks, they start lifting their heads, which are half their body weight, and at a few months, she can rip out a fistful of your chest hair with one hand. They love pro wrestling too.

Stick Her Tongue Out At You
While she is largely missing the attitude she will muster as a five year-old, your baby can learn to stick her tongue out by imitating you. Work on it with her in private to get it down, and then take her on tour with your childless friends. They will be very impressed.

Sleep on Your Chest
You get home late, stressed out after a bad boss day at work. The baby is fussy and mom's had it. Life sucks, right? No, because on this night, after walking your baby for a while, she falls asleep on your chest, this little warm package all sacked out, breathing deeply, sleeping like an angel while your heart lays down a thumping back beat. Life does not get any better than this.

Other things your baby can do that only you will appreciate include:

- Listening to you sing and liking it
- Totally buying your brand of politics
- Loving your favorite sports team
- Never complaining when you beat him at poker
- Sucking both of his big toes at the same time

More Things to Know About Babies

There is a great deal to learn, of course, and a few more lessons from the front lines of daddyhood are as follows:

My 8 month old little girl, sitting in my buddy's lap, grabbed his placemat with a glass, heavy plate and utensils on it, and just whipped it out and left every-thing on the table. An awesome show of strength for such a pretty little thing.
Veteran Dad

I used to dip her big toe in ice cream and then she would pop it in her mouth. I looked around and she had attracted a crowd of admirers. Such talent.
Veteran Dad

You Already Have a Little One to Protect

With a baby growing in mom's tummy, you already have taken on major responsibilities of fatherhood. While gearing up for her birth and homecoming, make sure she is well protected and cared for inside mom. Take extra care when driving, fix any loose steps or rails or slippery throw rugs at home. Take care of yourself as well, as your baby will need her daddy.

Fathers Have a Lot to Offer Babies

The most surprising thing was how natural fathering is.
Veteran Dad

We are more than an extra set of hands, although that alone is a huge help with fussy babies. Our approach is different from mom's. It compliments hers, because there are some things we will just be better at. Since babies learn a great deal from their parents, our unique personalities and styles alone broaden their horizons (especially our private discussions about sports teams).

Babies Can Be Boring, Frustrating and Irritating

Babies can be a wonderful source of joy and fulfillment, but they can also be boring, frustrating and irritating. It just goes with the territory, especially if you're unsure of how to care for and play with them. The more you do, the more you will know, and the more positive and constructive you will be in raising your child.

Babies Love to Play

Playing is their job and how they learn, and we are their designated playmates. Enough said. Make playing and adventures with your child job number one, and you will never have any regrets as a father.

They Grow Fast

The major regret of our fathers' generation is that they missed out on spending time with their kids. Career demands, waiting until the baby is older, the playoffs, feelings of inadequacy, etc. easily get in the way, and before you know it, something precious is lost forever.

The antidote is to develop a habit even now, a commitment to connect with your child every day in some way. Before he is born, just thinking about him will get you started in a direction that you both will greatly appreciate over the decades to come.

The Best That Life Has to Offer

From experience, we know that given the opportunity, your baby will grab hold of your heart, provide you a new and serious source of strength, and add dimensions to your life that for now are unimaginable. Of course, one of these dimensions may be having nothing else to talk about but this special little angel who takes all your partner's time and energy, won't let you sleep through the night, regularly tosses his lunch and screams at all hours.

There is a reason that we sacrifice so much for our children. We experience our baby's warmth, snuggling, smiles, coos, and the amazing depth of her eyes as she gazes up at us. Falling asleep on your chest, warm, soft and secure in your arms, she clearly needs you and you know that no one else will look after her and protect her like you will. When she turns her head to you, or reaches out when she hears your voice, you know you are very important to her.

The reason is that children provide us the best that life has to offer. No title compares to "my daddy" uttered with pride and a smile by your little one who thinks you are the biggest, best looking, strongest, smartest, coolest dad on the planet.

No endeavor is more important than consoling your child who is upset over a nightmare, showing your frustrated kindergartner how to hit the ball off the tee, or reading that fairy tale one more time. No adventure measures up to the satisfaction of seeing his excitement in catching his first fish, or reaching the summit of a mountain with your teenage daughter.

Fatherhood is about sacrifice, dignity and honor. Our children bring out the best in us as men, and the pride and fulfillment we experience by doing this challenging job feeds our souls.

The key is developing confidence before she arrives, and jumping in with both hands once she does. Get involved, give it time, and keep it up. What you give your child, and receive in return, is up to you.

What have I treasured the most?
Rocking Samantha to sleep in my arms, knowing that that moment in time is singular and unbelievably a precious treasure.
Veteran Dad

The things we could do when we had no children are not missed, because they are replaced by things 1,000% better. I love my daughter with all my soul. I really love getting and giving 100 hugs a day.
Veteran Dad

4

Becoming a Family

Having the baby in our life has added so much more, I can't even begin to tell you. We lie together in bed at night talking about our dreams for our child and how much its brought us together.

Veteran Dad

As a new father, your most serious challenge is not comforting a crying baby or figuring out how to pay for everything, but learning to work together with your mate to form a family.

You need to know that a first baby has a profound and often negative impact on a man's relationship with his wife. Intense and pervasive change is mandatory for her, and in turn, her needs and demands can become overwhelming as you try to adjust to your new life. And then she gives birth to your baby, who proceeds to overwhelm and exhaust you both for months.

Having a baby was like throwing a hand grenade into our relationship. We were a classic case of opposites attracting, but with the baby, we just couldn't seem to agree on anything.

Veteran Dad

If you learn to work as a team, a baby can seriously enhance your relationship. Talking, understanding and working together on caring for and raising a child brings you together. Sharing the rewards, for which the words joy and pride seem very inadequate, is exquisite.

The challenge a baby presents to your relationship cannot be overestimated. By understanding the powerful and often conflicting forces at work as you take on fatherhood and a family, you'll increase your prospects for pulling through and coming out the other side a stronger man, with a stronger marriage, and a family that makes all your efforts and sacrifices incredibly worthwhile.

Given what's at stake, this is this book's most important chapter.

Family Planning

I had what I call the "three M's" all in one year: marriage, mortgage and maternity. Got married, two months later bought a house, then during escrow I find out my wife's pregnant and I'm going to be a father. Talk about a…shock.

Rookie Dad

Did you plan to have this baby? About half the babies born in America are planned, so either way, you have lots of company.

If your baby was not planned, well surprise, surprise. Life can throw us curveballs, and an unplanned baby can really put one through the ringer. She can also be a God-send, all at the same time.

Having a baby is sort of like getting on a roller coaster, which starts off slowly and then speeds up and throws you through a lot of twists and turns. You get through it in one piece, and before you know it, the rough part is over. This "jump in the deep end and swim" approach works well for most, since planning a baby does little to actually prepare you for a child. You just start by accepting the fact that you are going to have a child, and go from there.

Among the toughest circumstances are those in which the baby was planned by mom alone. This happens. All of a sudden, you are going to be a father, and you suspect, or may know, that she chose to do it without your knowledge.

Feeling blindsided and trapped makes it very hard to take a positive approach. Even if you acquiesced to your wife's desire for a baby and feel you have given one to her, you may find it difficult to take full responsibility as your child's father. If so, you and your baby may both miss out.

But you have a son on the way. Or a daughter. Time to get over it. Time to get on with forming a family. Easy to say; tough to do. Lingering issues over a "surprise" pregnancy are debilitating to all involved. Talk about it with people you trust. Talk about it with your mate.

> ### Babies Come Tough and Easy
> Your baby may scream with colic for months, or sleep through the night within a week, or have a temperament somewhere in between. Some babies are easy on mom and dad; some are not, and this factor alone can make a huge difference. Even the toughest ones typically turn into happy babies within months, and they have an upside for dads in that they require involvement and afterwards, having delivered when it counted, you have a stronger connection with your child that can last for decades.

If you planned your baby, you and your mate may have worked hard and long at getting a pregnancy to take. If so, you have likely spent a lot of time thinking about your baby and hoping and planning for the future. As a result, you may be better prepared than most.

You may have also experienced a good deal of stress in your relationship as you struggled, and may be surprised at the added strains a new baby can bring. You will want to make it work out no matter what it takes. Especially after what you have been through.

If you and mom decided to go for a baby and it took right away, well, congratulations. In fact, congratulations to all – you are going to be fathers.

The baby was a surprise. I am really looking forward to having a child, but I don't know where we are going to find the time. We both need to work, and we are real busy as it is.
Rookie Dad

The responsibility of providing for a family hit me hard just as soon as she told me she was pregnant. We talked about it for a few minutes and I felt like I was just floating. I went outside and started chopping firewood and I damned near worked myself into a frenzy while thinking I wanted to keep the house warm for the baby.
Veteran Dad

Tough Transformation

Your first child is one of the greatest challenges you and your wife will face. Financially, emotionally, physically and sexually, no aspect of your marriage is exempt from this trial by fire.

Many couples approach parenthood in the mistaken belief that having a baby will repair their relationships. Although some do get better, most do not, and couples get caught in a cycle of disappointment, misunderstanding, frustration and conflict.

A variety of studies have found that about half of couples with a new baby experienced a moderate to severe decline in marital satisfaction. They reported declining feelings of love and decreasing communication, combined with increasing conflict and ambivalence.

Thirty percent of couples reported no significant change in their marriages, and about twenty percent reported that their marriages actually improved. This is where you will want to end up, of course.

The first month there are a lot of changes going on with everybody. I was learning how to be a dad and help out. My wife was learning how to be a mother. And both of us were trying to figure out the different cues our baby was sending us…My wife was also going through hormonal changes.

Veteran Dad

Babies Can Push Us Together or Apart

No matter how much two people love each other, the process of becoming a family tends to polarize you and your partner.

Men and women become parents in fundamentally different ways, and in different timeframes. Mom tends to fall head over heals in love with her baby early on, while dad is inclined to take a slow, get-to-know-you approach with his son or daughter.

Differences in values, family background, personalities and priorities come to the surface and are intensified by the demands of caring for an infant and the issues involved in raising and shaping one's own child.

Babies also divide parents by overwhelming mom directly with physical, emotional and lifestyle changes while leaving dad relatively unscathed. Many moms resent these circumstances and feel that dad is not doing his "part," which of course he cannot.

It is tougher for new parents today because times have changed and moms and dads do not know what to expect of each other, or often of

I found if I get frustrated with the situation, I need to go downstairs and calm down because otherwise I just get more frustrated.

Veteran Dad

themselves. The gender wars of the past decade have added new dimensions, and intensity, to normal conflicts.

Being unprepared for the divisiveness of raising a young child, many couples start to experience a decline in marriage quality. Parents expecting their baby to bring them closer are surprised and angered when they find themselves drifting apart.

> **Every Mom, Dad, and Baby Is Different**
> Keep in mind that every mom, dad, and baby is different, and each family combination is unique. Each one is a moving target, as they constantly are going through changes. Sorting your issues out will take time, and all the expert advice in the world will not sort it out for you. You will have to work it out together.

First Babies Can be Very Tough on Moms

If all goes smoothly, the baby is easy and your mate takes to motherhood like a duck to water; great for her and you. But the reality for most mothers is quite different, and it is important that you understand what she is going through so you are prepared to deal with it.

The happiness and excitement of learning she is going to have a baby is the first of some almost delirious highs. Seeing and holding her baby for the first time after carrying him, feeling him grow inside, and knowing she has finished giving birth, must be pure ecstasy.

She can go through some very serious lows as well. The physical impacts of pregnancy alone are immense: morning sickness, gaining weight, losing energy and mobility, medical problems like backache (for which pain medication options are very limited), not to mention actually giving birth, which sometimes involves surgery.

The emotional lows can be even more distressing. Her life begins to transform steadily and inescapably as she is swept up into a whirlpool of events driven by her bringing forth a new life.

Take an "MTV bred," contemporary career woman and throw her back into the 1950's with a baby programmed to alternately cry, nurse, and poop at all hours. Add a mother's innate, intense focus on her baby, and you will likely have some real stress and even misery. And don't forget the hormones, which supercharge her feelings both up and down, exhausting and disorienting her.

Even though you know your partner well, and you witness her every step along the way, it is very hard for you to imagine what she is actually experiencing. It is important that you do your best to comprehend, even as you experience your own ups and downs. She needs you to lean on, to help her through, and to understand.

New Moms Can be Tough on New Dads

Her body, emotions, identity, sense of worth; her very being gets wrapped around her baby, who alternately enthralls and exhausts her for months, even years. How much energy and attention will your sweetheart have left over for you?

And your love life? The doctors say six weeks and she is good to go. Actually, she will be good to go when she feels like it, which means when she is feeling rested, attractive, good about her baby, good about her life and good about you. This could take a while.

You go for super husband, dive in and read the books, paint the nursery (twice), rub her back, go to all the appointments, and what do you get? No matter how good you are, it may not be good enough. Her appreciation may be limited by the fact that her needs, and by extension, her expectations of you, can be overwhelming, incomprehensible, and virtually impossible for you to meet.

And whose fault do you think this is? You are supposed to be partners, right? Except she is the one who is getting dumped on, while you worry about your golf game (her view). While she is feeling bloated, tired and nauseated, you go out for a run like your life has not changed. Which, of course, relative to hers, it has not.

Evolving expectations about the roles that fathers and mothers play have also set you up. You are supposed to share equally in the care of your child, which is very tough during the first months for guys who work and do not breast feed. Her friends may expect you to lag, and she may focus on what you don't do and ignore your contributions. It can get to the point where you wonder why you bother. Be careful it does not become a self fulfilling prophecy.

Finally, something that you can be good at: she needs to exorcise her frustrations in some way, and you make a convenient target. Being her punching bag is part of the deal. It is just the way it is.

"Children of happily married couples are simply happier. They have more advanced social skills, do better in school, aren't as likely to succumb to depression during stressful times and act out less."
Pamela Jordan, Ph.D., co-author of Becoming Parents: How to Strengthen Your Marriage as Your Family Grows

One time I dumped on my wife due to frustration over the baby. It wasn't going to work, because she definitely had the harder part in this. But other times, it's true. I do need to stand my ground, because there are times when my wife is tired and doesn't know what she's saying or doing.
Veteran dad

This too will pass. Keep in mind you are getting a child, and a mom who will unconditionally love and care for him from conception. And if you hang in there, you will get your sweetheart back.

Stress Debilitates Kids
Happy marriages are beneficial to children, conflict distresses them.

Even at three months, babies of parents who enjoy each other have a higher capacity for joy, concentration and self-soothing. Research in Germany found that preschoolers raised in homes with "great marital" hostility had seriously higher levels of stress hormones. At fifteen, the kids of troubled marriages had significantly higher levels of truancy, depression, peer rejection, low school achievement, behavior problems, anger and aggression.

Apparently when children are raised in homes where they feel safe instead of stressed, they are better able to handle stress themselves and approach the world in a more positive manner.

What We Have Here is a Failure to Communicate

Communication, understanding and teamwork are the keys to success. If you do not regularly talk things over with your mate, it is essential that you start now.

Don't assume that you have to agree on a parental philosophy and strategy for your child's upbringing right out of the box. Common issues that will get you off to a good start can include:

- Your dreams and concerns regarding your new family
- How you can help each other do your best
- How you will balance work and family

Focus on learning to talk about the issues first, learn to understand each other's perspective, and then learn to compromise, negotiate, and agree to disagree. At that point, you'll be ready to take on naming your baby.

The very common alternative is you and mom tiptoeing through a minefield in sullen silence, and periodically blowing your tops. At a time when communication becomes more important than ever, it often starts breaking down. If this starts happening in your relationship, recognize it for what it is. And deal with it.

Both mother and father take a back seat to the baby. Communicate and work together as a team. Words of wisdom from Veteran Fathers

Remember, mom is likely so focused on the baby she is oblivious to relationship issues. All she is thinking is that when she needs you most, you are not there. Be proactive, be creative, write her a letter if words don't work. Buy her flowers when she least expects it. Take the initiative; you will be glad you did. She will too.

Sources of Conflict

While moms and dads expect a new baby to result in more work, they aren't really prepared for what's involved and tend to fight over it. Maternal employment and feminism have made today's moms expect and feel entitled to a substantial amount of involvement from you, regardless of your work hours. You may have a different perspective.

In addition to the division of labor, new moms and dads usually fight over the following:

- Money: both spending and earning
- Relationship, or lack thereof: fighting over making love is highly counterproductive
- Social life: mom won't leave the baby; doesn't trust any baby sitter

In relationships that are strong, both partners work to resolve these issues. Moms and dads try to understand each other and do the little things that count. Those who go the distance are happier. Unfortunately, the opposite is also true – those who don't follow through are miserable.

> **Six Characteristics of Happy Parents**
> Jay Belsky and John Kelly, authors of *The Transition To Parenthood*, found that couples that successfully overcame the polarizing effects of a first baby shared six common characteristics. Understanding these and striving to implement them in your relationship may help you and your mate weather the storm. These couples:
>
> 1. Surrender individual goals and needs and work together as a team.
> 2. Resolve differences about division of labor and work in a mutually satisfactory manner, and argue constructively.
> 3. Attempt to keep up a pool of common interests, despite priorities that are branching off in different directions.
> 4. Understand that their marriages will never be quite the same after the baby's arrival. It will be different.
> 5. Continue communicating in a manner that sustains and supports the marriage.
> 6. Each handle stress in a way that does not overstress their partner or their marriage.

A month after the baby was born things got so bad that I contemplated divorce. No matter how hard I tried I couldn't make my wife happy and I got frustrated because I wasn't getting my needs met. But then one day when I was holding my daughter I asked myself, do I want another man in this house taking care of our baby? And the answer was no!
Veteran Dad

The most important thing is teamwork. Before my son was born we discussed how we're going to take care of the baby and what we're going to do and it seems like that's paid off.
Veteran Dad

Building a Parenting Team

Children thrive when mom and dad have a strong relationship. So do mom and dad.

You two can burn a lot of scarce energy fretting about who is not doing one thing or another. The need to expect change and learn to work together is a no brainer. Teaming up to raise children is a great deal more efficient, an essential issue given the enormous amount of work involved.

Expecting that arguments are likely to occur prepares you to take a constructive approach. This enables a positive attitude to get you through the tough times and helps you enjoy the good times even more.

Marriages that are enhanced by a baby are those in which mom and dad understand each other's needs and do their best to meet them. Dad strives to be his wife's "Knight in Shining Armor," even when mom is too fatigued to appreciate his efforts.

You have to decide to make the sacrifices, even though you are not required to do so. (In most situations, biology requires moms to do their part; you have a choice.) Hopefully mom will recognize that your desire for some attention and affection is reasonable and necessary if your new family is to thrive.

The good news is that every day you will learn a little more about your baby, yourself, and your partner. At about 2-4 months, you'll understand your baby's needs, likes and dislikes. And, perhaps best of all, your baby will be sleeping most of the night. A more rested mom and dad make the household a lot calmer and friendlier. Also at this time, pregnancy hormones begin to subside, baby blues become a memory, and confidence sets in.

You have weathered the storm, together.

Teamwork: I don't know how single parents handle it. It takes two people working 110%, 24 hours a day and even then it ain't easy!
Veteran Dad

Career Path Convergence

Having a baby in the 1950's was a lot simpler for most. Dad worked, mom stayed home. You and your mate face a lot more choices now.

If you are the major breadwinner, mom wants to stay home with the baby, and you can afford it, cool. Just don't get cut out of your child's life like many of our own fathers. Also, be aware that many of today's moms find this new role very confining, especially after they've tried it for a month or two. In this case a part time, flexible job for her, combined with limited day care, may be the ticket.

If she is the major breadwinner and you want to stay home, and you can afford it, cool. Be aware, though, that you may find this role confining, and given the tradition of men bringing home the bacon, you may need a thick skin to make this work. Some sort of part time, home-based business may work for you.

She is a doctor and I am finishing medical school. With a baby on the way, typical medical careers for both made no sense. We thought it through and decided we will both work 3 1/2 days a week. We can share the baby, have a career, and earn plenty for a new family.
Veteran Dad

If you are a two-career couple and both of you want or need to work, well you have lots of company today. Juggling jobs and daycare is tough, it works a lot better if you understand that your mate will not be able to work full time and take care of the baby full time. A lot of guys, particularly those who earn more than mom, don't get this, and it is a major source of relationship turmoil.

Work with your partner to expand your options. Think them all through, particularly with regard to what you consider essential expenses. Maybe a big mortgage is not appropriate for your new family. Maybe your baby's welfare is not dependent upon an expensive new SUV. Take your time to sort it out, and stay flexible. Really flexible, as mom (and perhaps you) may have different feelings once the baby arrives.

And the last thing that is important is what someone else thinks. Ultimately, you will want to do what works best for your new family as determined by you and mom.

If You are Not Married

Are you married? If not, you have lots of company, and additional challenges. If you are, skip to the next section.

About a third of babies are born to parents who are not married. About half of these parents are living together and another third are romantically involved but living apart. Roughly three quarters of both new moms and dads report an even chance or better of getting married. While some feel good about their relationship and see no reason to marry, most plan to do so with a child in the picture.

However, like your married counterparts, you and your mate are likely oblivious, at this point, to the divisive impact a child will probably have on your relationship. And since yours is inherently weaker on average than those with a legal commitment, you face bigger risks.

No, you don't have to get married; that is entirely up to you and your mate. But given the circumstances, you should want to work hard to build your relationship. With mom focused on the baby, the ball is mainly in your court.

Ask yourself about the strengths and weaknesses of your partnership. What has kept you from getting married? Most unwed moms report the barrier to be the economic stability and emotional maturity of their mates. If this is you, it's time to step up.

How about you? Not ready to settle down? Want to wait until …? Is she nagging you about …? Bottom line is, ready or not, you are going to be a father and she will be the mother of your child – for life. The picture has changed and so will your relationship, for better or worse. Not responding is like sailing into a storm without battening down the hatches. The forecast for sinking is high.

The prospects for your baby bringing you closer together are also high – if you take advantage of this important opportunity. Being unmarried, she will be even more concerned about whether you will be there for her and the baby. People around her will ask her whether you will stick around. Expectations for you might be low, so if you do respond and step up, it will be a pleasant surprise that will score big points. You will find her response gratifying; it is nice to be appreciated. As she sees you caring for and playing with your baby, she will know that her baby has a father who will be there. More big points, and another reason for her to love you.

It's a great opportunity; you have nowhere to go but up.

I don't want some other guy raising my kid.
Veteran Dad

Use Your Resources

Your family will take on ultimate importance to you. Meeting your family's needs will become your basic responsibility in life. With mom focused on the baby, you may need to be your family's resource manager. Don't forget to use all available resources when it will help. The wide range includes:

- Free or low cost medical services
- Medical information
- Employment training
- Marriage counseling
- Social worker at the hospital

Find available resources by asking. This may be uncomfortable to you at first. Ask your friends, church, librarian, doctor, county social services, etc. Scope them out, and be assertive in going after them. Don't be shy; you are not asking for yourself, you are doing your job as a dad and taking care of your family. (Also see *Learning More/Getting Help* in the Resource Guide in Appendices).

Laughing Beats Crying

Keep a sense of humor. Work, family and marriage all add up to more than 24 hours, and there are places you have to give. There is no perfect formula [for maintaining] a constant balance. But if you keep a sense of humor, you can find the fun in just about everything.
Veteran Dad

Keep your sense of humor intact, and if you don't have much of one, get one. When stress and exhaustion take their toll, nothing beats despair and the blues like a good laugh.

There is a good chance she will lose hers, and you may have to learn to make her laugh all over again. What you both previously laughed about may not be funny anymore; you may have to find new material.

Recommended Reading
National Lampoon's Managing Editor, Mason Brown, has produced a book, *Breathe: A Guy's Guide to Pregnancy*, which can help you maintain your sanity and sense of humor. Breathe will show you how to laugh it all off. Show it to mom, and if she has any sense of humor left, she will laugh with you. For the record, this book is so over the top, we cannot technically recommend it as the politically correct enforcement squads would have us strung up in no time.

Tough World Out There

Are you pleased with the prospects of the world you are bringing your child into? Most of us do not even like to think about it. Regardless of your outlook, you will want to build a family in which everybody looks out for each other, and equip your children to handle whatever challenges they encounter.

This starts with you and mom looking out for each other. When things get tough, us against the world, back-to-back in the foxhole, it sure beats every man for himself. Looking out for each other will get you through the tough times early on, and as your children grow, they will join in. This is what a family does.

When they leave the family nest, your children will still look out for each other, and will do the same with their friends and mates. They will be ready to take on the world, no matter how tough it is.

Make A List of the Things You Like to Do Together
The "list" has become standard advice at Boot Camp. Your baby will likely overwhelm you and your mate, to the point that you have neither the time nor the energy to have fun. Perhaps to the point you even forget how to have fun together.

As a simple investment in your parenting partnership, sit down with your wife and make a list of the things you like to do together. After life with a baby settles down, pull out the list and pick out something to do. Even if your options are still limited, it will remind you both of what you had together. Don't wait until the last month of her pregnancy to do the list because you may have already started forgetting.

Becoming a Family

With all the day-to-day changes, confusion and uncertainty new dads and moms encounter, it is easy to lose sight of your goal of becoming a family. It is important that you not do so, because the rewards of a family are what make your sacrifices along the way incredibly worthwhile. Keeping your mind set on what your family can become will help give you the determination and strength to get there.

As words cannot do justice to how much your child will mean to you, the same goes for your new family. You will just have to trust us veterans that nothing else can equal the fulfillment and happiness one brings.

You can look forward to thousands of magical moments as your family grows:

Having a child and a family is the greatest thing in the world...It puts life in proper perspective for me. I realize that money, cars, and material things such as careers are far less important than I previously thought. At my son's age, he doesn't care if we live in a mansion or a one-bedroom apartment. He just wants love from his mom and dad.

Veteran Dad

- Can you imagine your one year-old taking tottering steps towards your open arms, and developing a huge smile when you scoop him up in a big hug while you congratulate him on being the best walker ever?

- How about your one year-old daughter looking at you and smiling, responding to your hug and smile with great pride and an enthusiastic string of "da-da's"?

- How about you and mom silently smiling at each other when the child you made together makes his first friend, reads her first words, wants to help you wash the car, or about a billion other wonderful things kids do when they are loved and cared for?

- Can you possibly imagine your one "in the oven" growing up and handing you and mom your grandchild, pointing out how he has your eyes?

I want to be my kid's role model so he won't have to look somewhere else to look up to someone.
Rookie Dad

A baby can provide his parents new opportunities and mutual respect. The result can be a renewed sense of unity, the feeling of being a family, the shared challenge of working together to care for him, and the wonderful sense of fulfillment that comes from building something important together that will last for the rest of your lives.

Families are the basic building block of humanity. The struggles, even the sorrows, make a family richer. You and your partner are doing something momentous, which is easily lost when you are both dead tired and perhaps wondering who should get out of bed this time to care for a screaming baby.

Take it one day at a time, and remember where you are trying to go. God speed.

5

Becoming a Mom

Understanding your mate's transformation into a mom is essential if you are to work together to form a family. This is very difficult to do since new mothers, as powerful events force them to adapt to a very different life, rarely understand what is happening to themselves.

Health care professionals and the popular month–by-month guides portray their extraordinary development as a progression of physical and emotional events, from morning sickness to mood swings to giving birth to postpartum depression, rarely explaining the overall impacts within the woman we love.

Our society loudly debates stay-at-home versus working moms, the benefits of breastfeeding, and merits of medication during birth. But it is also largely silent about the all-embracing changes brought on by motherhood.

This leaves it up to you to understand that over the initial year, motherhood will change her to her core. Your mate will, in essence, be reborn as a mother as she steps up to her awesome responsibilities. The more you understand, the better you can help bring out the best in her as a mom, and as a partner. You will find that in time she does the same for you as a dad.

When you come home from the hospital, you don't come home with one new person. You come home with two. My wife changed a lot after giving birth to our baby.
Veteran Dad

Our Unique Perspective

The experience of many thousands of veteran fathers looking back and comparing notes provides a fresh and unique perspective on new moms. Some of the basics:

- Next to procreation, the metamorphosis of young women into mothers is the most remarkable of all human experiences.

- Much of this change is beautiful: your carefree mate grows over just nine months into a mom who unconditionally loves and commits herself to the well-being of her - and your - child.

- She experiences a long, tough and tumultuous ride, a physical and emotional gauntlet of thrills, pain, fierce love, depression, exhaustion, assurance, anxiety, and on and on.

- They innately reach out to other mothers, especially their own, who offer the comfort of having been there and the reassurance that she is a good mom.

- As she copes with her own and her baby's tremendous needs, she will no longer have the time or energy to be as concerned with yours.

- Even surrounded by you, her family and medical professionals, she can still feel stranded and utterly alone.

Motherhood adds a whole new dimension to her; a new component to her personality and character, which she steadily embraces as her baby grows inside her and she builds confidence in her new role and responsibilities.

The girl you love is still there, and in time, you will get much of her back. You will also get a loving mother for your child, a part of her you will come to love and deeply respect.

Different Trajectory

Our mates typically played with dolls while we tended towards guns. She has toyed with notions of motherhood for perhaps 2-3 decades, while most of us never even thought of being a father until recently.

The physical impacts of pregnancy hit her quickly and often hard, and the realization that her baby is growing inside her can be thrilling, harrowing, amazing and staggering in quick succession.

From the moment she learns she is pregnant, all this kicks into gear, launching her on a steep trajectory of change as she moves quickly along the path to motherhood. She begins contemplating a wide range of issues including what kind of mother she will be, changes in her career, marriage, body, friends, the birth, and what her baby will be like.

Typically, we're months behind. We warm up to the notion of fatherhood more slowly, taking a much flatter trajectory as we begin mulling over the issues and changes we will face. We can be surprised

The experience takes a great physical and mental toll on moms, but don't forget the mental torture moms put new dads through. If a man isn't in touch with his feelings before the birth, he's in trouble. And he won't be in touch with these feelings if he doesn't know what to expect. If anyone talked about it, they glossed over it.

Veteran Dad

that the first changes we notice are those occurring in our relationship with her.

Some new moms may also appear to be flat. She may keep the issues of pregnancy and a baby at arms length to maintain some notion of control over her life, and may be reluctant to talk about it. Keeping her thoughts and emotions private may be her way of initially dealing with impending motherhood.

Most new moms experience a more moderate course, but at the other end of the spectrum, some get so involved in their pregnancies that they seem to lose their perspective and go overboard. Another normal reaction for a woman new to motherhood.

Window of Opportunity

When asked what is most important for rookie dads, veteran fathers will say that no matter how difficult your circumstances are, focus on supporting mom. They will also tell you that the birth is when the rubber needs to hit the road, because not only is this when she needs you most, your support once the baby arrives is what she will remember in the years ahead.

The first few months are the toughest for new moms, when the demands on her are often overwhelming, and her confidence and capabilities as a mother are just developing. In comparison, pregnancy is like the preseason before regular season games. You want to do well, but if you do not meet her and/or your own expectations, the games that really count are still ahead of you. Most anything you did prior to labor kicking in, good or not, will be archived in the recesses of her mind, much like who won or lost in the preseason.

Bottom line is that your performance during this crucial post-birth period will form the basis for her new perspective of you - as the father of her child, and her partner as a parent.

The long-term potential of your actions during this intense process will easily justify any effort you can muster, and then some. You may need to go beyond anything you can conceive of in terms of effort and exhaustion to get the job done. Mom may be inundated by the baby's needs as well as her own. If she has a cesarean birth, plan on pushing the boundaries of your endurance for at least the first two weeks. If your baby is fussy or becomes colicky, plan on it for three months.

This is your window of opportunity with the new woman in your life — the mother of your baby — and you will want to be there for her. In time the demands upon you will pass, but the job you do will set the tone for your relationship for perhaps decades.

Her Extraordinary Bond

I wondered sometimes why my wife was overreacting to the baby's cry. I'd say the baby is all right and she'd say but the baby's crying. But she's the mother. She's got a chemical bond with the baby who's been inside her for nine months. It's something I can never fathom.

Veteran Dad

Millenniums of evolution and socialization take effect when our mates become pregnant. They are hard wired to love their babies and develop an intense bond which drives them to sacrifice a great deal as they carry, give birth and care for them.

Her phenomenal commitment assures your child's well being, if not survival, and your support and encouragement will help her thrive in this role. As she does, you will come to honor and respect her for it, as there is nothing more important to the welfare of your child. (You may also become frustrated, as her focus on her baby comes at the expense of her attention to you.)

A mom's bond starts developing early on, takes a leap once her baby is born and in her arms, and then grows continually. After her pregnancy is confirmed, the incredible reality of a baby developing inside her captures her full attention, and she begins imagining what her baby will be like. She will likely begin day dreaming about what he will look like as a baby, and perhaps as a little boy, a kindergartener, or even teenager, fantasizing that he has the ideal traits she chooses. (Ask her what she thinks your child will be like; she'll be glad you did.)

My biggest challenge was dealing with a hormonally unbalanced spouse who believes one germ will kill her child. The complexity and passion of a spouse's emotion for her new child in unnerving.

Veteran Dad

Mothers are as connected to their babies after the birth as they were before. This may seem impossible when you see her joyfully holding her belly and feeling him kick inside her, but her bond deepens over time as she inherently responds to his needs, and as the baby responds to her love and care. As her child grows, when he needs her she will respond, no matter how old he is. (This explains a lot of 30 year old "kids" living at home.)

As veteran fathers witness this connection, we are struck by the fact that a mother's love for her baby stands no matter what, and there is no limit to its depth. The only thing that can match it is the often untapped potential of a father's love.

A Baby's Impact on Mom

Upon conception, a mom cedes control over her body, emotions, time, career – her very life. Her bond with her baby essentially requires her to focus upon his needs, as hers are superceded by her new need to mother. This bond tethers her to an inexorable force that dictates how her life will be.

Some mothers would have it no other way. They begin beaming when their pregnancy is confirmed, and never seem to stop. They have a new purpose and love in their life that fulfills a powerful drive and instinct. Being a mom just fits.

But for most, it is a roller coaster ride of ups and downs. A mom's love affair with her new baby can be euphoric at times, and exhausting at other times. Her feelings and focus on her baby can be so strong that she can barely think about herself, let alone anyone else.

The impacts of a first baby on mom include:

- Physical changes are flat out amazing if you really think about it. They take a toll in terms of weight gain, stretch marks, etc., not to mention her wardrobe.

- Persistent feelings of nausea, back pain, birth pain, exhaustion, or sore breasts.

- New, confusing, powerful, biologically driven emotions, contributing to sharp and unpredictable mood swings, and sometimes major depression.

- Discombobulated career plans.

- Her personal sense of worth may diminish as her world compresses to caring for a baby in isolation at home.

This loss of control over her own life is often the worst aspect for moms having a tough time. They may feel they cannot escape this new responsibility, and there is no turning back. Trapped with no choices, they feel virtually chained to an infant who demands their continual devotion. This can result in serious anxiety bordering on panic.

A cranky or colicky baby, of course, adds a whole new dimension to her precarious situation.

Patience, Patience and PATIENCE! Both with a new mom going through changes I only particularly understand, and also with the new baby who knows so little but is changing so rapidly.

Veteran Dad

I wish I'd learned more about self-sacrificing before the baby came. I didn't know how selfish and insensitive I was toward my wife until months after the baby was born.

Veteran Dad

What Happened to My Wife?

You may at times wonder what ever happened to your wonderful, loving mate. Pregnancy and motherhood do not always bring out the best in a woman as far as dad is concerned. In fact, at times you may feel like you want to hand her a broom to ride.

The impacts of motherhood will result in fundamental changes in your wife over a short time period. You are well behind her on the learning curve, which means that while she is getting hit hard, you remain virtually unscathed (she is unlikely to be sympathetic that you are no longer the main focus in her life).

These circumstances can make it tough for you to sort out what is happening, especially if you are taking her apparent rejection personally (it happens to the vast majority of us dads). If you feel like someone who has lost his mate, welcome to the brotherhood of fatherhood. You are not alone.

Keep in mind what she is going through mentally and physically, and try to keep your sense of humor. You may feel like her punching bag at times, which in essence is one of your new roles. Your job is to take it and hang in there, being as supportive as you can. Her moods, which she can barely control, will come and go. You may as well roll with the punches since the alternative is not particularly constructive. It will also get you ready for after the baby is born, when mom will be worn thin and the punches may fall harder.

Again, your sweetheart is still there inside her, and if you hang in there, you will get her back.

Are We Scaring You Yet? (This May Not Happen to You)
Even though we are telling it like it can be, it can be alarming for a rookie father to read about how tough new moms often are for new dads. This is not a hazing ritual for newbies and we certainly are not ragging on new moms (our great respect should be clear to all). We just want to be sure you are prepared for whatever might come your way. Much of the potential downside of new moms may not happen to you, but if it does, you will be ready. If not, consider yourself a lucky man.

A New Mom's Take on New Dads

Witnessing your mate's transformation into the mother of your child is ultimately wonderful, but there are many rocks along her path. One way most dads find out is when she seems to start picking the rocks up and throwing them at you. Since her predicament is clearly your fault, you need to learn to duck, as throwing them back is not an option.

Common landmines in this alien territory can include:

Low Expectations

Moms may have low expectations for you based upon their own experience with fathering and what they have seen or heard from their friends. Hey, a lot of guys are not doing their part, and early missteps by you may confirm her worst fears. You can find yourself in a hole before you are barely outside the gate.

The Only One Getting Dumped On

With a new baby on the way, she has forgotten why she loved you in the first place, and is interested only in what kind of partner and parent you are going to make. With all she is going through, it is improbable she will like what she sees, as there is no way you can keep up. When she is experiencing the downside, she feels that she is the only one getting dumped on.

He Doesn't Care

After the initial enthusiasm over the pregnancy, mom begins planning and preparing. Dads tend to set the issue aside and let it percolate, as nine months is a long time off. As moms become focused on the incredible changes a baby brings to them, they often perceive their mates to be unconcerned, uninvolved, and uncaring. They begin to wonder what kind of father you will be and what kind of support you will provide. Many fathers report mom consuming every source of information on babies available, and wanting them to do the same. Not going to happen.

He's Not Going to Be There for Me

As the physical changes brought on by the baby constrain and even pain them, a mother's desires of her mate are unlikely to be met by his performance. Whether it is repainting the nursery, or providing rubs to relieve back pain throughout the night, or just attention to the issues she's concerned with, men often fall short of a pregnant moms'

I'm afraid that I might not live up to my wife's expectations when it comes to caring for the baby.

Rookie Dad

The thing about new moms is that they are going through a lot of changes; and the whole trick is to form a team with your wife and become family.

Veteran Dad

Moms get very frustrated, and they can take that frustration out on us.

Veteran Dad

expectations. While aware that demands will increase once the baby arrives, these mothers wonder whether dad will be there for them or their baby.

He Wants Me to Make All the Career Sacrifices
For a new mom with a fulfilling career, after a generation of feminism, her sense of self worth may be tied to what she accomplishes outside the home. Her pregnancy brings career issues into question for her alone, which is unfair. While many career moms choose to focus on motherhood, the public battles of stay-at-home and working moms may be ringing in her ears.

Other Potential Landmines Along the Road
The baby's actual arrival opens up a new set of possibilities, including her thinking that:

- You are worthless around the baby
- You are purposely working longer hours when I need him here
- All you want to do is get back in the sack

It just goes with the territory. When she is having a tough time, no matter how good you are, it may not be good enough. It helps to remember what she is going through, and perhaps trying to imagine what it is like to give birth.

Getting Between You and Your Baby

A major factor in your involvement with your child will be whether your partner encourages and facilitates your hands-on care. If she becomes possessive of "her" baby, she may actually come between you and your child. But only if you let her.

I focused on my job. She handled the girls. Several months ago, it dawned on me that I was no longer part of my own family. There was nothing left for me.
Veteran Dad

Gatekeeping
"Gatekeeping" is a term applied to possessive moms who restrict a father's access to his child. It comes in varying degrees and is common. This can be a new mother who develops a compulsive, highly protective focus on the baby and distrusts anyone else, including dad, to care for him. Or it can involve a mate who is irritated or angry at you for any reason, and ends up taking it out on you and ultimately your child by interfering with your relationship. Or a variety of other circumstances that fall in between.

Gatekeeping often manifests itself in her micromanagement of your interactions with your baby. For example, constantly hovering around and criticizing or correcting your every move. She might say, "Kate doesn't like to be held that way," when Kate is clearly comfortable in your arms. It is just not the way she likes to hold your daughter.

It is driven by her feelings; in most cases mothers do not make a conscious decision or are even aware they are hindering dad's involvement with his child. Interestingly, if her relationship with her own father was poor, she will be more likely to support and relish a strong one between you and your child. Twins, colic and mom going back to work also diminish this problem by simply leaving mom with no choice but to accept you as a parenting partner.

The Real Problem

The bottom line is that your efforts to engage your child are frustrated rather than facilitated. The real danger is that her behavior will cause you to lose (or never gain) confidence and actually back away from taking care of your own baby. During those trying first months when you are unsure of what to do, it is easy to conclude that "if she wants to do it all, let her." Once established, this becomes a very hard pattern to break for both mom and dad.

Real Solutions

First, understand what is happening. A gatekeeping mom's whole life is wrapped around that baby; she may need something to call her own to just feel a sense of purpose in her life. Second, don't take the easy way out of your child's life by succumbing to the comfort of sitting on the sidelines. Stand your ground and get involved:

- Demonstrate to her that you are capable of caring for your child when the opportunity presents.
- Be sensitive to her needs and ask for her "advice" on how to care for the baby. Be patient when she calls five minutes after she leaves you home alone to ask "how is the baby doing?"
- Use your trump card: explain that "her" baby will greatly benefit from the very relationship with you that she is undermining.

Finally, you don't need to ask her permission to care for your child. Take advantage of the many opportunities you have when mom is asleep or in the shower, and encourage her to get out on her own.

You might also experience the gatekeeper phenomenon that occurs where mom is watching you like a hawk. You're not holding the baby right or she may not like the way you're bouncing the baby. You feel like challenging your wife but it may not be the best thing to do. Just say…okay honey!
Veteran Dad

How to Support Her

First, don't take anything your partner throws at you personally. It is very normal and you have a great deal of company.

Next, a generous dose of patience will considerably ease your circumstances. Take deep breaths, count to ten, blow off steam with your close friends or brothers. (It is best to work on developing patience early, as kids require lots of it).

And then get involved. Go to your baby's first doctor appointment, and to as many as you can after that. Get educated about what new moms experience as they leave their former lives behind and endure the highs and lows, exhaustion, anxiety, pain and change. (There is reason this manual makes understanding and supporting moms the highest priority).

Remind her that she's beautiful and encourage her by telling her that she's going to be a great mom. After your baby arrives, continually look for new reasons to compliment her on her role as a mother. It is easy to take for granted all the little things she does, like waking up several times a night to nurse your baby, Don't take any of it for granted. Tell her how beautiful it is to watch her take care of your child.

You also need to support mom first by showing her that you are capable and willing to take care of your baby. She needs to know she can count on you, especially once her support system at the hospital, a full staff of doctors and nurses, is reduced to you once you get home with the baby.

Talk to Her

Talk to her a lot. Even if she seems to be handling it okay, you do not want to underestimate the impact upon her.

Both of you are going through a lot of changes. While most of it is for the better, change inherently creates conflict, and talking is how we resolve conflict; communication is the essence of how we process problems and come together as a couple.

Focus on her issues, for obvious reasons. But get to yours as well. You have your own things to deal with, and your best defense against your own anxiety is to talk to your mate.

Talk to Her Doctor

If you are worried about your partner as she experiences this trial by fire, share your concerns with her physician. The downside of new motherhood is very real and can be very serious, and you will want to make sure it is handled.

Honor the Mother of Your Child

The more we learn about new mothers, the more we appreciate the contributions and sacrifices they make for our children. Because there are many millions of moms doing what they do, it is simply expected of them. In fact, she herself will take for granted what she does best as a mom, while dwelling on any inadequacies she may feel. (Moms will often feel they are not good mothers if they do not know why their baby is crying, or even if they have any less than saintly thoughts about their screaming baby.)

Therefore it is up to us to let them know they are doing great things, and we greatly appreciate it. Tell her that you can see the incredible bond she has with your baby, that you are grateful for the sacrifices she is making, and that you understand (some at least) how tough it can be.

Being appreciated by you (no one else over two feet tall counts) makes all the difference to her and helps make the downside of motherhood worth it. Your baby will essentially do the same for her, and together you can make her motherhood a beautiful experience.

Respecting her as a mom, and loving her for what she does for your child, will also serve as the foundation of your new relationship with her. As your child grows, look for reasons to do so, and you will find them.

You will also find that what goes around comes around. Your honor and respect for her as a mother will result in her doing the same for you. No one can encourage us more as parents than our mates, and the better we both do, the more we appreciate each other, as well as ourselves.

When two people are covering each other's back when they have it coming at them from all directions, they develop a very strong relationship. This should be your plan.

I have a phenomenally new respect for my wife…that as much as I love her…the respect I think is different and for what she went through - to give birth - and her amazing ability to be a mother is incredible and very hard to put into words.

Veteran Dad

6

Becoming a Dad

A father, at his best, is awesome. His integrity, courage, love and strength serve as both foundation and pillars for his family. Every father is irreplaceable; no other man, no matter his wealth, can be more important to his children.

His children are also of ultimate importance to him. Watching them grow and learn to walk and talk, teaching them to catch a ball and read, preparing them to carve out a productive and fulfilling life; they give his life meaning and purpose. This is why fathers don't mind working so hard to provide the best life possible for their kids.

It is a long adventure of course; you are just starting out, and the initial weeks and months with your baby will be challenging. You pay a lot of dues on the front end as you become a dad.

There will be highs, there will be lows. Seeing him born, holding your son as he looks up at you with intense curiosity, telling him, "welcome to the world, I am your daddy." It may not hit you right off, but these feelings go right off the charts. Of course, so does sleep, romance, attention, friends, time, money, Saturday mornings (let's stop here; a general rule of thumb is never add it all up).

You will get through it. Maybe just barely, if you have an infant with colic. But over several months time, your new baby will get easier and you will become more proficient in caring for her. Mom will also lighten up as she develops confidence and gets used to her new responsibilities.

So now, after babies, families and moms, it is your turn. You may as well get comfortable with your new position in the pecking order, because at least for the next six months, this is just the way it is.

Starting Point: Our Own Fathers

Our experiences with our fathers differ dramatically; some were great; some were not there at all. Stepfathers, coaches, or other men may have had positive impacts on us, but for most, the legacy of our own fathers is our starting point for becoming a dad.

It is ironic that a distant or absent father can benefit us now, but the more we missed out as children, the more desire we bring to this job. Of course, the more we received, the more prepared we are to connect with our child due to the example set by our dads.

What Kind of Father Will I Be?
A great question to ask yourself, as it focuses you on a positive, constructive approach. How do you want to be the same or different from you own dad? Was he involved with you as a child? Did he provide warmth and respect? How about your friends' dads, who may provide good models for how you want to approach fatherhood? How do you want your kids to feel about you as they grow up?

Connecting with Your Father
As we become fathers, we take on an extraordinary role that we share with our own fathers. This provides the basis for a new relationship with him, one that can get beyond the normal constraints felt by fathers and sons. He sees you in a new light, and you may be wondering how he felt when he was just starting out. This can also bring up issues about his experience as a father, so you may have a lot you can talk about. Look out for the opportunity, or just ask "dad, how did you feel when you became a father?"

My dad worked hard, but when he was home he liked to be with me. I could always talk to him about stuff; I still can. I hope to raise my son the same way.

Veteran Dad

He also may enjoy being hands-on involved with a baby. If he missed out on you, he can have a second chance as your child's grandpa. We are just beginning to explore these issues, but we believe there is a lot to gain from connecting father-to-father with your own dad. Maybe someday fathers will mentor their sons in fatherhood like mothers do for their daughters in motherhood.

Connecting with Other Dads
As Boot Camp for New Dads has demonstrated for well over a decade, we can learn a great deal from each other. The problem is that, for the most part, we don't. Rookie dads don't ask, and experienced fathers don't tell – unless asked. Break the ice and ask other dads for their suggestions and frank advice. Ask them what they found to be most important when they were just starting out.

They may be caught a little off guard because no one asked before, but most fathers would be honored and would give you their best words of wisdom from their heart. It is a great way to both compliment a man and learn from his experience.

Reporting for Duty

Being a father is as serious as it gets. And it comes all at once. One day you pretty much have yourself to take care of, and the next you have a family to look after. If you asked some veteran dads what to be ready for, this is what they might say:

First: The Good Stuff
You should be hearing about the joys of fatherhood and hopefully you are experiencing some. Learning you have one on the way can be thrilling, this new adventure with your partner can be blissful, and thinking about doing things with your child as he grows opens all sorts of possibilities. If this is what you are feeling, enjoy it. If not, give it time.

Lots of Change
Relationships, finances, free time, night time, in fact, most everything outside of work changes, and even careers can take a different direction due to a baby. The compelled, required, no-choice-but-to-do-it kind of change, and there is no turning back.

You Will Fail at Times
No matter how good you are, you will have your bad days as a father. We all fail our mates and children at times. Worse, we will fail in meeting our own expectations, running the risk of losing our confidence and drive to do our best as fathers. Good thing tomorrow is always a new day with kids.

On Your Own
According to the norms of your new world, relative to the needs of your baby and mate, your needs do not even register on the scale. So don't expect any help or empathy. You are expected to support mom, not the other way around. New mom networks sprout spontaneously and programs for moms are plentiful, while support for fathers is rare.

Ups and Downs
Mom's changing moods are going to have an impact, and you are going to get hit by the downdraft. Add in your own highs and lows, and a roller coaster ride would seem boring compared to the lives of some guys during this period.

Your Child Will Help You Clean Up Your Act

Not only do you have to give up your perfectly good life, you will also need to undergo sudden maturation from a somewhat self-centered, fun-loving guy to a self-sacrificing paternal role model. As a father you are expected to set an example for your child and give up all activity that you would not want your child to witness or emulate. May as well start by repeating the Boy Scout Law (for those who did Little League instead, it goes "I will be trustworthy, loyal, helpful, friendly, courteous, kind, obedient, cheerful, thrifty, brave, clean and reverent"). Don't try to do them all at once.

In all honesty, all of us want to be better in some way. Our children give us both a reason and the strength to overcome the challenges we face. When you are struggling with something, pick up your baby, look in her eyes and ask yourself what you would like to be able to do for her. Then try doing it for her.

Lessons From The Front Lines

There is a lot to know; here are some more of the important lessons from those who have been there:

The Long Learning Curve

No matter how good you are, becoming a dad doesn't happen overnight. While the learning curve is sharp at first, it tapers off and extends for decades. You have a nine month warm up period, then hell week that lasts a month or three, and then you will find your groove for the long haul. So focus on getting over the hump, and then set a pace for the long term. And don't wear yourself out before your baby is born.

Everyone's Situation Is Different

While the fundamental transformation of men into dads remains the same, our differences mean that there is no set formula and each of us needs to figure it out for ourselves. Every new father's circumstances are unique. You may have a calm or colicky baby, an in-home baby nurse, or no help at all, a partner who was born to be a mother, or one who struggles with her own transition.

It Can Get You Down

You will find a good deal of information about baby blues and depression commonly encountered by new mothers, but you should also know that about 30% of new fathers also experience significant

I have been married 10 years and never even held a baby until I had my own. I knew nothing about babies and never really wanted to hold babies. I thought they were real fragile and would break and wasn't comfortable around them at all and then I had two. It's like everything else if you put your heart into it and work hard, you ask a lot of questions then you will learn, you will learn by doing and you can get good at it.

Veteran Dad

depression. It stands to reason that with all the stress involved us guys can get down as well, so if you find yourself feeling low, understand that you have a good reason. Deal with it the best you can, and know that it will pass.

There is No One Way or Right Way to Be a Dad

The right way is the one that works for you and your new family. Feel queasy about cutting the cord? Don't cut it. Does your staying home to take care of your baby while your partner builds her career work best for your family? Do it. It is easy to get caught up in doing what others, or society, expects of you as a father. You decide what works best for your child; no one else could possibly know.

Don't Turn Into an Assistant Mom

You will be surrounded by women who inherently know how to take care of babies and will naturally want you to do it their way. Do it your way, because fathers bring unique strengths to families, and a child needs a mom and a dad, not two moms.

Don't Be Accused of Being Jealous of Your Own Baby

A typical scenario: your wonderful mate becomes enamored and fully focused on the baby and has little time or energy left for you. You miss her and the life you had together and suggest that maybe you two spend more time with each other. This may be interpreted as you being jealous of your own baby, which is demeaning and embarrassing, rather than what it really is: grief over lost love. If anyone suggests otherwise, let them know you love your baby, miss your wife, and feel she could use a little balance in her life.

Don't Lose Your Friends

You need your buddies for balance in your life, and to blow off steam when pressure builds. Most men do not make friends easily. After a baby arrives, we tend to lose touch with those we have, and prospects for new friends are often limited to the mates of the moms our wives befriend as they network. While your play time will be severely limited, stay in touch with your pals, even those who might be a "bad influence," as most of them eventually grow up and have babies too.

Stand Your Ground

Keep in mind that a century of paternal tradition is changing, and you are on the leading edge of this change. This poses basic issues regarding your role. Make sure you and your partner are clear on your plans for being an involved father. It is not uncommon for new moms to become so immersed in the baby that they become the "gatekeeper" regarding dad's participation. If this happens, be patient and understanding, but make sure you are not pushed out of your child's life. Ditto with your mother-in-law, boss and friends. Many men who have worked hard to provide for their families have been surprised to find out down the road that they were not really part of their children's lives.

You Have No Idea How Important You Will Be to Your Child

You will understand how much your baby means to you only after you feel it. The flip side is true as well; you will become incredibly important to your child, but you will only appreciate this once you can see that she feels it. If you trust us veterans and assume that she does, it becomes a self fulfilling prophecy. Many fathers don't know this, and never find out.

Common Feelings, Fears and Concerns

You are going to have issues, and it helps to understand those that men normally encounter as we become fathers. Your counterparts in childbirth class may not express them (hardly the environment for men to spill their guts), but rest assured these issues are churning in their minds as well.

After the initial shock and/or excitement of the news of a baby on the way, you may experience doubt, fear, second thoughts, even panic. You may not know why you are feeling the way you are. Remember, no matter what is going on inside, you are not alone.

Men often become downright scared regarding their responsibility for a new family, and commonly experience a range of strong emotions ranging from euphoria to dread and even depression. This life changing transition can stir up a physic thunderstorm that dredges up all sorts of issues and exacerbates old insecurities. So if you find yourself freaking out inside, take a deep breath and understand that it is normal.

Also, if you worry that you are all worked up over nothing, don't, because there is a lot to get worked up over. Most of what you hear about the downside of initial daddyhood can come true. But maybe not for you, as everyone's experience is unique.

At the real risk of giving you more to worry about, here is a sample of the things that frequent the minds of men "meta-morphing" into fathers:

Hey guys can we stop talking about mom. Hey, I don't know about you guys but I'm riding an emotional roller coaster too!

Rookie Dad

Fear of the Unknown

Even though you are going where billions of men have gone before, it is largely unknown territory for you. *What am I getting into? I don't know the first thing about babies. Doing this was not my choice. I am not ready to be a father.*

Fear of Failure

I will faint or throw up in the delivery room. I will blow it as a birthing coach. I will drop the baby. I won't measure up. I will not be a good father. One of the big ones, fear of failure can be a serious obstacle that prevents you from focusing on preparing for the challenges ahead.

Fear of Becoming Your Father

He may have bailed on you, or worse. Or maybe he was an all around great dad who raised the bar very high for you. Or a combination. We tend to have strong and mixed feelings about our own fathers that surface as we head down this road.

Fear of Losing the Life You Know and Love

This baby was a surprise, maybe a mistake that I will regret for a long time. I don't even like babies, they're messy and their crying grates on me. I loved my wife the way she was. I worked hard to get my act and life together, and now this.

Worried About the Wife

Or fear of losing the wife you know and love. *Can she handle this? How much pain will she be in? Will she ever get back to normal? Will she be a good mother? When will my sex life return? Or for the lucky 10% - will she ever leave me alone?*

Worried About Money

A big one. *I work 60 hours as it is. We barely make it now, and she wants to stay home. I can't afford a bigger house, another car, etc. How much is baby stuff going to cost? How can I work enough to pay the bills and also spend the time I want with our baby?*

Worried About the Baby

Another big one, if there is the slightest indication anything might be wrong. Towards the end, with no sign of trouble whatsoever, your list of desires for your baby may whittle down to *I just want him to be okay.* Even weeks after your perfectly healthy baby has arrived and is sleeping like an angel, you may find yourself checking to make sure she is breathing.

Weird Stuff

Your trip into this uncharted territory starts with a lot of things running through your mind, not all of it rational. The thought *"Is this baby really mine?"* when you know better is surprisingly common. No matter what pops up, there are many other guys that can top it.

Relative Fears

Mothers-in-law. Enough said, with good reason, as one study found that in-laws were the number one complaint of new fathers (they must not have asked about sex). Particularly mothers and sisters-in-law who interfere with your relationship with your partner and baby.

Chemicals at Work

If you like the certainty of science, you will be pleased to know that your strong feelings are partly driven by biochemical reactions to your new experience as a father. While male hormonal changes are minor compared to what new mothers experience, recent research confirms that they do occur during pregnancy, and particularly when you hold your baby for the first time. Like those energizing endorphins that kick in when we exercise, hormonal changes as we become fathers also serve a purpose - predisposing us to want to care for our babies.

Remember also that many other men are ahead of you on this path. Seek out fathers you can trust and talk to them. It helps to hear other guy's stories and vent your feelings. Knowing that they went through similar issues will help you work through your own.

Balancing Act

Being a dad has a lot to do with choices between competing priorities (you might have noticed). You want to take several weeks off without pay when the baby comes while one of your major concerns is how you are going to pay for all of this. Nobody can tell you to make these choices; each new father must figure out how to make it all work on his own.

We generally have a full life before our first baby comes along. Our careers are usually building or in full swing. We have developed broad relationships with our mates, spending time together and sharing common interests. We have friends, hobbies, outside activities, and physical endeavors that fill out our days. In many cases, long work hours have already stretched us to the limit.

I'm concerned about how I'm going to meet my financial responsibility as the breadwinner of the family, and my moral responsibility as a father. I work long hours… already. Now, with the baby coming, I don't know how I'm going to find time to be a dad.
Rookie Dad

Of course, your child will require a large amount of time. A small amount of "quality" time doesn't cut it with kids. It is very unlikely this extra time is readily available to you, and so you must reorder your life.

Some men faced with tough circumstances get proactive early on. It is increasingly common to find fathers-to-be taking major steps to assure they can make their family their first priority by:

- Changing jobs or careers to enable more time at home
- Moving to reduce a long commute or large mortgage
- Cutting back on expenses or selling their "toys" - motorcycles, boats, sports cars - to reduce debt and financial demands

Many men, though, have little flexibility regarding work commitments. In addition, good choices are hard to make when you are dealing with an abstract notion of what your child will mean to you. Once the stork has landed and after your life has settled down a little, you'll be in a better position to assess your options. It is important that you remember to make the hard choices and not simply get comfortable in an untenable position in which you are not a significant part of your child's life.

The bottom line is that your baby must become your priority and you have to figure out how to make this happen. It's good to take your time in considering these issues during your mate's pregnancy; otherwise, you might get hit like a ton of bricks when your baby arrives.

Long Work Hours

Today's economic realities create difficult circumstances. Many careers demand long work hours, your new baby is going to add to your financial requirements, and your mate is going to be out of commission as an income generator for at least a while. You may run your own business on thin margins with no backup. Taking a month off when your baby is born may be as much an option as going to the moon; making sure you're available for the birth itself may be difficult.

Many veterans faced such circumstances, and you can learn from their ideas:

- Set the tone that you are here to be a player. Get involved early (change that first diaper!). Make the time you have count as much as possible.

- Strive for solutions that enable you to spend time with your child. Be creative. Figure out how to work from home, if possible.

- Play a strong role in providing emotional support for mom (such as calling her from work and asking how she is doing or letting her know how proud you are of her).

- When you are home, spend a good deal of time alone with your baby. Don't let your inexperience preclude this. Learn to do it by sending mom out with some friends; just do it.

- Make sure you are there for the birth. Many hospitals offer beepers for this purpose or will call on your cell phone.

- If you simply have no choice, do not allow yourself to feel diminished because you can't spend lots of time with your new child. Your work and income is your family's lifeline.

It is an ongoing challenge, as two-thirds of fathers report that they would spend more time at home with their children if they were financially able to do so.

I usually take over when I get home from work, but I'm tired and it takes a lot of patience not to become short-tempered with the baby.
Veteran Dad

Limited Finances

Many young families have to face the reality that there simply isn't enough money to go around. The cost of baby equipment and supplies alone can be startling. Advertisers regularly proclaim the fact you must spend a fortune just to get one child through high school, let alone college. You can feel like you are failing your offspring before he even gets out of the chute.

With new moms focused mainly on the new baby, dads are often left on their own to face the financial challenges, and can feel quite alone in doing so. Add in some of the following factors and dad can definitely feel like he's the one left holding the bag:

- Mom opts to stay home with the baby for an extended period, reducing income while costs rise.

- Mom spends money you do not have "on the baby" for discretionary items, oblivious of the budget.

- Dad responds by working longer hours, and mom resents dad's lack of involvement at home.

Being an avid photographer and camera buff I had saved up enough money to buy a 35mm camera. Well after the baby was born, I had to use that money to buy a bedside crib. For a while my wife thought I was bitter about the whole thing. But I told her that I accepted the fact that our son needed the money more than I did.
Veteran Dad

The stress this causes can be debilitating for a father who has inherited the expectation that he will be his family's provider. Extended work hours, justified by the added financial demands, can also lead to guilt as a new father grapples with the lack of time left for interaction with his child.

Developing Patience

The most important thing you need to have is patience with the baby and patience with your wife. I always thought I was a really patient guy until the sleep thing - lack of it - starts kicking in and it's your turn to get up and take care of this person who is just screaming, it is real easy to feel yourself get frustrated.

Veteran Dad

When veteran dads are asked to list the top three most important things about becoming a father, one of the first things they say is patience. Most men can find themselves frustrated, irritated and even angry when trying to cope with a crying baby when her reason is not apparent, or when responding to a critical spouse whose needs exceed any man's capacity for support.

While most new fathers expect the baby to become the main priority in the family, many are stunned at how little wifely attention or affection is left over for them. Dads also become frustrated with themselves as they struggle to both provide and participate.

It is particularly tough when you feel totally out of control, trapped and swept along by events. The temptation is to throw in the towel, and go have a beer with your friends. Which may not be a bad idea if that's what it takes to blow off some steam and regroup.

It's a long and frustrating road for the father who is not naturally endowed with a strong dose of patience. Step one is recognizing that this is one of the most important issues you will face.

So how do you develop composure and not sweat the small stuff? The best advice from veteran dads:

It has been the most wonderful as well as the most frustrating time of my life. You need to keep your sense of humor.

Veteran Dad

- Don't take it personally, it happens to most guys.
- Think constructively – come up with a plan.
- Find someone to talk to and vent – get it all out.
- Give yourself a break.
- Exercise is a good way to burn off stress.

Don't expect immediate returns; just hang in there. It will get better, much better.

Protecting Your New Family

Mom-to-be will be feeling vulnerable, and she and the baby she is carrying will be at times. Part of your job will be to protect them, and since men have done so throughout history, the intuition to do so comes naturally to new dads. If you find yourself worked up and angry at the driver tailgating you and your pregnant partner, or at the stranger who offered her some unsolicited advice, chalk it up to instinct. Just don't overdo it.

This is no time to be shy of course, so join your billions of ancestors, pick up your proverbial spear and ward off any threats that may come your way. Opportunities to protect her and your baby may include:

- <u>Poor drivers, including yourself</u>. Drive with an extra margin of safety and get a little compulsive about checking out the condition of her car. Remember that if you find yourself getting angry with any driver who does anything remotely dangerous, road rage does not protect your family, it endangers them.

- <u>Falling or toppling over</u>. Her baby and belly will continually grow, shifting her center of gravity and creating the danger of a fall that could hurt her or the baby. Clear out anything she could trip over on a night time trip to the bathroom. Use nightlights and make sure steps and railings are secure. Don't let her pick up anything heavy, and hold her arm to help her balance on walks.

- <u>Well-meaning relatives and friends</u>. Her own mother, your mother, her sisters, friends all want to help, and this networking is essential to mom's peace of mind. But sometimes one will go too far with inappropriate criticisms of how she is handling her pregnancy, to the point that it hurts. You may need to step in and, in the nicest way possible, tell them to back off.

- <u>Her own emotions and fears</u>. She can get upset and scared, and can feel incredibly alone even when surrounded by people who love her. She needs you more than anyone else to hug, comfort and reassure her. Even when it hits both of you that it's too late to turn back, she needs you to tell her it will be all right.

Keep Your Baby Safe
Little is worse than your child being seriously hurt, particularly if you could have prevented the injury. So after he arrives, keep your protective instinct honed and operational. Take care of the obvious, such as his car seat and baby proofing the house, and learn to be

vigilant about potential dangers such as sharp corners on the coffee table or a popped balloon he may eat. Make it your permanent role; while part of being a father is to teach your child to take risks, you also want to show them how to be smart and minimize the dangers.

Keep Yourself Safe

For your child, little is worse than something bad happening to dad, and of course you will want to be around to finish the job. Male pre-baby behavior tends towards risk-taking macho, so you may need to rethink some of your activities and tendencies. Many dads continue to jump out of airplanes, dive to serious depths in the ocean, and climb high mountains. It's just that those who do get fully trained, strictly observe weather guidelines, and set their parachutes to open above 1000 feet. For most of us, dad safety has to do with more mundane matters such as moderating our alcohol intake, assessing our driving behavior, and following safety precautions around equipment. Be careful out there.

Welcome to Serious Manhood

It's an incredibly awesome thing because you're constantly thinking about the responsibilities that you're dealing with. You're faced with the reality that you're going to be raising something and you're going to be an influence on a new person in the world.
Veteran Dad

Becoming a father is the ultimate rite of manhood for those who step up to the challenge. It is an individual event – we are not part of a team in which commitment and solidarity with our buddies is a driving force. Whether we succeed or fail is entirely up to us. Add it all up and a more rigorous trial could not be developed.

It clearly takes a man to raise a child. Staying up with a crying baby, working without sleep, changes in your relationship with your mate, needing to earn more and still do your part at home, rarely having time for yourself, the demands of protecting, guiding, and being a role model to our children - there are times you must dig deep for strength just to get through. And at times, having failed, you must dust yourself off and get up and try again. And again, if necessary, as this baby will always be your son or daughter.

Fatherhood is indeed an awesome responsibility, and presents each of us, no matter our size, age, education or income, a unique opportunity to be a hero to someone we love. The true measure of a man is how well he performs as a father, and ultimately, we measure ourselves in terms of our effort. As men, at some point in our lives, we want to know what we are made of. As a father, you will get your chance to find out.

Welcome to serious manhood.

7

Pregnancy: The Warm Up

The time between hearing "Honey, I'm pregnant" and "Oh my God, I think I felt a contraction," is a warm-up period for the rest of your life.

Remember that most men start off slowly, sorting out and thinking through all the implications, while moms quickly ramp up to light speed. The circumstances are similar to being left in the dust in with the planning of the wedding after she accepts your proposal for marriage. Both events take about nine months, except this time she wants you to be very involved.

Keeping up with the pace she sets is impossible. Since burning out and quitting is not a viable option for you, the answer is to stay in the race by taking shortcuts. Like the runner who took a cab for parts of the New York Marathon, you keep track of the race, show up periodically and make sure you are there at the finish line. All's well that ends well during the warm up period, as long as you are ready to go into action once the baby arrives.

The hormonally driven physical and emotional impacts of her pregnancy may be intense, and she will depend on you to help her get through the rough patches on the road. It may just be up to you to save her from herself as she's started on the second jar of pickles, or if she's sneaking a cigarette in the bathroom.

Raging Hormones

The hormones will likely drive her, and in turn, you, to distraction. Essentially, her chemical composition changes and she becomes – well – different.

Pregnancy alters her hormonal makeup and her reactions may be all over the board. Large releases of hormones include progesterone, which may make her tear up at the slightest provocation, and estrogen, which may make her smile.

There I was at the ice cream shop, reading off all the flavors into my cell phone, while she waited to hear one that triggered a new round of cravings. They should develop a pregnant mom flavor with pickles mixed in; it would save us guys a lot of time.

Rookie Dad

I have also learned to have patience with my wife; she's got a lot of hormones running through her and has a lot of apprehensions too. I'm the one with the easy job of being able to kind of sit back, and she is the one who is actually pregnant.

Rookie Dad

Not every new mother suffers severe mood swings with unexplained bouts of sadness or anger and uncontrollable urges to eat chocolate. All of this is normal, some cases are worse, and in many cases the happy couple gets along just fine as they anticipate their new child.

But many women do suffer moderate to severe mood swings. The thing to know is that your mate is not taking the opportunity to be a psycho brat. There really are major physical changes happening to her body.

Hormones also have their positive effects – in fact, they are creating the ideal environment for your baby to grow and thrive. Some hormones improve her health and even looks. Many women feel energized and positive during their second and third trimesters. Hormones also can cause her senses to be heightened. Some women actually find that their self-confidence soars – even as their body image collapses towards the end.

Don't Write It All Off as Hormones
A woman entering motherhood will experience powerful thoughts and feelings, and writing them all off as hormonally driven can be very frustrating for her. Encourage her to talk about those she feels strongest about.

Her Fears and Concerns

Most new moms find this a tough period of time, because in addition to undergoing physical changes, their lives have been turned upside down. They are expected to perform proficiently in a role for which they generally have little experience, and they tend to worry about everything.

Intense fretting about the health and safety of her developing baby is common. The slightest indication anything may be wrong will weigh heavily upon her, requiring your reassurance that everything is OK, regardless of your own concerns.

If your partner has already experienced a miscarriage, the threat of another one may hang like a boulder precariously perched over your home. Again, reassurance is required, particularly if she is bottling up her anxiety inside. Remind her that most women who have miscarriages go on to have successful births.

Moms also worry about the impact of motherhood, especially if her career is in jeopardy. Other fears concern the extraordinary responsibility of having a baby. Due to the mandatory changes occurring in her life, she can lose her sense of identity, which can be very scary. Talk to her, tell her what a wonderful mother she is going to make, and that you will help her get her life back by working with her to raise your child.

It seems rational that she accept the fact that her figure is history for awhile, along with her wardrobe. But this does not come easily to a pregnant woman who is surrounded by beautiful and skinny cover girls on every magazine she sees. Tell her how beautiful she is.

Expectations
As her baby's birth draws closer, a mom-to-be typically draws up mental blueprints that feature her ideal notions for the baby's personality and characteristics. These might also lay out what she perceives as the ideal role for you, as a dad, and for herself. The pregnancy provides a long preparatory process for well defined expectations; they rarely meet reality, of course, particularly for moms who envision a peaceful and angelic baby and end up with a fussy one. Dads also rarely meet her idealized expectations, and her expectations of herself usually fall apart within the first few exhausting weeks as a mom.

Scared About the Birth
In the last months before delivery, a mom's fear of giving birth occupies a large piece of her mind. A wide array of normal fears visit almost all mothers to be. They include having a stillbirth, not being able to bear the pain, the baby getting stuck or having to deliver the baby alone. Her fears can show up in nightmares; some moms report dreams of giving birth to puppies or kittens. (Moms will always win the weird worries contest.)

The absolutely best antidote to fear and anxiety is for both of you to attend childbirth education classes. You can also watch birth programs on the TLC Channel. If her worries are so intense that they trouble you, suggest that she consider some counseling, or mention it to her doctor or the nurse.

Her Highs and Lows

In addition to the worries, she also has a lot to be happy about, and with hormones supercharging her ups and downs, you can be in for a real roller coaster ride with a lot of ups and downs. Be ready for her mood swings, as she can turn on a dime.

The highs include the feeling of creating a baby, a new life inside her and the love affair that begins to develop. Hearing his heartbeat and seeing him on a sonogram make this love more real, but nothing compares with feeling him move inside her.

She may feel him faintly at first, a flutter easily mistaken for a rumbling stomach. As he gets stronger, and she realizes that what she is feeling is her baby, healthy and strong, she may swoon with excitement and even relief. When she first says "put your hand here," be patient because you likely won't be able to feel him at first. "I think I felt something" and a hug is an appropriate response.

Later on when you do feel your baby move, a genuine "wow" works well. Still later, when you find it amazing how hard your baby can kick, it will be "wow," indeed.

And of course the biggest high of all: your baby's birth. After all the worries and the pain, this one is indescribable.

Showing up means being there, sharing the experience and enjoying her highs. Don't blow it off because it is not be happening as intensely for you. Take any opportunity to thank and congratulate her for nurturing and protecting your child, and tell her she is going to be a wonderful mom. More hugs.

Try to roll with the punches that come with the lows. And don't take them personally. One of the most prevalent comments at Boot Camp, after the rookies share their stories of what's up with mom, is "I thought it was just me" who was getting a raw deal. Having a lot of company in common misery makes it eminently more endurable. And when it is suggested that "part of our job is to serve as her punching bag" to help her exorcise her frustrations, the rookies take it on as a challenge.

Getting Ahead of Her Curveball

New dads are generally way behind moms on the pregnancy learning curve. Moms are out of the blocks and halfway down the track before us men figure out that we have a lot of ground to cover. Some conflict is inevitable, particularly if you are not exactly thrilled initially with the news. To make the best of these new circumstances, you need to devise your own personal strategy for getting into the game on your own terms.

Think It Through
Keep the big picture in mind, which is the ultimate well being of your baby, your relationship with your wife, and the job you do as a father. Many issues during pregnancy are blown out of proportion (amplifying Mozart through mom's tummy, book length birth plans, designer nursery furniture, etc.). Others are beyond your control, and you won't be able to fix them (e.g., moms moods are chemically driven reactions to her pregnancy, and they will go away on their own).

Save some energy for when it really counts – after the contractions hit and the two of you take your baby home alone. This is when you want to be hitting on all cylinders; don't burn your energy up being ticked off at her.

Little Things Count
And they count a lot. She wants to know you care, and little indications reassure her that you do. Choose your targets, and regardless of her (or your) mood, periodically try something like:

- A backrub out of the blue.
- A trip to the store for something she needs or wants.
- Ask her about her pregnancy symptoms (insomnia, swollen feet) and let her talk.
- Note issues that make mom nervous and make sure they are addressed at the next doctor visit.

You will never keep up with her reading, but if you scan one of her favorite books, you will surprise her with your knowledge. You'll know more than she would ever expect you to.

Ask Her to Be Specific
The predominant complaint of first time moms-to-be is that their mates are not "involved." This can mean a lot of different things, so ask her to tell you exactly what she has in mind. Specific ideas are much easier to deal with, and asking her to come up with them will help her understand that there is no way that you can be as involved as she is.

Don't Be a Spectator On the Sidelines
It is easy to get overwhelmed, pushed aside and bewildered. with all that is going on. The result is you lose your bearings and end up going along for the ride – a spectator on the sidelines, waiting to be told what

In the last three months I have discovered more emotions than I even thought I was capable of. To add to what others have said about being scared, I would add the word shitless!

Rookie Dad

to do when you need to help lead the charge. It happens, but when it does, focus on getting back into the game. Find your own path, the one that works for you.

What to Expect by Trimester

We are cheating by giving you the rundown by trimester, so consider this the Cliff Notes for *What To Expect* and remember every word (even if you are reading this in the third trimester).

First Trimester
From the point of conception, her body begins to react even though her pregnancy is not apparent. A wide range of symptoms can accompany pregnancy; some of the physical and emotional changes that she is likely to experience in the first three months are:

I went thru morning sickness, food cravings, weight gain, etc. It was weird, but it made me feel closer to her.
          Veteran Dad

* Nausea and vomiting
* Frequent urination
* Tiredness
* Breast tenderness
* Mood swings
* Odd tastes, cravings
* Heightened sense of smell
* Weight gain

During the first trimester it is imperative for mom to take care of herself. No smoking or alcohol, good nutrition, prenatal vitamins, moderate exercise, and plenty of rest make for a healthy pregnancy. If she does not have one, she needs to find a doctor (ask around). She should make an appointment for her first prenatal visit at about eight weeks. If at any time you have concerns about your mate's condition — unusual pain, bleeding, etc. — call her doctor.

Prenatal care is essential as this is the most crucial time in your baby's development. This is also when he is most vulnerable to harm from alcohol, x-rays and other toxins, so help her stay informed and protected.

Second Trimester
In the next three months, some of her first trimester symptoms like nausea and fatigue tend to subside, although not entirely. They are replaced by a variety of new symptoms:

* Renewed energy
* Emotional contentment

- First fetal movements
- Headaches
- Heartburn, hemorrhoids, constipation
- Leg cramps, especially at night
- Swelling of legs, feet, and hands
- Skin, hair, and nails change
- Clumsiness, forgetfulness
- Impaired vision
- Faintness, dizziness
- Varicose veins

I can always tell that a guy has attended a Boot Camp class. He displays more confidence in caring for his baby and partner.
Laura, Maternity Nurse

Her body is definitely taking on a pregnant shape, and she'll probably need to start wearing loose or maternity clothes. She should have her energy back, and with it a sense of emotional well being. She may feel a return of libido (enjoy it while you can!). She'll be feeling the baby move now. Wait a few more weeks, and you will too.

Third Trimester

In the final three months, her previous symptoms continue and magnify:

- Frequent and urgent urination
- Hip and pelvic pains
- Backaches
- Sleeplessness
- Shortness of breath
- Impatience and frustration
- Braxton-Hicks (false alarm) contractions may begin
- Anxiety over approaching delivery
- Disturbing dreams about the baby

Although she's in the home stretch, she feels more anxious now than ever, with her energy level dropping and concerns about preparedness rising. She may waiver between feeling completely enthusiastic and completely anxious.

Birth preparation classes are standard and important, not only so you'll both have a better understanding of what to expect during labor and delivery, but also to ease your fears of the unknown.

During the last month, she will probably be examined weekly. This is a very exciting time, but also a tough one for those who are working during this period. (Doctors routinely place moms on disability at this point.) With everything that is going on, she may have no desire to go to work and will find it difficult to focus on her job. Her physical condition will also make it difficult. The final month may last from two to six weeks, with any extra weeks seeming like a month each.

How Dad Can Help

The fundamentals: talk to her, understand her as best you can, don't take her anger personally, and show her you care. Some moms-to-be could use a lot more, and you will want to focus on her symptoms for which you can do the most good. Suggestions include:

Nausea (Morning Sickness)
It hits most new moms, it comes early in her pregnancy, and can happen anytime of day. Take notice if she loses her appetite or can only handle a few bites, because this can quickly progress to losing her lunch. While food may seem to be the problem, eating food that she can handle is the antidote. You can help by:

- Help her get to the bathroom, and help her clean up.
- Brainstorm with her on foods she might try (fish, nuts, fruits, vegetables).
- Indulge her cravings by keeping them stocked.
- Encourage her to eat smaller meals more frequently, and to eat slowly.
- Help her stay hydrated by keeping bottled water around.
- A prenatal vitamin taken at night may alleviate symptoms of morning sickness.

Backache
Weight gain, a shifting center of gravity, inactivity, inability to stretch, and a growing baby pushing her pelvic structure open; all conspire to wreck havoc on her back. And painkillers are generally not permitted due to their effect on the baby. You can help by:

- Back rubs, using the most effective technique you can develop (with serious pain and permitted no drugs, she may literally beg for backrubs every couple of hours at night).
- Help her find support straps for pregnant moms that lift her belly.
- Look into other resources specifically for backache related to pregnancy.
- Buy her a body pillow so she can swing one leg and one arm over it.
- Ask her doctor what else you can do.

Lots of anxiety - we dealt with early contractions, extended bed rest, steroid therapy, loss of feelings of movement. We experienced an emotional rollercoaster.
Veteran Dad

We were overdue, and the weight estimate had the baby at a little over 10 pounds. The doctor said, "gee we have got to get this baby out one way or another," so they decided to get another ultrasound from the specialist, and she was guessing 9.5 pounds. We were very much involved in the decision making process the whole way, and it ended up that we induced labor and our daughter was only 8.8 pounds, and we had a natural birth. The point is to consider all the facts and decide things early.
Veteran Dad

Sore Breasts

They start growing early in pregnancy and keep growing, often causing pain and tenderness. You can help by:

- Encourage her to get a special pregnancy support bra.
- Offer to massage them, perhaps using her stretch mark prevention lotion. Stay away from her nipples.
- Pour her a warm bath.
- Be very gentle in love making; if she asks, place her breasts off limits until the soreness subsides.

Mood Swings

While they are a natural by-product of hormonal and lifestyle changes, her mood swings can be confusing to both of you. You can help by:

- Remind her (and yourself) of their natural causes, and that they will pass.
- Don't get sucked into arguments, practice patience, count to 10, count to 10 again.
- Help her get enough rest, time alone, and exercise.
- Reassure her it will all work out and she will be a great mom.

Ask the Guys in Childbirth Class

Or your friends or brothers who are fathers. Ask them what works with their wives. Trade stories about your own experiences and see what they suggest. Blow off steam and laugh it off. If the experienced fathers say they didn't have any problems, you are witnessing the mind's natural ability to repress traumatic events. Look forward to this yourself.

> **Borrow Her Bible**
>
> In the realm of the expecting, life is lived month-by-month. This has been officially decreed and is codified in the bible of Expecting Land, *What To Expect When You're Expecting* by Arlene Sisenberg and Heidi Murkoff, 1996. If you expect expecting life to be endurable, you should borrow her bible and review at least the highlights. It is best to review the month before it occurs, and pick out something to help her with or ask her about. Avoid reorienting your whole life into this month-by-month framework, as your weekends will no longer exist.

Use Your Imagination

Men tend to be creative, and this is definitely a time to be thinking out of the box. Call her from the ice cream store and read her off the flavors. Make a cradle for your baby if you can, or paint stars and rainbows on the ceiling in the nursery. Buy some tiny bootees and ask mom if she knows anybody they might fit.

Go to Her Doctor Visits

This is probably the single most important thing you can do during the pregnancy, as visits with her obstetrician get you personally connected with what's going on both with mom and your baby. Your being there lets her know she is not alone.

Important Visits
Her appointments will likely be monthly for the first five months and then ramp up to weekly visits during the last month. Go to as many of those that occur early in the pregnancy as you can, since you never know what you might miss. Later on they become routine. Important visits include:

- The doctor's confirmation of her pregnancy.
- Hearing your baby's heart beat (third month or so).
- Seeing him on the sonogram or ultrasound (about the fifth month). Visual confirmation kicks feelings of fatherhood in for most guys; be sure to ask the technician for a picture. Ultrasounds for non-medical reasons, such as those offered at shopping mall kiosks, are not recommended due to potential risks.
- Make sure you are there if an amniocentesis or other procedure to test for birth defects is necessary, or if there are any concerns regarding the health of your baby. The implications are enormous; she will likely be scared and will need you to be there with her.

If you are unable to go to any visit, be sure to ask her what happened.

Talk to Her Doctor
When you are with the doctor, don't be shy about asking questions. If you are being ignored, get assertive. This is your family the OB is dealing with. Keep the focus on mom, and first make sure she is getting her questions asked and answered. Important questions include:

- Concerns about mom or the baby.
- What should I be looking out for regarding mom?
- What should I encourage her to do (or not do)?
- Concerns you personally have regarding the birth.

If you get to know the OB and nursing staff, they will help you get fully engaged in the process during pregnancy and birth. Asking how you can help makes you part of the team, and they will be happy to help you out if you request their advice. During the birth, effective communication, especially if problems arise, is much easier if you and the doctor know each other.

You Do Not Need to View Everything

At some point during the visit her doctor will conduct a pelvic exam with her lying on her back with her feet in stirrups. This is not prime time for your involvement, so if either you or your partner (ask her) are uncomfortable with your being there, step outside the room. If you remain in the room, station yourself at head of the table, where you can be a welcome distraction and a source of comfort for your partner.

We did not need or want time apart. We wanted to go through this pregnancy together until delivery.

Veteran Dad

Remember it Is Her Doctor

The relationship between a pregnant woman and her doctor is a special one that requires a high degree of trust and some confidentiality. You do not need to be with her at every moment. Consider asking her if she wants to talk with her doctor alone. Respect her wishes.

When to Call Her Doctor

It is also important to clarify the circumstances under which you should call the doctor. Ask what conditions (e.g., bleeding, serious illness) should prompt a call. When should you call? What is the best way to communicate on non-emergent issues? (email, phone) What kind of issues can the nurse handle?

I'm really worried about my wife and baby's health. I've been to all the doctor's visits. My wife's gone through all these tests to make sure the baby's okay. But I still worry about some of the things that might go wrong in the delivery room. I really don't care if the baby is a boy or girl. I just want it to be healthy.

Rookie Dad

The bottom line on when to call the doctor is whenever you have serious concerns about mom's or the baby's health. If you or mom "aren't sure and don't want to bother the doctor," you may end up with serious regrets. If you call too much, the doctor will know how to handle it. Be respectful regarding when you call, of course.

If you are seriously concerned about mom's state of mind or behavior, call the doctor, or at least talk to the nurse. Avoid embarrassing mom to the extent possible, but make sure the important issues facing your new family are effectively handled.

If something happens, such as a fall or excessive bleeding that requires an emergency visit to her doctor or the emergency department; immediately drop everything and go with her.

Mom and Your Baby's Health

Pregnancy is a great motivator for breaking old habits and getting fresh air and exercise. A baby in her womb places great responsibilities on mom regarding her personal health. As soon as pregnancy comes into the picture, she needs to abstain from a variety of pleasures, and perhaps adopt a health regime that a vegan might find extreme.

You have responsibilities as well, and if mom has difficulty dealing with hers, you have even bigger ones. The tougher issues you may have to deal with include:

Smoking

I use to smoke two packs a day. When my baby was born, I walked out of the hospital and threw the cigarettes away. Every time I wanted to smoke, I would pick my daughter up and look into her eyes.

Veteran Dad

Toxins in cigarette smoke enter a mother's lungs and bloodstream, and then pass through the placenta to the developing fetus. Smoking increases the risk of miscarriage up to 80%, and causes low birth weight, developmental delays, diabetes, obesity and colic. This includes smoking marijuana as well as second hand cigarette smoke. A baby provides mom a great reason to quit. Give her some tools and suggestions to help.

Alcohol

Recent research has shown that even small amounts of alcohol can be dangerous for a developing fetus. Drinking during pregnancy can cause developmental and neurological problems, including deformities of the face and limbs, and brain abnormalities. This can happen even after one drinking binge, especially early in the pregnancy. Mom needs to clear any use of alcohol with her doctor, and you may need to help her stay within the limits by passing on the drinks yourself or taking her to the movies instead of the party.

Drug Abuse

Casual drug use by mom, with a baby in her womb, is by definition drug abuse. Any problem with drugs is critical to the health of your child and needs to be handled. Drugs used by mom during pregnancy and breastfeeding cause all kinds of damage to babies, including being born addicted. Mom, after her baby is born and her motherhood instincts are fully engaged, will never forgive herself. This in itself may jeopardize her ability to care for your child.

Other Drugs

There are many prescription and over-the-counter drugs that may be off limits to mom during pregnancy and breastfeeding. This includes many that seem vital - like pain medication for serious back pain as birth nears - which can make her life very tough. It can also include simple decongestants, cough syrups or constipation medication. Be sure to read the warnings on the label, encourage her to check with her doctor, and be prepared to help her get through whatever is causing her to want the medications. (Her doctor should give her safe non-prescription medications for colds, coughs and fevers.)

Dads Need to Handle Business Too

Regular partying is one of the casualties of fatherhood. Drug and alcohol abuse, whether illegal or not, is definitely out, as they are fundamentally incompatible with raising children. If you smoke, now is the time to quit, as second hand smoke is no better than the first hand variety. Easier said than done of course, but a baby can provide a strong motivation to get it handled. Especially when one considers the likelihood of passing such habits on to your kids.

Other Potential Dangers for Pregnant Moms

There are many, and include:

- Dieting, especially fasting, can deprive a baby of needed nutrients.
- Weight gain to the point of obesity.
- Exposure to toxic cleansers, pesticides, and insecticides.
- Exposure to hair dyeing chemicals, nail lacquers or paint fumes.
- Handling hamsters or cleaning the cat's litter box during pregnancy can result in serious problems from parasites.
- X-rays, even dental x-rays are linked to underweight babies and other problems and should be avoided unless absolutely necessary.
- Hot tubs, saunas and steam rooms can lead to overheating. A body temperature above 102.6° in the first trimester can harm a fetus.

Be protective of her, particularly with toxic substances or anything else that might endanger her or the baby.

Hazing of Pregnant Mates

From the moment she announces her pregnancy, she will become a target for unsolicited advice and birth horror stories that must be part of an ancient maternal hazing ritual. Perfect strangers will feel free to feel your mate's belly in the check-out line at the supermarket like she is public property. Look out for her, and if necessary, protect her.

Making Love

The bottom line is that morning sickness, fatigue, fear of hurting the baby, extreme emotions, and her changing body will severely cramp your spouse's sexual desire. It might resurface in spades during the second trimester, only to dissipate once again, and then expire altogether at birth, after which it may slowly resurrect over a long period of time.

If you have a strong sex drive, you are likely in for a long, frustrating time. While her declining interest and ability regarding sex are driven by the fact she is carrying your baby, you are still a red blooded male with needs.

Now that we have your attention, let's work on how to make the best of a tough situation, as a less than constructive approach will make it worse. Education is key.

Safe Sex
It is generally safe to continue intercourse throughout the duration of the pregnancy, as long as it's comfortable, there's no sign of bleeding, and there are no continuous contractions. In fact, her doctor may okay sex as a means of inducing labor. Make sure you ask about limitations or cautions. Be gentle and avoid aggressive, deep thrusting.

Many Factors at Play
Most pregnant couples experience a growing gap in their intervals between intercourse. Sex gets more complicated and problematic due to a variety of factors. The physical factors, including a growing baby in very close proximity, sickness, fatigue and major weight gain, are apparent. Less so are diminished desires due to pregnancy hormones, and her changing emotional makeup, which are the basis of most women's sex drive. All factors count.

Your Issues May Be the Issue
While some men are aroused by the changes wrought in their mates' bodies, others are turned off. You may have to try harder to maintain a mutually enjoyable sex life during pregnancy. Shifts in desire for both you and your partner throughout a pregnancy can contribute to feelings of being out of sync with each other.

Understanding and Patience are Essential
First, don't take it personally, as she is not rejecting you; she wouldn't want to make love to at least 24 of *People Magazine's* "Sexiest Men Alive" either. Try to maintain your perspective on what is most important – she's carrying your baby. Try exorcising your frustrations with exercise in the form of sports, work outs, long runs, and perhaps long, hot showers.

Lots of Affection

Affection that does not lead to sex (a quick kiss and hug and then walk away, a walk holding hands) shows you love and care about her, and should be part of your basic support strategy for your pregnant mate. Such "warm-ups" also set the stage for a romance; make sure you take time to do it right with a focus on her needs, which includes making love versus having sex.

Get Creative With Comfortable Sexual Positions

In the last half of the pregnancy, the weight of your body on top may be too heavy for her swollen belly and tender breasts; and in fact it may be harmful. Try it with her sitting on top, an alignment that works, is fun and gives her a sense of being in control. Also try spooning, or any position that may work, and be prepared to laugh at the logistical challenges. Take time for foreplay as in kissing and massage, and keep it fun and lighthearted.

You Might Get Lucky

Her interest in sex may pick up in her second trimester. She might end up chasing you. Really. With increased blood flow to the pelvic area, many women experience greater sensitivity and heightened, more powerful orgasms during this period. Pregnancy hormones can also make her feel sexier than ever. If it happens, indulge her and enjoy it while it lasts.

If She Asks You If She Is Getting Fat

She will likely wait to ask until she is waddling around like a walrus. No matter how many times she asks, no matter how big she gets, and regardless that there is no other conceivable answer than yes, the answer is "no, you are more beautiful than ever." She simply does not want you to acknowledge the obvious no matter how obvious. She wants to be wanted. Be creative with new responses; otherwise she may think you are not being honest with her.

See Chapter 18, *Re-Igniting Romance*

Romance is a huge issue for new parents, and your approach during her pregnancy will be a predictor for how it goes after the baby arrives. A comprehensive discussion of romantic challenges and strategies is provided in Chapter 18, *Re-Igniting Romance*, and education is your best bet for a strong, ongoing love life.

The most difficult times were the countdown and passage of time as we marked off the calendar to the improving chances of a successful full term delivery. Also - "no sex"!

Veteran Dad

Countdown to Delivery

As her due date nears, and as she focuses on her hopes and fears regarding the baby and delivery, your wife will likely become introspective. Don't worry if she isn't very talkative; it's like she is getting psyched up for a big game, and they don't get any bigger.

You on the other hand may be ready to talk about issues that have been percolating in your own mind for a while. Call a friend or brother; this might be a great time to connect with your father.

After nine months of waiting, myths about triggering labor may become a semi-serious topic she will talk about – even horseback riding may seem like a good idea, especially if her due date comes and goes. Indulge her by acting on a myth or two – try salad or sex, but keep her off the horse.

As D-Day Approaches
The last few weeks are when she needs you the most. The bigger her belly gets, the more she will need help doing even the simplest things, like tying her shoes. Make sure she does not try to pick up a heavy object or carry a bag of groceries. Mostly she needs to know you will be there for her.

Plan on spending most of your time with her, avoid trips away if possible, and stay in touch by phone. Make sure she knows how to contact you immediately if she needs to.

False Alarms
False labor (Braxton Hicks contractions which stretch the uterus to accommodate a full term baby) is common and can be frustrating. You get excited thinking "this is it," and then go back to waiting. They feel like contractions to her because they are, but she experiences no labor pain and they stop. To play it safe, contact her doctor's office.

Getting Ready for Your Baby

In addition to hearing her heartbeat and feeling her kick, spend some time doing things that will help you connect and feel ready once your little one arrives:

My wife has had a good pregnancy; we have done Lamaze class, breastfeeding class, and I thought I was really ready. Then I came in here (Boot Camp) and saw those babies. My hands started sweating, and I was like "Oh God," so I am not really ready for this. I know it is going to happen and I have seen all the films but until I have a kid of my own I don't know what I am doing.

Rookie Dad

- Get some experience with a baby, any baby, especially alone with another father you know. Just hold the baby for a while, talk to him, and check out how he will stare at you and fully check you out. Try calming him if he's fussy by rocking or walking with him.

- Go out by yourself and buy something for your baby. A birthday gift just from you. It can be inexpensive; perhaps booties to keep her tiny feet warm.

- Think of doing things together with your child as he grows up.

Finally, visualize yourself holding your brand new baby, looking down at him in your arms, saying "I am your father". Amazing.

PART TWO: RUBBER HITS THE ROAD

8

Getting Ready

You will need to be prepared to help your partner through the birth and to care for your baby once at home. Prior to the delivery, there are things that need to be done: we suggest you include the priorities outlined in this chapter.

Preparing for fatherhood, of course, goes way beyond building the nursery and packing for the hospital. The most important preparation will take place in your mind, so give yourself plenty of thinking time.

She came 5 weeks early. We were not even close to being ready.
Veteran Dad

Getting a Handle on Finances

Sort through your family's income and expenses so that you can get a handle on making ends meet. Put a simple budget together. If mom is spending money you don't have on baby clothes, a budget in black and white may be your best line of fiscal defense.

When you first run the numbers, if costs outweigh revenue, consider it normal. Most couples find that adding a baby's costs to a current lifestyle, while subtracting mom's income, doesn't add up. One way or the other, though, they work it out and have enough to meet their family's essential financial needs.

One or Two Incomes
About half of new moms return to work within a few months after their babies are born. On the other hand, you and/or your partner may want her to quit her job and stay home to take care of the baby, and do without her income. Either arrangement can be tough, at least through the first year, with serious tradeoffs involved.

Get ready for a roller coaster ride. You try to plan, but your baby will rule.
Veteran Dad

Think it through and talk to her about available alternatives. She and/or you may want dad to stay home and take care of the baby, and do without your income. Perhaps she (or you) could work part time with a flexible schedule, with the baby in day care a few days a week. Or perhaps one of you could work out of the house.

Alternatives regarding work for moms and dads evoke strong societal pressures and many people may have an opinion. The only one that counts is the one you and mom develop as you determine the best way to support your new family. Keep in mind this may not be fully resolved until well after the baby arrives, and even then it may change, so keep your options open.

Big Changes May be Appropriate

If you have a big mortgage that is dependent upon two incomes, you may want to reconsider being house rich even with a baby on the way. If you have a long commute that adds hours away from home on top of a long workday, you might want to look at employment or housing alternatives. Moving or changing jobs is increasingly common during the ramp up to "D-day."

Trading the sports car in for a van (serious pain here) may be necessary. On the other hand, since you and mom are going to be spending more time at home, a big screen TV may be a prudent purchase (make sure her favorite movie is playing when she first sees it).

Addressing these challenges together will get you on the road to working with mom to form your new family.

When Money Is Tight

Figuring on the new costs and reduced income, coupled with a tenuous job market, could cause you to wake up at three a.m. in a sweat. Financial worries are an inescapable fact for most fathers. The average cost of raising a child to age 18 is about $180,000. But there are many things you can do to keep your budget from becoming a runaway train:

- Talk with your partner about your concerns and map out a plan to stretch the dollars after the baby is born. Do it now, as it will be very difficult to find the time, energy and emotional focus to do it afterwards.

- Make sure you have health insurance. If your employer doesn't provide it and you cannot afford to insure your child, there are public programs that will help. Ask the hospital for information.

- Buy baby furniture second-hand, or borrow it. There are a great number of stores that recycle baby items – from clothing to strollers and car seats to cribs and playpens. Lots of it is brand new – castoffs from baby showers or duplicate gifts.

I liked living near the beach, but we moved to reduce my commute as well as our mortgage so Mary doesn't have to go back to work for a while.
Rookie Dad

My wife and I are really concerned about our financial situation. We just bought a new house and didn't consider the cost of caring for a baby…Things like diapers, clothes, accessories into our budget. I guess it's time to sit down and really crunch the numbers and find a way to cut down on our expenses so we can make it work.
Veteran Dad

- Buy carefully. Remember that most baby furniture and equipment outlives its usefulness after only a short while. A cradle may be obsolete in a matter of months, and while some babies never get tired of their swings and floor gyms, many never take to them at all (why the second-hand stores are so full of nearly new items).

- Mail out baby announcements to everyone you can think of. Many will want to send gifts, gift certificates or money. Make sure you have registered at a baby store or big department store so people will be able to get you what you want and need.

- Register with online sites, such as www.babycenter.com and you'll not only get great information, you'll also get coupons and discounts on baby stuff.

Health Insurance for Your Baby
Enacted by the U.S. Congress in August 1997, the state Children's Health Insurance Program (CHIP) is designed primarily to help children in working families with incomes too high to qualify for Medicaid but too low to afford private family coverage. All states and the District of Columbia offer health coverage through CHIP and Medicaid.

Preparing for the Unthinkable

As new parents, you will have the very heavy responsibility of making arrangements in case something happens and you are not there to care for your child. While doing this ahead of time is prudent, mom will be very sensitive to the notion of leaving her baby without a mother, so use your discretion. Major tasks include:

- Make out a will and arrange a living trust. If you have access to legal assistance, take advantage. If not, inexpensive on-line resources are available.

- Specify who will care for your child if you are both unable to do so. This may take some time to work out if an obvious choice is not available. Write it down and make sure that person knows they have been chosen and agrees to do it.

- Consider purchasing life insurance. Ask yourself how your family would support themselves if you were unable to do so.

See Appendix – *New Family Finance* for additional information.

Being a father is a commitment for life. The biggest one you'll make. You can say this, and agree with this, but it isn't real until you've had your own child for a while.

Veteran Dad

Getting Your House in Order

Building the Nursery
They call it nesting, and like birds, moms need the comfort of knowing a safe, warm place is ready when their baby arrives. Dads can really get into this as well, as it offers you an early opportunity to make a tangible contribution to your baby.

If you have a room that can function as the nursery, you've got your work cut out for you. Mom will have lots of ideas – you may have a few of your own – go with a plan that makes mom happy. This plan may change, of course.

If you don't have a spare room available, sit down with your wife and discuss options for how you can accommodate the baby. There are various alternatives; while your child is unlikely to notice the difference whether you build a Taj Mahal or put a laundry basket next to your own bed, mom will. Try to indulge her.

Some practical suggestions:

• Check out the room with the baby in mind. Is the window drafty?

• Visit it at different times of the day to check on where and when light from the sun hits (you don't want the sun to wake your baby or make him too hot).

• Also check on light from street lamps at night which may keep your baby up.

The basic list of furniture for a nursery includes a crib, changing table, chest of drawers, and a rocking chair or glider (with footrest).

Nursery Safety
The bottom line when building a nursery is safety and comfort for the baby. Be careful with used, hand-me-down, and foreign-made baby equipment. In some cases, these items are unsafe for your baby, both because of ever-changing safety guidelines and defects from use (such as missing parts).

Make sure the furnishings are safe for your baby. The Juvenile Products Manufacturers Association (JPMA) sponsors a safety-certification program; check for their seal. Sometimes an item that was

Get as much done as you can ahead of time. Getting the baby's room together and other stuff takes a lot out of you. A big mistake we made was not buying the mini-van before the baby was born. I tell you - going around on weekends with a newborn and talking to salesman - it's something you really don't want to go through. Get things done early so you can spend more time with your baby.
Veteran Dad

originally thought to be safe is far from it. For information on recalled products, call the U.S. Consumer Product Safety Commission hotline at 1-800-638-2772 or visit their website at (www.cpsc.gov)

Other safety considerations include:

- Pads for the changing table should have straps to keep the baby from wriggling off onto the floor. The table may also be equipped with safety rails.

- Avoid floor-length curtains or drapes; once your baby begins to crawl, he may grab them and pull them down on top of himself.

- Blinds with long pull-cords are also a no-no, especially looped cords, as a baby can easily get these wrapped around her neck.

Also, check out the house for loose railings, outside steps that are slippery in snow, exposed outlets, etc. It's difficult to regain footing while carrying a baby.

Crib Safety
If a crib is used, check it out for:

- Corner posts are dangerous because your baby's clothes can get caught on them. If posts are present, you can saw them off, making sure to sand the splintered edges. If your baby's crib has high posts for a canopy, they may not pose a problem. Use your best judgment.

- Bumper pads protect your baby from head injuries, but some experts warn against them. If you prefer to use them, make sure they fit around the entire crib, and snap into place in at least six places. Remove them once your baby can pull herself into a standing position.

- Use a snug-fitting mattress. You shouldn't be able to fit more than two fingers between the mattress and the sides of the crib, and avoid decorative cutouts that can trap the baby's head or limbs.

- Make sure the slats or posts are no more than 2-3/8" apart so your newborn doesn't get jammed in or slip through.

- If the crib has been painted by its previous owner, make sure the paint isn't lead-based, as babies do tend to chew on whatever's handy.

- Don't overlook cribs at grandma's or other babysitters' homes - the same rules apply.

Checklist: What Else to Have On Hand

Setting up the baby arsenal prior to his arrival is a basic dad duty. A checklist of what you may want in addition to nursery furniture is as follows:

When will my wife stop buying stuff?
Rookie Dad

Highly recommended by Boot Camp veterans
- Diaper Genie – eliminates the smell
- Bouncy seat (with sound and lights) – entertains and gets babies tired.
- Swing (battery operated) – puts your baby to sleep
- Soft chest carrier - feels great and puts babies to sleep
- Battery operated stick-on touch lights – convenient, not too bright for a baby or sleeping spouse
- Digital camera and/or video camera (See Resources-*Recording Your New Family*)

Standard Items
- Car seat (properly installed and ready to go)
- Bassinet or cradle – basically a small moveable alternative to the crib
- Baby bath tub with insert that helps hold newborns
- Mobile to hang over the crib
- Baby monitor – to hear your baby while in another room
- Boppy pillow – helpful for holding the baby while nursing or feeding
- Bathrobe for mom – a nice big, soft one
- Extras of everything – blankets, washcloths, pacifiers, hats, burp cloths, bedding, etc.
- Bottles and extra nipples
- Breast pump for nursing mothers
- Stash of diapers, wipes, diaper rash ointments
- (Apparently an incredible amount of designer baby clothes are also standard.)

Brace yourself for your first visit to a baby store, where it will become overwhelmingly clear that babies were invented as a marketing ploy, and your wife is the willing target. Your role is to pay for whatever she wants, carry it home and put it together (or figure out how it works).

You Buy Something for Your Baby

This may seem ridiculous if you are dealing with a runaway credit problem, but try going out by yourself and picking out something for your baby. Small and inexpensive if fine, as junior won't care. Perhaps some tiny booties, which are amazingly small, or her first baseball mitt,

Being a father has given me as incredible feeling of love that's really unique. It's deep, it's different, it's rewarding, and it's very special.
Veteran Dad

or whatever might mean something to you. Consider it an early bonding exercise.

Build Something for Your Baby
Men tend to like working with our hands, and building things can be reassuring when we're worrying about the challenges of a new baby. If so inclined, refinish a cradle, build a sled, or add a room (just kidding). Previously unfinished projects around the house can be disconcerting with a baby in the house, and you will have a lot less time to finish the job after junior arrives.

Getting Educated

Education is the key to being prepared: classes, books, talking with your mate and networking with other fathers all offer opportunities.

Childbirth Classes are Essential
Childbirth classes are a rite of passage, your transition into the parallel world of parenthood, and yes, you have to go. The more you know about the birth process, the better you will be able to help your mate handle your child's birth and the more you will be able to handle it yourself. So pay attention even if it's the end of a long day and the class material seems surreal.

Don't expect to know it all!

Veteran Dad

Going in knowing that your primary role is to provide essential and critical support to your partner will help you focus. When the time comes, she may be frightened and in serious pain. You will need to advocate for her and support her any way you can. If you understand what is going on and know what to do, you will be ready to do your part.

What You Can Expect to Learn
You'll learn about recognizing the signs of labor, when to call your doctor, relaxation and breathing techniques, the logistics of labor and delivery, pain medication alternatives, hospital procedures, surgical births (c-sections), basic breastfeeding information, and what to expect from a newborn. Most classes will show videos of a vaginal birth and a c-section, give you a tour of the hospital's birthing facilities, and the better ones will do a good job of outlining your role. You may also learn things about the female anatomy that you never imagined.

Get to Know Your Classmates

Reach out to your fellow class attendees, who are going through the same thing you are. Making the effort to get to know them can really make things more pleasant, and you and your wife will get the most out of the classes. You will find yourselves trading ideas and information with other couples and getting different perspectives, which will help you clarify your own.

Make New Friends

Many long term friendships start from sharing the experience of having a baby, and for a while you will have more to talk about with couples you meet in your childbirth class than your own friends. Consider inviting your new acquaintances to get together outside of class, and plan on staying in touch after your babies arrive.

Other Classes to Consider

Fathers have essentially been required to go to childbirth courses, but attended few other classes. Times are changing, though, as men conclude that any preparation for caring for a brand new baby is probably a good idea. Those who have attended the classes suggested below are glad they did.

Boot Camp For New Dads - Nothing beats sitting down with experienced new fathers who hand you their babies to practice on while they tell you what they have learned. Men who have attended consistently say this was the most helpful class they took.

Newborn Care - Having an expert show you and mom how to change, bathe, feed, and care for a new baby will give you a common set of skills and sense of confidence. This class will mean no "deer in the headlights" look when you are first home alone with your baby.

First Aid/CPR - The likelihood that you'll need to give your baby CPR is very, very small, but knowing how gives you a sense of being prepared for anything. First Aid is another matter, especially since a dad's role with his baby typically includes being lead rough-houser. At the minimum you will learn how to patch him up before mom finds out her baby got hurt.

Do I Really Need to Read All Those Books?

No. Reading this book will put you ahead of most guys, and reviewing one or two of your mate's books will put you way ahead as well as score you big points with her. We can suggest a few other books, depending upon your needs and reading capacity. Most books are designed as references, so just skim through them and become familiar with what they contain in case you ever need to find some information.

Here are a few book and websites that we can recommend:

Books For Dad
The Expectant Father: Facts, Tips and Advice for Dads-To-Be by, Armin Brott & Jennifer Ash, Abbeville Press, 1995/2001. Presents information for new fathers during pregnancy in month-by-month format made popular by the *What To Expect* series.

Breathe: A Guy's Guide to Pregnancy by, Mason Brown, Simon & Schuster, 2002. Will help you laugh off the tough stuff, and Mom may find it funny as well; get her laughing and it is all downhill from there.

Pregnant Fathers, Becoming the Father You Want to Be by, Jack Heinowitz, Ph.D., Andrews & McMeel 1997. An honest and down to earth look at coping with the concerns and deep emotions of fatherhood.

Helpful Websites For New Dads
Many web pages for fathers are actually just token offshoots from motherhood sites. Here are a few that fathers should find helpful:

www.newdads.com - The companion website to this book where you will find complementary and updated information.

www.babycenter.com - Lots of information with articles targeted at new fathers. Chat rooms for dads overrun by moms, though.

www.fathersforum.com - By Bruce Linton, a psychologist who has conducted classes and worked with new fathers for over a decade.

www.slowlane.com - A website for and by stay-at-home fathers.

Arranging Time Off Work

About 60 percent of new fathers are able to take time off work after their baby's birth, and of those, 75 percent take off 1-4 weeks. Since most time off is unpaid (unless there is vacation time owed), it can take some serious planning to figure out how to be there for your new family and get the bills paid at the same time.

Recommended Resource The National Center for Fathering provides a wealth of information for fathers of children of all ages. You can find them at www.fathers.com

I worked half time for 4 weeks rather than taking a strait two weeks off. We had some help at first but she was still exhausted in those last two weeks and I hate to think of how she would have handled it if I had not been there for at least half a day.
                    Veteran Dad

Consider Your Alternatives

If taking weeks of unpaid leave is not an option, consider the following alternatives:

- Save up and use your vacation time.
- Work half days, which can stretch out limited time off.
- Take off one midweek day each week for 1-2 months, which gives you time with your new child and gives mom a break she can plan on over a period of time.
- Ask other recent dads, particularly fellow employees, for their insights and suggestions.

Even if you can only get one day off, make the most of it, and make nights and weekends at home count by pitching in all you can with diapers, feedings and holding, rocking and walking your crying baby.

Negotiating With Your Employer

According to the Family and Medical Leave Act (check out www.dol.gov/dol/topic/benefits-leave/fmla.htm) companies with more than 50 employees must offer up to 12 weeks of unpaid leave for the birth or adoption of a child. Small companies are exempt from this law, and there are some other exceptions. Leave can be taken anytime in the 12 months after the birth, and it may be spread out rather than taken at one time (e.g., two weeks at first and then one day a week for a while.)

State laws apply as well, and many companies offer their own benefits, so ask around. Some suggestions for getting the best deal from your employer:

- Try working overtime now in exchange for time off when the baby arrives.
- Talk to your boss as far in advance as possible about using accrued vacation time.
- Ask your HR department or manager about other benefits your company might have.
- Check out your state laws and union benefits.

Consider Your Employer's Needs

A CEO of a small company who attended Boot Camp suggested that you put yourself in your boss's shoes and think of mutually beneficial solutions. Come up with ideas that enable you to get your job handled and take care of business at home, and your manager will likely provide you more flexibility.

I decided to forgo any promotions because I wanted to be a more involved dad. I used the Family Medical Leave Act and combined them with my vacation days so I could spend the first two months helping my wife take care of our new baby girl. I'm so glad I did because we got to spend some real quality time as a new family. Great thing about it was that my employer supported my decision and didn't have a problem with me taking so much time off work.
Veteran Dad

It is better to come to your employer prepared to be flexible than to simply say I am going to take X weeks off; and your employer will be more likely to work it out. It is about solutions.
Veteran Dad

If You Cannot Get Time Off Work

There are two major reasons new fathers want to be home for a while when their baby arrives:

- To help mom in caring for the baby, as two pairs of hands are definitely needed.

- To be part of your new family, right from the beginning, when a new baby, a new mom and a new dad all get to know each other.

Not all new fathers are able to take time off work to be with their partners and babies. Circumstances range from military obligations to the demands of your own business to simply not being able to afford it. If you are not able to do so, you will need to make sure the above issues are handled. The first is simple; make sure mom has enough help with the baby when you are at work, and pitch in when you are home.

The second is much more complex. A lot is made of dads bonding with their babies. But an even more important issue is the bonds a new family makes together, especially when they are first together. Mom needs to know you are her partner from the start, and more to the point, you need to feel like you are her partner and part of your new family.

Be there as much as you can. And when you are home, make the most of it, especially in caring for your baby. Make something important, like giving your baby a bath, your thing. Take her for walks in a stroller, or better, on your chest in a Snugli or something similar. Let mom know you wish you could be there more, and how much you appreciate her hard work in caring for your baby. Look for opportunities that will enable you to be home more.

> *We are expected to work 60 hours a week. One new father at my company quit and got another job. I am thinking I may have to as well.*
>
> *Rookie Dad*

Planning a Birth

The great thing about births today is that there are many choices of settings, pain relief, personnel, etc. You can basically plan a birth like you plan a wedding. The downside is that while most weddings go off according to plan, births tend to take on a life of their own. As a result, managing yours and especially your mate's expectations regarding the birth has become an important factor (e.g., even with an epidural, she may experience significant pain).

The Birth Plan

With so many options, determining and communicating her wishes (even more than a wedding, the birth is her show) requires that they be written down. This is called a birth plan, and it should accompany you into the hospital to be used as a reference for attending medical personnel.

The birth plan can address any issue that you want to be clear on with those involved in the birth, including whether she wants to have an epidural, who you plan to have attend during the birth, your wishes on a C-section, etc. Childbirth education classes will provide a great deal more information on birth choices and planning.

My mother-in-law and sister were in the delivery room with us. So it was kind of tough for me because I felt like all the women were watching me. And I'm the guy: if I make a mistake I'm going to be judged. But that went away real quick when I started focusing on my wife and the baby.

Veteran dad

Remember the birth plan is a "plan", and be prepared to deviate from it. Your wife may develop a different view on abstaining from an epidural as the labor progresses. Most doctors or midwives will adhere to a birth plan, but under certain medical conditions they may make the call to deviate where they see fit. But a plan is crucial, especially so you can be clear about your partner's and your own desires. It will be up to you to advocate for choices once it's time for the birth.

For a sample birth plan, and to fill one out online, visit http://birthplan.com

Define Your Choices

You have some options for participation as well, and the birth plan provides an opportunity to think them through:

- Do you want to cut the umbilical cord?
- Are there other ways you would like to participate in the birth?
- How soon after the birth do you want to hold your baby?
- Would you like the doctor to hand you the baby so you can give her to mom?
- If your baby needs to be taken anywhere, do you want to go with him?

Who Do You Want in the Birth Room?

The birth plan should incorporate guidelines you and mom set on the role of friends and relatives at the hospital. This is a special time for mom and dad to share, particularly with a first child, and the medical personnel provide all the necessary assistance. Stick with the guidelines and do not let anyone intrude. The nurses will be very helpful in this regard, as long as you ask them for their support.

It may seem like fun to have relatives or friends there to take pictures and video, but think carefully. It's difficult to ask people to leave once they are there. Birthing can be a messy, arduous, frightening process. A woman is exposed and not in control. If you both desire to document the great event, it might be wise to assign the task to a trusted and sensitive friend or relative and let all the others meet the baby after he's safely in his mother's arms.

Is a Doula Right for You and Your Partner?

In your childbirth classes you will hear about the benefits of hiring a doula, a professional labor assistant that provides supplemental assistance in the birth of your baby. A doula can be well worth the added cost ($200-600 depending upon region and extent of services), particularly if you have special needs regarding the birth, such as:

- Mom really wants to labor naturally, without analgesics to minimize the pain.
- Mom is scared of birth, and experienced assistance would give her needed confidence.
- Mom is delivering twins or triplets, or is trying to deliver vaginally after a previous cesarean birth, or there are other worrisome clinical issues.
- Dad, due to job requirements, may not be able to be there.
- Dad is scared of the delivery, and is worried that he won't be able to provide adequate assistance to mom.

Feeling helpless is one of my worst fears. Not knowing what to do when something unexpected happens.
Rookie Dad

Couples without special needs also use doulas, of course, with the upside being that mom is supported by a professional "coach," versus an amateur (you). The doula will take on your role as coach, which enables you to be an active participant but without all the responsibility.

The downside is that with a professional on hand, there is not much demand for an amateur. While some fathers-to-be may view this as an intrusion, most have reported they are able to relax and enjoy the birth experience knowing that mom is being taken care of.

This tradeoff may or may not be important to you and mom. If you decide to use a doula, interview them together, go with one that you both feel comfortable with, and make sure she is aware of your wishes regarding your role in the birth. If you have any concerns, seek out a couple of fathers your doula has worked with, and ask them about their experience and advice.

Talk It Over with Mom

An important aspect of a birth plan is that it requires you to discuss with your partner the major issues of the upcoming event. Communication between you and your mate is so important that anything that puts you in a situation where you have to talk is a good thing. This catalyst for communication cannot be over emphasized, and you should take full advantage.

The ride to and from childbirth classes also provides a great opportunity to talk with your wife about the issues raised, her feelings and concerns about the birth and a new baby, as well as your feelings. The classes will focus your attention on the realities of your baby's birth, and the more you talk them through, the more confident and prepared you both will be.

Making Arrangements at the Hospital

Pre-Register

One of the main tasks of preparation is hospital pre-registration, and most hospitals offer it. Make sure you do it. It allows you to fill out all the required paper work beforehand so that when you do arrive at the hospital with your baby on the way there are no forms to fill out and no waiting for admission. You'll be able to show up and very quickly be admitted and go directly to a labor room. Things to check on when you pre-register:

*   Health insurance – ask about any out of pocket costs or limitations.
*   Accommodations for you to stay with your wife at night.
*   Your baby's social security number application (called "Enumeration At Birth" for some bizarre bureaucratic reason). It will arrive several weeks after your baby does, and can actually be a pretty cool confirmation that you are really a father.

Become Familiar with the Place

Many hospitals will also include a tour of the hospital, including the labor delivery rooms and postpartum areas. It will enable both of you to get familiar with the surroundings. Fear is often the result of not knowing what to expect. Getting a handle on what is going to happen goes a long way to reducing anxiety for both of you.

You will probably get to see the birthing rooms and the surgical center for Cesarean births. Also the post-delivery room and the recovery rooms for Cesareans. Some hospitals have sleeping facilities, whether it's a cot or fold out couch. Some may have showers or even Jacuzzi tubs. The tour leader may also have literature with ideas on what to bring and comments about what will be happening through the whole process.

Ask Questions

The employees associated with the hospital's/mother-baby floor like to help people, so don't hesitate to ask. You can get detailed information on everything from hospital policies and procedures to where to park, where to enter the hospital (this can vary at different times of day and night), and what reception desk to go to.

Get an idea about where food is served. While mom will have meals brought to her, dads usually do not. So get an idea of the cafeteria facilities and the hours of operation.

Packing Your Hospital Bag

Pack for the hospital well in advance, because your baby may come early. Being ready a couple of weeks ahead of your due date is prudent.

Prepare a List

Get a list together of the items you want to bring and keep the list with your bag to double check before you head out. To put a list together, get ideas from the hospital staff and through birthing classes. Talk to other expecting couples or someone who recently delivered. Many of the books on pregnancy will offer suggestions on what to bring.

We can offer a "starter" list below for you. Add and subtract as you see fit:

- Everything your partner needs.
- Everything the baby will need, such as an outfit and blanket for the trip home.
- A few copies of your birth plan.
- Change of clothes, toothbrush and shaving kit for you.
- Comfortable shoes as you may do a lot of walking.
- Something to read to her

- Bathing suit for you — to help mom take a shower or bath to ease labor pains.
- Something to eat and drink; power bars and juice are suggested.
- Champagne—put your name on it and ask nurse to store in refrigerator.
- Camera (we suggest black and white film during delivery).
- Make sure you have some cash on hand.
- Have a folder ready with important documents – insurance cards, pre-admission forms and any other documents.
- Small boom box with her favorite music (if not provided by the hospital).
- Pen and pad of paper.
- Any pain easing tools recommended at your birthing classes – balls to squeeze, hot or cold packs, massagers, etc.
- Address book/list of phone numbers to announce birth.
- Calling card (you may not be able to use a cell phone inside your room).

Making a Dry Run

As the due date gets closer, make some practice driving runs to the hospital. Get an idea of how much time it takes to get there. Also be aware of traffic patterns. Determine if rush hour traffic may be a factor on your route and the hours when it may be thickest. Have an alternate route planned in case there is a traffic jam.

As you near the date keep your gas tank topped off. (A worst case scenario would be timing your wife's contractions in line for gas during rush hour.) While there is usually more than enough time to get to the hospital, a little bit of foresight can avoid making an exciting event into an overly stressful one, especially for a mom in labor.

Make sure your car is in good working order. Check the:

- Tires
- Battery
- Brakes
- Windshield wipers

Park in the visitor's lot; it would be very unfortunate to leave it in a restricted area and find it has been towed when you are ready to take your baby home.

Drive Gingerly and Watch the Bumps

Your trip to the hospital is not a NASCAR event; your practice runs and the real thing should be as smooth as possible because a woman in labor is extremely sensitive to sudden moves and even small bumps. A calm drive also helps mom stay calm and focused.

Install the Car Seat Early

Hospitals require your baby to be in a car seat for the ride home. This is no time to be fumbling with instructions and adjustments to the straps on these confounding things, while mom sits tired and waiting, perhaps with a crying baby. Install it early and get used to adjusting the straps; you will want to look like a pro when getting your baby situated for his first ride home. If you have any concerns about installing the seat correctly, consult a certified expert at a car seat fitting station. Visit www.nhtsa.dot.gov/people/injury/childps/CPSFitting to locate a station near you.

Final Checklist

You know where you're going, and you're packed and ready to go. Now is the time for some final preparations. While your doctor can name a due date, many times with very good accuracy, it is still just an estimate. The baby can come early or could come late. So put yourself in a position to be able to go at a moment's notice.

- Make sure you are able to be contacted at anytime during the day. Having a cell phone or pager is recommended. And have it on at all times. Getting a cell phone, even if temporarily, for your wife could be a good idea, too.

- Make arrangements with your work in terms of time off, transitioning workload or possibly designating someone to cover your load. If it is possible avoid traveling.

- Work out a policy for in-laws and friends regarding visits to the hospital and home and "help." Make it known in advance. Plan your help's responsibilities ahead of time. You don't want them to be holding the baby while you or mom cooks and cleans.

- Plan on putting a message on your phone answering machine announcing the baby's name, size, time of birth, eye color, etc. Ask callers to leave a message and understand that you are busy and it may be a while before you get back to them.

Be sure that when you go to the hospital to pick up mom and baby, you've made a trial run. When my baby was ready to come home, I had the car seat, but it wasn't installed. I got mom and baby down to the car and found that we weren't prepared for the ride home! The baby sat in the car seat on the sidewalk (under the hot sun) while we fumbled with the seat belt and tried to figure out how this car seat thing was supposed to work!

Veteran Dad

Bring your vitamins with you, or Gatorade, or whatever. I was up for three and a half days straight.

Veteran Dad

- Pre-arrange pet care, if needed.

- Keep the doctor's phone number handy.

- Have a watch with a second hand to count contractions.

- Enjoy as much time alone with your wife as you can manage, as it might be a while before you are able to do this again.

The Circumcision Decision

Another decision you should make before a baby boy's arrival is whether you want him to be circumcised. The procedure is usually performed in the hospital before baby departs for home, so don't put this decision off until after the delivery.

It's a Guy Thing
While the decision to cut or not to cut may not rest on your shoulders alone, chances are this is one area where your mate will look to you for guidance. You may not be consulted on which types of diapers junior will be wearing, but it's a sure bet that the eventual state of his male appendage will require serious input from you.

Like Father, Like Son?
For most couples, the decision is fairly simple: Like father, like son. If you are circumcised, it's likely you will want your son to "follow in your footsteps" in every way possible. Similarly, if you practice the Jewish or Islamic faiths, your beliefs dictate the necessity of male circumcision. One thing is certain. The procedure, which is usually performed on a healthy baby in the first few days of life, is much safer when done in infancy. The simple surgery — in which excess foreskin is removed from the tip of the penis — is somewhat riskier if performed later in life.

Changing Recommendations
The American Academy of Pediatrics (AAP) used to recommend circumcision for health reasons, and it was generally performed without pain medication. Doctors believed that infants did not feel or would not remember the pain. A new AAP policy statement recognizes that while circumcision does have "some potential medical benefits," the benefits are "not compelling enough" to warrant routine circumcision. The policy also recommends analgesia as a safe means

to reduce the considerable pain that infants otherwise would experience. Check with the person who will perform the circumcision and ask if they use analgesia.

Pros and Cons
There is still some justification for circumcision. Among the benefits: a slightly lower risk of urinary tract infections, a lower risk of contracting cancer of the penis, a lower risk of being infected by sexually transmitted diseases, including HIV, and prevention of phimosis, in which the foreskin cannot be retracted.

Although circumcision is generally safe, complications occur in a small number of cases. Most are minor, involving mild bleeding or local infection. Some opponents of circumcision argue that foreskin removal reduces future male sexual pleasure, but there is no evidence to support this claim.

Boys left intact must be taught to clean the penis thoroughly each day. The foreskin produces a cheese-like substance called smegma, which must be washed away daily for good hygiene. In this regard, circumcised males have the advantage in that their personal hygiene is easier.

For more information regarding your circumcision decision, visit the web site of the American Academy of Pediatrics at www.aap.org. Follow the links to "You and your family," "Advocacy," and "Publications" for more information. And certainly discuss the matter with your physician.

Nothing you do in life is permanent. If you don't like your job you leave. If you don't like your marriage get a divorce. But the relationship you have with your child is forever.

Veteran Dad

Preparing Yourself

Preparing yourself is mostly sorting through the many issues involved and developing a positive, constructive approach to the challenges you face. Easier said than done, of course.

Questions For Yourself
In the final month before the big event, you may find it helpful to take a sort of checkup quiz to see where you are on some basic matters. If you don't have an answer that satisfies you, focus on developing one.

- Are You Engaged, or Along for the Ride?
  Are you doing your part? Are you sharing in the decision making, or is she driving the whole process? Are you working as a team?

I do not believe that anyone can truly prepare you for the massive and pervasive effect that fatherhood has on virtually all aspects of your life, but I think that the message that should be conveyed is to at least begin to prepare yourself for this change.

Veteran Dad

- Do You Have a Constructive Plan?
  Is there something big worrying you? Do you know how you will deal with it? Do you know what your alternatives are?

- Have You Talked About Your Needs and Concerns?
  Does she know what's on your mind, or are you keeping it to yourself? Do you have someone else you can confide in, someone who understands?

- Are You Ready for the Birth?
  Are you ready to help your wife through it? Are you afraid of something bad happening? If it does, do you know what you will do?

- Are You Ready to Care for Your Baby?
  Do you feel any connection with the little thing in mom's stomach? Do you feel confident about being able to care for him?

- Do You Feel Good About Becoming a Father?
  Do you think you will be a good father? Are you excited about meeting your son or daughter for the first time?

I'm a career oriented guy, a bit of a workaholic, play a lot of tennis, and enjoy the finer things is life. I'm not sure how I'm gonna handle this new lifestyle change that comes with having a baby. But I'm willing to give it a try.
Rookie Dad

How to Handle an Emergency Birth

Are you as ready as you can be? Actually, there is one more thing.

The chances are slim of it happening these days, but there is always the possibility that you will need to assist with an emergency delivery of your baby, either at home, in your car, or somewhere else. It can happen that her labor kicks in so fast and hard that that there is barely time to call the doctor, let alone get her to a hospital. Knowing what to do is not a bad idea, and it provides some reassurance (for you, not her), and one less thing to worry about.

You Know It's Too Late If
- You can see the baby's head at the vaginal opening
- Your mate says she can feel the baby coming
- She can't stop pushing

If this is happening, take a deep breath and remain calm; it is time to go to work.

Call 911
If you're at home, don't attempt to get her into a car and to the hospital. Call 911. If you're home alone, call a friend, a neighbor, to assist. Call her doctor. If you're in your car, make sure you know how to tell them where you are – the address or cross streets. Pull over, put on your flashers.

Calm Her and Slow Things Down
Reassure her, tell her that everything's fine. "The baby will be ok; we can do this. Babies have been born for millions of years outside of hospitals. You know how to do this, I'm here with you. We'll do this together." Help her breath through the contractions instead of pushing. She may just be able to hold off long enough for the paramedics to get there.

Get Her In Position
Try to get your partner into a comfortable position lying down, instead of standing or squatting. This position is also safer. Babies come out fast and they are slippery, making them hard to catch. If she is lying down and the baby slips through your hands, he will land on the soft cushion.

Get a Blanket
Blankets, clothing, towels, your shirt – something you can wrap the baby in once he is born. Grab two in case you need them.

Get Positioned to Catch Your Baby
Get into a position to catch her. Carefully – she will be wet. If possible have your body wedged underneath in case she slips out of your hands. As the baby is being born, try to get your partner to stop pushing and to just breathe, or pant lightly.

Place Your Baby on Mom
Wipe the baby off quickly and place her naked on her stomach or side on your partner's abdomen. Then cover her. Make sure you can see her face.

She Should Start Crying
Babies usually start crying within a few seconds of being born. If she isn't, rub her back or chest briskly or slap the soles of her feet. That should do the trick.

Clear Your Baby's Airway
Make sure the baby's nose and mouth are clear of mucous or any

other material that might impede breathing, and make sure her face is not buried under blankets or against your partner's body.

Don't Worry About Cutting the Cord
It will not hurt anything to leave it until the paramedics or doctor get there or until you can get to a hospital.

Start the Baby Nursing
If the cord will reach, place the baby at your partner's breast and let her start suckling or nuzzling. This will help assure mom her baby is fine.

Wait for the Paramedics
If they are not available, carefully drive your new family to the hospital's emergency entrance. Do not rush and keep your eyes on the road.

Now you are ready. Get some sleep. You're going to need it.

9

Your Baby's Birth

Birth is when the rubber hits the road, the moment when everything changes.

Two generations ago, fathers were not allowed to witness the birth of their children. They were expected to sit in a smoky waiting room, nervously pacing the floor, out of the loop, waiting to hear. A few of these fathers said no way and forced the issue by chaining themselves in the delivery room so they could be with their wives when their babies were born. They helped open a door for the rest of us.

You will be taking your wife to the hospital, and may be loading the bags and making calls to the doctor, the hospital, relatives, friends, or your boss. You may run into problems, such as stalled traffic or an overloaded delivery facility. But no matter what happens, this is the point when you need to take control. And in doing so you will let your partner know that you are there for her and she can depend on you.

She will need you. She will need your support, your caring, your patience, your hand, and maybe your shoulder. She will need you to be strong, to look out for her and protect her and your baby. If a punching bag is what she needs, remember to roll with her punches. This is the time to suck it up and draw on your own reserves of inner strength and self-restraint.

Your baby's birth can be both nerve-wracking and exhilarating, but one thing's certain: you're about to witness the most remarkable event in human experience.

This is also the moment when you become a father and meet your child for the first time. Life does not get any more real than this.

Her Lion at The Gate
A woman in labor needs her husband to be a man - if she needs to bite on his hand to get through a contraction, or squeeze his arm until it bleeds, he needs to take it. She needs to know he is her "lion at the gate".
Roslyn Bernhardt, Doula, St. Croix, U.S. Virgin Islands

> **This Chapter Does Not Repeat What You Learn In Childbirth Education Classes**
> This book provides only supplementary information for fathers regarding birth and assumes you have or will complete a childbirth education class. They provide a great deal of essential information, so listen up and learn when you are there.

Ready As You Are Going to Be

By the time mom's labor kicks in, if you haven't prepared to the extent that you or others wanted you to do during the pregnancy, you have a great deal of company. Expectations of new fathers, particularly our own expectations of ourselves, have soared in recent years. We want to be the best fathers possible for our children, but very few of us find it possible to get totally up to speed in time for the birth.

The reality is that you are as ready as you are going to be, and what really counts now is how you perform from here on out. If you let disappointments, feelings of inadequacy or your fears get in the way, you will not be able to do your best. So no matter what has transpired up to this point – now is the time to focus on your new family's needs and take care of business.

When her labor starts, purge from your mind any notion that you've already screwed up by not doing everything you could have. Just go for it. Your instincts will tell you much of what you need to know, and the nurses, your mate, and even your baby will fill in the blanks.

When It's Time to Go

Your childbirth classes will have prepared you to recognize the onset of labor; the major things to keep in mind are as follows:

Out of the blue she said "I think I just had a contraction" I was stunned for a moment. Then I said "tell me when the next one starts.
Veteran Dad

Most women know without a doubt when labor has begun, but in some cases the early signs are subtle and it's hard to be sure. Other pains, such as cramps, may be mistaken for a contraction, but once the real thing actually kicks in, there is no mistaking what it is.

Is It the Real Thing?
False labor, characterized by "Braxton-Hicks" contractions, is not uncommon, but it may be uncomfortable and it is often difficult to differentiate from actual labor. False labor contractions occur at irregular intervals, in contrast to true labor contractions, which occur at regular, gradually diminishing intervals. Braxton-Hicks contractions also last less than 60 seconds. They are likely to disappear if your spouse gets up and walks around, or even if she changes position, while movement has no effect on true labor contractions, and in fact can make them seem more intense.

Logging Her Contractions

Once her contractions get going, one of your initial tasks will be to log them. Don't forget or blow it off, since you'll need to be able to tell the doctor the duration and interval of the contractions. You don't want to delay going to the hospital because you couldn't give the doctor the right information. And the log makes a cool addition to the baby book. Get your watch out and if you want, go about it like you are tracking a launch to the moon. Get a pad of paper and make a table as follows:

Start	Stop	Duration	Interval

Write down the start and stop times to the second. Subtract to determine the duration. The interval is the time from one start time to next. You will quickly learn to report that "the contractions are lasting _____ seconds and are coming _____ minutes apart". Once she is experiencing contractions every 3 – 5 minutes for about an hour, most doctors will tell you it's time to go to the hospital.

Contractions occurring more than four times per hour prior to 36 weeks warrant a call to the doctor, as this may be a sign that the baby is being born early. She does not need to sit around or stay in bed after the contractions start. In fact, movement, especially walking, is a good thing. Take her arm and encourage her to keep moving.

Call Your Physician

After noting the specifics of the labor, call your physician. In many cases, especially with a first delivery, you will be advised to remain at home until labor progresses to a certain point. If you are uncertain of how things are going, however, it is always best to err on the side of caution and call the doctor again. Always call the doctor immediately if your mate's water breaks, if there is relentless pain (which does not subside between contractions), or if there is actual bleeding. (Some slightly bloody mucus, called show, is normally discharged either several days before or at the onset of labor and is no cause for concern).

Your Cue to Take Charge

Given the ever-increasing burden she's been carrying, she may initially greet the onset of labor with a sense of relief. As things progress, she will most likely become, to varying degrees, nervous, excited, frightened, joyous, maybe agitated, maybe hysterical, maybe serene. But she is about to have a baby, and every cell in her body is centered on one thing – giving birth.

A Calm, Capable Partner

Once it is apparent that your baby is on the way, take a deep breath and remain as calm as possible. This will reassure her that she can count on you. If the doctor's office doesn't tell you what she wants to hear - it's time to come to the hospital – assume the role of her advocate and ask specifically what will be required.

Taking Charge

Real labor is your cue to take charge, as your mate will be totally focused on what is going on in her body. Taking charge means assuming responsibility for making sure everything she needs gets handled. Take care of everything else as well. From here on out everything is about mom. Pay attention to her. Reassure and indulge her in any way possible.

Going to the Hospital

Once you get the go-ahead to proceed to the hospital, calmly load your pre-packed bags, make any necessary calls (e.g., Will someone need to be notified to care for pets?), check the house (You don't want any nagging suspicion that you may have left the stove on or the bathtub running), then drive her to the hospital. Needless to say, you'll want to drive very carefully, despite the powerful urge to make like NASCAR. Remember that even little bumps on the road are painful for a woman in labor.

Going to the Hospital Too Early

Do not be overly distressed if your physician determines, after examining her cervix, that labor is not, in fact, imminent. First-time expectant parents often end up making two trips to the hospital before actual labor, requiring a stay in the hospital, sets in. During the examination the doctor will assess the progress of labor by noting the effacement (thinning out) of the cervix and its dilatation (opening up).

When delivery is imminent the cervix will be "fully effaced," with 10 centimeters of dilatation.

If she is willing, take her for a walk, which can speed up labor and get her mind off the painful contractions. Or go to a movie, or do something else that distracts her from focusing on the clock. Take your cell phone and don't travel too far from the hospital.

At the Hospital
Get her checked in and settled. Your objective is to determine what she wants and make it happen. Hospitals have lots of rules, but keep in mind that you are the paying customer. Ask for the nicest room available. If they are busy with lots of births, get clear answers about how they will handle her needs. This is when you'll be happy you wrote up a birth plan with your partner.

Nurses and Doctor are There to Help
You will be assigned a nurse who will have the responsibility of getting mom settled, hooking up appropriate equipment, monitoring your mate and baby's progress and condition, and helping her deal with labor. She is there to help, and you should quickly establish communication and a constructive relationship with her. You should ask for her suggestions and advice, and if there is anything you can do to help. If a shift change occurs, do the same with your new nurse, and take the same approach with the doctor or midwife.

Once we got to the hospital, she had 26 hours of labor and I stayed with her the whole time. I didn't take a shower or go to sleep. I wanted to share it as much as I could. I couldn't take on her pain, but I could be there for her. She was great.
Veteran Dad

Review Your Birth Plan
Form a collaborative alliance with the medical staff, which will help assure the best support possible. Everyone involved wants the same outcome: a healthy baby. Review your birth plan with them and ask if they anticipate any issues in meeting your desires. Be flexible but insist on what is most important to you, keeping in mind that hospital policies may vary.

Your Role as Her Birth Coach

Not that long ago men were not even allowed in the delivery room. Now you are in charge of "coaching" your mate through her pain, amidst the tumult and uncertainties of delivery, to giving birth to a healthy baby. Just remaining standing can be a challenge.

Many pending fathers ask, "How will I know what to do?" Childbirth classes, which prepare you and mom to work as a team, help a lot.

The doctor and nurse will also be available. But there are always a variety of unknowns and possible twists and turns on the path to childbirth.

Attitude is Everything

There is no way you, as a first time father, will know everything that you might have to do, but the right attitude can often get you through. Going in with the dedicated purpose of providing critical support to your wife will make most things you need to do come naturally. Whether its fluffing a pillow, getting more ice chips or counting out her breathing during contractions, if you focus on your wife's needs, they will become apparent and you will rise to the occasion.

Key Roles

Like a coach of a skater, or better, the manager of a prize fighter, your role as her birth coach includes encouraging and guiding her, massaging her cramps, and making sure she gets all that she needs. Managing communications with the medical staff, particularly if problems arise, is also your job. You are her husband and the father of your baby, roles which bring intense responsibility if medical problems develop.

Reassure Her

Reassuring your mate with your constructive actions, attentiveness and attitude is essential. She has enough on her mind. Make sure she knows that you are in control, are handling things, and that you will make sure she gets all the care she needs. This will allow her to concentrate on delivering the baby, free of worry about what's going on around her.

Support Her

The nurse will come in and out of the labor room, so while your mate is on the ride of her life, you are her real support team. Support includes:

- Keeping ice chips handy for her to suck on.
- Massaging her back and anything else she might like. (If her labor is long, you might find this physically exhausting, so hang tough.)
- Reminding her about drinking fluids and emptying her bladder.
- Taking her mind off the labor by reading to her, or engaging her mind in other ways.
- Helping her take a bath or shower.
- Taking her for a walk.

Unconditional support is in order; no matter how tired or frustrated you are, don't wait to be asked.

Listen to Her
She might or might not have a clear idea of what she wants, and it may or may not be what you learned in childbirth class. Listen carefully to her requests and instructions, and then do your best to get it handled the way she wants it. If she is shy about making requests, ask her what she wants – regularly.

Encourage Her
Build her confidence. Tell her how proud you are of her, how brave she is, what a great job she is doing. Tell her you love her, over and over. If there ever was a time to turn into a sappy romantic, this is it.

Take Her Best Shots
Your mate might blame her pain on you (who else to blame?), and might find your assistance (guidance with breathing, for example) to be irritating. "She grabbed my shirt and ripped it and began calling me every name she could think of." If this situation occurs, back off and don't take it personally. Just get back in the saddle with an offer of ice or a backrub.

Help Her Go the Distance
It can be a marathon, especially for first time moms. Cheer her on, tell her how far she has come, how close she is to finishing. "You already went through half of this contraction, it's almost over." Pace yourself, eat and drink regularly to ensure you can go the distance with her, every step of the way.

Monitor the Equipment
You will naturally want to monitor the monitoring equipment used in childbirth. Get familiar with anything that is being used, and ask the nurse what to look for so you can alert her if something comes up. You will also be able to track the duration and intensity of your wife's contractions, and she may appreciate your letting her know when they have peaked. If you like equipment, you may find yourself in a tracking a launch to the moon mode; remember to focus on her needs though.

Not a Camera Man
You can't be in the action and film it at the same time. Focusing on mom through a viewfinder just won't cut it. If you bring a camera, try to arrange for someone else to use it, such as a visitor or even a doula. The best photo ops occur after the baby is born and in mom's and your arms for the first time, and taking a few pictures or a little video at that time won't interfere with your job as your partner's labor coach.

Highlight of Your Life

Right after the birth I broke down crying and kissed my wife.
Veteran Dad

The birth is also your first chance to be part of your child's life, and a proactive approach will enable you to make this incredible event all the more powerful and fulfilling for you personally. Most men report that witnessing and participating in the birth of their child is one of the highlights of their life. Seize the day and go for it!

Be Your Wife's Advocate

This is no time to be shy.

I wanted to make sure that everything went smoothly in the delivery room and that we'd have a healthy baby. I guess you could say I was a little over protective.
Veteran Dad

From here on out your main role is to serve as mom's advocate. Pursue her every request regardless of whether you think it is necessary. If she has specific requests, express them to the staff and intervene as needed. Present your birth plan to the labor nurse and remind the rest of the nursing staff of its core elements.

Be assertive, but not obnoxious. She needs to know that you are going to bat for her, but if you get into unnecessary conflict with the medical staff or appear to lose control, it will scare her. Besides the helplessness she feels, she will also feel incredibly alone when she needs to count on you more than ever.

Speak Up for Her
Your mate will be preoccupied with having a baby, and at times experiencing intense pain, so you will have to be engaged and aware of what is happening in the birthing room, how the birth is progressing and how she is doing. She will need you to speak up for her. If mom wants to labor in the bath or shower, let them know. If she wants the lights dim, let them know. If she wants an epidural, ask them to set it up early.

Make Sure She is Heard
When she is in pain, she may be able to manage only a whisper in your ear about something important. She may feel the baby is coming quicker than the medical staff realizes. Let them know in very clear terms. She may want more "juice" in her epidural. Let them know she needs it yesterday and make sure she hears you.

Managing Friends and Relatives
Closely manage any issues with friends and relatives in the birth room. Your partner might have wanted to have her parents, her sisters and a

best friend in on the birth, but as the labor progresses she may not be up to having a 'crew' in the room. Hospital policies limiting the number of visitors may do the job for you, but if not, be sensitive to where she is at; if she needs some space you will need to politely let visitors know it is best if they wait outside. If they are intruding, or if other problems develop, be firm and ask them to go to the waiting room.

Your New Family's Protector
You should be comfortable with looking out for the needs of your new baby and partner:

- If your doctor is late, insist on his or her appearance. Ask about alternatives if he does not arrive on time.

- If medical problems arise, ensure that they are effectively communicated so that you and your mate know what is going on and are as prepared as possible to make necessary decisions.

- If the nurse is clashing with your mate, or ignoring her needs, ask that another nurse be assigned.

Remember that she needs you to be her "lion at the gate."

How to Avoid Fainting or Worse

Fainting, throwing up or losing your temper while participating in childbirth can happen, and it can put a major damper on the experience for you and perhaps mom. There are several things you can do to avoid problems, and if they occur, how you react will make a big difference.

It Will Be Messy
Childbirth is not pretty. You are probably well aware of this, having viewed at least one training film in a childbirth class. All the fluid that nourishes and protects your baby during pregnancy will come out during delivery. It will be bloody, especially if she needs an episiotomy. If your partner hasn't had a bowel movement, that may come out too. It's all natural and normal; her body is simply doing its job.

Anticipate and Plan
There's no shame in being uncomfortable around the gore. Many men are. If you get squeamish, you may want to evaluate the extent to which you wish to participate. Seeing your baby's head begin to

emerge for the first time can be very cool, but not if you pass out, hit your head and end up hospitalized yourself (it has happened). You be the judge of your own level of tolerance.

If you anticipate having a problem, think it through and go in with a plan. Some fathers watch their baby emerge, help catch him, and cut the cord. Others focus on talking mom through the birth and stand at the head of the bed, sharing her view of a beautiful, semi-cleaned up baby. Remember that the form and extent of your participation is your choice. Either way you are right in there; choose the path that works best for you and mom.

Prevent Fainting
If you're at all squeamish, your prevention plan should include:

- Make sure you eat – the prolonged intensity of childbirth on an empty stomach can drop the strongest guy. Don't forget to eat amidst all the excitement, and eat bland foods that are easy on your stomach. Replenish yourself if her labor is extended. Make sure you have some nutritious snacks and drinks available, and consume them even if you don't feel hungry. (Keep in mind that the sight or smell of some foods might bother mom).

You learn pretty quickly what has to be done.
Veteran Dad

- Focus on mom – Position yourself at your partner's head (stay nose-to-nose with mom in OB nurse speak) and don't take in the doctor's view at the foot of the bed. If a Caesarean birth is necessary, and you are allowed in the operating room, stay with mom on the other side of the drape. Feel free to decline opportunities to help catch your baby or cut the cord.

- Plan a safe landing – When you arrive in the labor room, plan on what you will do should you feel lightheaded and in danger of fainting. Find a chair with a back to quickly sit down on and place your head between your knees. If one is not available, find a place on the floor to sit on where you will not be in the way. The nurse can give you an ammonia capsule if you need it.

It Will Be Intense
The normal emotional turbulence you are experiencing as a new father coupled with the intense drama of childbirth can push you to your limits of self control. Unexpected problems can push you over the edge. Major challenges include:

- Seeing your wife in pain – She is hurting and may even cut loose with some primal screams. Very tough to witness, especially if you feel she wants you to make it stop, which you cannot do. If you believe an epidural should have eliminated her pain, which it does not, it is easy to lose it with the staff.

- Problems with the baby – If problems occur in the delivery, especially something affecting the health of your baby, the pressure you feel can be enormous. Since your mate may be out of it due to pain and exhaustion, you may also feel very alone.

- Not following the script – While your birth plan outlines the specifics that all add up to a beautiful experience, when it gets down to it, your partner, visitors or the hospital staff may not exactly stick with the roles you laid out for them. Since you are on edge already, your response may be less than constructive.

Prevent Losing Your Temper
Becoming angry and berating the medical staff over your partner's pain (again, epidurals do not eliminate all her pain), or their failure to follow the birth plan, is highly counterproductive. It may unnerve mom while she is in the middle of labor and erode the constructive collaboration you need with the medical staff should problems with the baby arise. If you feel you are losing it for any reason, step outside the room, take a deep breath to get a hold of yourself.

Get Back In the Saddle
If you do faint, when you come to, shake it off and get back in the game. Your mate and baby still need you, so do not let any embarrassment prevent you from doing your job. Take the same approach if you just lose it; a quick apology and assurance you have it under control will do. Make it a temporary problem and get beyond it. All's well that ends well; particularly when it is the birth of your baby.

Helping Her Deal With Pain

As you learn in childbirth education class, there are alternatives for reducing the pain she experiences in childbirth. The method for dealing with pain is her call, and she may change course in the midst of labor. Your job is to help make the method she chooses works as well as possible.

Even if she decides on an epidural or other drug, she may still experience significant pain. This might scare her because it can seem like the epidural is not working. Make sure her needs are communicated to the medical staff. While there are limits to how much medication they can give her, it will comfort her to know that you are making sure they are doing everything they can as soon as possible. (Remember, it is OK to be assertive, but don't be obnoxious.)

She may want to use practiced relaxation techniques to deliver naturally, without analgesics. If your mate was adamant about wanting to avoid drugs during delivery and she starts asking for them soon after her contractions begin, encourage her to hang in there and try to help her deal with the pain.

With our first baby, she went natural, but after 20 hours of labor, she gave in and asked for an epidural. Then the anesthesiologist was called away to an emergency. On our second, I asked for the epidural to be started before the pitocin (to induce) was turned on. I scored huge points.
Veteran Dad

When she is experiencing pain, use the pain relief techniques you both learned and practiced in childbirth class. Key pointers include:

- Start pain relief techniques at the first indication of pain, so she is up to speed when it really kicks in.
- Use the combination of deep breaths and short fast ones (panting).
- Count her through her contraction; let her know when the monitor indicates it has peaked.
- Help her establish a focal point.
- Continual support: take her for a walk, give her ice chips, a massage, and encouragement.
- Try anything she suggests that might work.

Remember she will be feeling birth pain for the first time and may react in unexpected ways.

If She Decides to Go With a Pain Killer
There's no shame in abandoning visualization and deep breathing for modern pain intervention. After initially encouraging her to hang in there, ask her if she is sure that she wants an epidural, and if yes, request it ASAP. Tell her you are proud of her for even trying to go natural, but you think the epidural makes sense too, as childbirth is not an endurance contest. Keep checking on the availability of the anesthesiologist, focus on the pain relief techniques, and continue them even after the drugs start working. On the other hand, don't try persuading her to go for pain relief just because you are having a hard time watching her experience pain.

Hard Labor

Labor and birth are very benign terms for what women go through in childbirth. In reality, after nine months of growing a baby the size of a small watermelon, her belly convulses with increasing intensity for hours until it forces it out through a passage normally one-tenth its size. Although her body is designed to birth babies, this will still seem like she's in a heavyweight title fight with nature, with a lot of intense pain involved. And of course, this being her first baby, she has no experience.

But she does have you in her corner. You need to keep your head on straight and be her safe haven and a grounding force. She needs to see in your actions that you are going to help her through. Be patient and be prepared for the long haul. Although some women breeze quickly through labor, most first-time mothers tend to spend a good number of hours in labor before delivering. Focus on remaining resourceful, flexible and calm, no matter what.

Active Labor
By the time she is admitted to the hospital, your partner will be at least in the active phase of labor (remember Stage 1, Phase 2 from your childbirth class). It can last from 20 minutes to many hours. Her contractions are becoming more intense, they are about 3 minutes apart and lasting about 45 seconds to 1 minute.

Her Fear Factor
Fear is a huge factor for first-time moms. The way her body takes over during labor, going beyond her control - even taking her to a different dimension -can be scary for her. It may scare you as well, but you are her anchor and will keep her from feeling like she will not get back. Most women reach an I-can't-do-this-anymore point. Reassure her that she can. She will get through it; you can take comfort in knowing that humans have been doing this for many thousands of years; she won't.

Help Her Through
Get in there. Help her get up and sit down. Be her support physically and mentally. You are her main coach and cheerleader. Ask questions. Read your partner's face. What does she need? Take her for walks down the corridors. Tell her your worst jokes, or read to her. If the hospital provides a warm bath, encourage her to take one. Reflect on the ideas you got in your childbirth education class and try them out.

She was incredibly brave. I didn't think she would be able to handle it, but she did better than me and I was just watching.
Veteran Dad

The whole birthing experience - she goes through the whole range of emotions: happy, excited, tired, etc. You have to be your wife's supporter. She is going to get testy…
Veteran dad.

Breathe With Her

Now is the time to put into practice all the breathing and relaxation techniques you learned in childbirth classes. Remember to show her how to breathe rather than telling her. Encourage her to breath through the pain, and remind her that it's a contraction and that it will be over soon. Use the second hand on your watch to count out the seconds. The real thing is much more intense than when you practiced in birth class; with a really tough contraction, you might find yourself breathing with her (just don't hyperventilate). Reassure her after every contraction.

Massage Her

Massage will help her feel better and relax, which will speed labor along. One study showed that a 20 minute massage every hour during labor helped women feel less pain and anxiety. Massage her head, neck, back and feet, paying attention to her responses. A very light fingertip massage over the abdomen and upper thighs, just hard enough to not tickle, can have a very relaxing effect after painful contractions.

Sometimes Silence is Golden

With powerful contractions she may focus intensely on just getting through them, and telling her how to breath or asking her how she is doing may break her concentration. If you sense this is the case, or she gets irritated, back off and give her space and quiet. You are still her anchor, there when she needs you, so let her handle it on her own if she can. You may find yourself in tune with her needs, not saying much at all.

Take Her Best Shots

Try what you think might work, and if she barks at you, remember it is her pain and frustration talking. Even if she reacts angrily, don't take it personally. If you do, you will be inclined to withdraw your support when she needs you the most. Never argue or debate with her, and most definitely don't sulk or mope. Just take the next opportunity to get back in there.

All the lessons went out the window. She basically told me where to stick the breathing. She was in a lot of pain - knowing I shouldn't take it personally helped.
Veteran Dad

If Interventions are Suggested

This can be a hectic time, and if things aren't going as planned the doctor might suggest an intervention, ranging from the use of forceps to a Caesarean birth. If it's an emergency, there will probably be no time for consideration, but if it's not, you can, and should ask questions such as:

- What can happen if we wait?
- Are there alternatives that are less drastic, less invasive?
- How will this affect the baby?
- What's the trade off?

Transition

Transition means her cervix is approaching full dilation (7–10 centimeters) and she is almost ready to give birth (This can last from a few minutes to hours though, so hang in there.) Contractions are 2-3 minutes apart and last about 1.5 - 2 minutes. Talk to her, tell her more jokes. She may feel a strong urge to push, but she shouldn't push yet. Breathing techniques now will help her keep from pushing.

She may experience one or all of these during this intense time:

- Nausea and vomiting
- Trembling legs with contractions
- Going to sleep with the end of each contraction

Many women have 20 minutes or so of calm at the end of transition before contractions return. Contractions actually slow down, and then gradually build as the baby descends, increasing in frequency, strength and duration. She has a very different sensation than she had during the first stage of labor.

If she is not in a birthing room, she will be moved to one at this point.

My wife went on and on for hours in the delivery room. Her contractions were off the chart and she was a bear to deal with. But once she got the epidural, she turned into a comedian and wouldn't shut up.

Veteran dad

Birth!

The moment is at hand! Her long, hard haul is about over and you are about to meet your child for the first time. Some things to keep in mind:

Stage 2 Labor: Pushing and Birth

Stage 2 is when the baby starts moving through the birth canal. Contractions are very intense, coming at 2-5 minute intervals and lasting 60-90 seconds. This stage can last from a few minutes to a few hours.

Things Will Speed Up

If your partner is not quickly moved to a birthing room, equipment and perhaps an extra nurse will materialize in your room. The doctor will have arrived and will run the show, with the nurse giving your mate

I told the nurse that the baby is coming, she said 'no, you have time', I said 'no, the baby is coming now'. The nurse checked, she was at 10 centimeters and the baby was coming!

Veteran Dad

directions regarding pushing ("don't push, push, keep your head down,"). Follow the nurse's lead and encourage your mate to follow the nurse or doctor's directions about pushing. If your partner wants to try another position, such as on her knees, make sure her wishes are known and honored.

There May be Problems

If problems with the delivery or baby develop, let the medical personnel do their jobs. Request an explanation so that you are not unduly worried or unprepared for an important decision that might be necessary. If your baby is taken to another unit for treatment, ask to go with him. Get back to your partner as soon as possible with news of what is happening.

The Basics of an Emergency Caesarean Birth

About a third of all births involve a trip to an operating room for a Caesarean delivery. Some are planned and the others are done on an emergency basis after a vaginal delivery is attempted and problems develop. If the latter occurs, your mate may feel as though she has failed in some respect, and it will be up to you to reassure her that she did everything she could have. Tell her that a C-section is another method of delivering a baby and it will work out fine.

Most hospitals allow fathers in the operating room for a routine C-section, and you can still participate by talking to your mate, who may remain awake during the procedure. Tell her that she and the baby will be fine, that you love her, and what is going on (use your discretion regarding the more graphic scenes) especially after the baby is born. Keep in mind the following:

- You may be separated from your mate while she is prepped for surgery.
- The experience may scare your wife (and you) - we're talking surgery here.
- There will be a drape hung across her chest so she (and you) will not be able to see the actual surgery. If you ask, they may let you watch.
- Immediately after the birth, your baby's lungs will be suctioned out to remove fluid that otherwise would be squeezed out during birth.
- You may be offered the opportunity to cut the umbilical cord, even though it was already cut during the caesarean birth.

Your baby may be taken immediately to the nursery to be checked out and cleaned and you will be faced with the choice of going with him or staying with mom. If you go, let her know you are going with the baby and will come back as soon as you can.

Her recovery from major surgery may require a good deal of you in terms of caring for her and the baby, so if help is available for a few weeks, take it.

Watching the Birth

If you want to watch your baby being born, go for it. The doctor will let you know when the head is visible (called crowning), which is your cue to look. If there is a mirror overhead, your wife can watch too; if not, let her know what is happening. Seeing your baby emerge is amazing. Blood and fluids quickly fade to the background as you focus on your baby's face for the first time.

Her First Cry

Nothing eases the nerves right after birth better than getting a positive signal that your baby's alive and kicking. For many fathers their baby's first cry is like an alarm that awakens a whole new part of them. Paternal instincts start to kick in, because all of a sudden the baby is real, and needs you.

Opportunity for You to Participate

Many physicians like to let dad cut the cord, although this practice seems to be declining due to hospital safety issues. Many fathers enjoy this, and if you like the idea, go for it. Talk to the OB and address it in your birth plan. Don't let anyone push you into something you are not comfortable with. Just say "no thanks" and focus your attention on mom. With your second child, your doctor may let you help with the actual delivery by catching your baby.

Cutting the Cord Can Mean a Lot: Practice On a Hotdog

You may have the opportunity to handle the last step of your baby's birth: cutting the umbilical cord connecting your baby to your mate. Initially suggested by doctors as a means of involving fathers, many men found it to be a little gross as it's weird to cut flesh. Over the years, the more we thought about it, though, the more meaningful this simple act has become. When a father cuts the cord, he releases a mother from total responsibility for their baby, and simultaneously accepts his responsibility for raising his child. In a sense, the moment he cuts the cord is the moment he becomes a father. So when you have the opportunity, think of what it symbolizes, rather than just how strange and squishy the cord feels. To be fully prepared, grab a hot dog and cut it with a scissors to get the squishy feel down; and then try the same with a rope because the umbilical cord is like one.

One thing that was weird for me is that you are in the birth process one minute, and then the baby is born. [Suddenly] mom's getting sewn up, and the baby is under the French fry warmer, and you don't know who to go to. So I kind of bounced back and forth trying to do both. Then as soon as they got the baby cleaned up and wrapped in a blanket I picked her up…and got together with my wife, and we kind of bonded together. You need to do it as soon as you can, but there's a conflict of where to go for the first half hour.

Veteran Dad

Make sure you take care of your wife after the baby is born, because she is totally exhausted. New moms want to take care of the baby, but they need to get rest...too.

Veteran Dad

Congratulations, Mom!

Ask the doctor to hand you the baby after the birth. Imagine taking a quick look at your brand new child, and then having the honor of presenting your partner with her son or daughter, for whom she has already endured so much. This is the moment she will truly become a mother, so remind her with a quick "congratulations, mom." (Congratulations to you, too.)

Your First Look: Remember Babies Clean Up Great

Don't be alarmed if at first look he is blue or even reddish purple, is covered in slippery white creamy material, or has a lopsided head, is scrawny, and has puffy eyes. All this is normal, and will change quickly as his flexible skull resumes its normal shape, his lungs start operating and he gets cleaned up. His head molds to fit the birth canal, and will round itself out in two or three days.

First Medical Checkup

Before you will be allowed to hold your baby for any length of time, the medical staff will want to whisk him away to a warming table to do some quick evaluations. (Ask to carry your baby to the warming table.) Some babies may require additional medical interventions, especially if delivered prematurely or born with congenital defects. In most cases you should be allowed access to your baby within about 30 minutes.

Mom's Not Finished

After the baby is born and is taken from her to be checked out, mom will remain on the birthing bed waiting for the placenta to be delivered and for any episiotomy to be sewn up. You now have a baby and a wife to look after, with one on either side of the room. Check on mom periodically to see how she is doing, and as you visit with your baby, give mom the high sign indicating everything is okay, blow her a kiss, and make sure she does not feel left out.

Meeting Your Baby

Her head popped out, her eyes popped open and locked onto mine - and wham, I was gone. It was incredible.

Veteran Dad

Whether your mate delivers naturally in record time, or endures a lengthy labor, or needs a Caesarean birth, the result will be the same. When it's all said and done you get to meet your baby for the first time. While many fathers report the birth of their child to be the highlight of their lives, many others report just being numb and are not sure what to think. It may take a while for the impact of your baby's birth to sink in.

Make Sure You and Your Baby are Getting What You Need

Go with him to the warming bed and check on what the doctor or nurse is doing. Ask questions. Place your hand on his tummy to reassure him that you are right there. Then place your little finger in your baby's hand and feel him grab on, both to your finger and to your heart.

Ask the Doctor About Your Baby

Some doctors point out the features, skills and preferences of babies to their parents and cite evidence that this practice enhances their confidence and care giving. It makes sense that knowing what is special about your baby jumpstarts the 'get to know you' process, which leads to 'I will always take care of you', and finally to 'you are the most wonderful thing on the planet'. So give it a try and ask your doctor.

The first moment of bonding for us was in the delivery room, when she (my daughter) squeezed my finger for the first time. It was great.

Veteran Dad

Intense, Surreal and Perhaps Disorienting

You may find your mind racing with disoriented thoughts in these circumstances. Things may pop into your head like "wow, check out the size of those balls" (a baby boys genitals are swollen at birth), or "bummer, I wanted a boy," or "she looks like my mother-in-law." All normal. Just be careful not to voice these thoughts out loud, as they can put a damper on an otherwise truly wonderful event.

A Father's Calming Effect

Your baby has had a rough time. Lying quietly in a warm pool, suddenly it empties and the walls close in, forcing her down through the drain and then out into a cold, alien world full of bright lights and noise. At birth, she will have a high heart rate, elevated blood pressure, and rapid respirations, which reflect how stressed she is.

You get that child in your hands for the first time and it has a calming effect. On you and your baby.

Veteran Dad

Take her in your arms and gently rock her. Talk softly and gently, as it will both sooth her and get her attention. She is definitely wondering what is happening, so tell her. Just being held by you and hearing your gentle voice will calm her. OB nurses report that as a father talks to his baby, the newborn's heart and respirations slow down, and she will often try to turn her head towards her father's familiar voice.

They Talk With Their Eyes

Holding your baby for the first time, and looking into her eyes as she looks into your own, is incredible. While new babies tend to look around in a fuzzy way, they can lock their eyes on yours and almost seem to communicate telepathically. As they talk with their eyes, they seem to say "Who are you?," and "Where am I?" As we look back and talk, they stare intently at us, hanging on every word. If she turns her head in the direction of your voice and stares at you, you then know that she recognizes your voice and understands that you are her dad. Her response to you is very powerful; this alone can cement your bond.

Welcome Her to the World

One of the most important things we fathers can do with our children as they grow is to simply talk to them. That first conversation will always be special:

- "Hello, Samantha. I am your daddy! You're my daughter. I love you."
- "I'm here. You're going to be okay. You're safe. Everything's going to be all right."
- "I am always going to take great care of you."
- "Welcome to the world!"

Get s Few Shots With the Camera

Don't forget the camera and make sure you or someone (friend or relative) gets a few quick shots with a camera or camcorder, as this is a now or never opportunity. Don't get carried away, as your primary responsibility is still that of your wife's birth coach. Her needs come first.

> *When it's your turn, make it you and her - alone. If necessary, just ignore anybody else or anything else going on. Grab your baby's hands, grab her toes, smooth her head, just touch her, squeeze her just slightly. Look at her, talk to her, knowing that you're doing her good and she'll like it. This is the best way to get a good start.*
>
> *Veteran Dad*

> *In a sense I felt like I bonded with my son as soon as I held him. He would kind of look up at me and I felt a lot of love for him right away and was really glad I had that time with him for just ourselves. It is kind of like a small progressive thing. You just realize that he is looking at you and responding to you and that it is a good feeling. It seemed natural from the first.*
>
> *Veteran Dad*

Start the Sports Bonding

According to research conducted by us fathers, our babies carry a gene that predisposes them to like our favorite sports, and especially our favorite teams. It is important to trigger the bonding this hardwired connection enables, and the earlier the better to enable them to reach their full potential as sports fans. So take the opportunity right in the birth room to tell her, "I got you a Raiders Nation shirt to take you home in," "I have a Shimano fishing reel with an Uglystick rod waiting for you at home," or whatever works for you.

Mothers tend to not understand this genetic link, and while they may interpret the look on your baby's face as a blank stare, it is actually awestruck wonder over what a cool dad they have. Our continuing research indicates this link extends to the music we like, as well as our favorite truck or car. Stay tuned.

If Things Go Wrong

If a problem develops, stay calm, ask questions of the medical staff, and let them do their thing. Keep mom informed and reassured as much as possible. While your own feelings can be overwhelming, your response to the needs of your family at this critical time will be crucial.

No matter what happens, several key issues that will be important are:

- Remain as calm and rational as possible. You may have to make decisions regarding your child and your family, and down the road you'll want to know you made the best ones possible.

- Trust your doctors. While some physicians can be lacking in "bedside manner," they are highly trained to deal with problems that may develop, and in emergency situations, you will need to trust them.

- Early on, moms are more closely bonded with their babies, and given the impact of pregnancy on them, are understandably likely to react very emotionally to problems. Be prepared for the possibility of a very strong reaction from mom; it will be up to you to comfort and perhaps calm her down.

- When serious problems develop, support organizations, such as grief support groups and neonatal support groups can be incredibly helpful. Talking to those who have experienced what you are going through can be very comforting and enlightening.

- While all of us want a healthy baby, it is amazing the meaning and joy a less than perfectly formed child can add to the life of a father. Take it one day at a time and keep the possibilities open in your mind.

- See *Babies With Special Needs* in the appendix.

Hang in there. This is when a baby needs his father the most.

Your First Day as a Father

After your baby is born, cared for and settled in a bassinette next to mom, they will spend a day or two at the hospital; add a day or so if she has a Caesarean birth. Spend as much time as you can with them, including staying overnight as accommodations permit. Take advantage of the opportunity to care for your baby while mom is resting up. Don't let her feel compelled to have the baby in the room all the time; if she needs some rest or just a break, ask the nurse if she can take the baby to the nursery for a while.

Become a Family

Your baby is brand new, your wife is now a new mom, and you are a new father. This is a very special time for you to get to know each other and bond as a family, so relish the moment by just being together, alone. Definitely do not let work or other issues intrude on your first days as a family. The nursing staff will handle most of the baby's needs, and there is even a primitive form of room service, so you can focus on resting, relaxing and just taking it all in.

Manage Your Visitors

A few low key visits is cool, but don't feel pressured to have lots of visitors, or let visitors stay for more than an hour, as they can easily intrude on your family's needs. The best excuse for limiting visitors is: "she is exhausted and needs to sleep," which is generally the case anyway. Make arrangements for them to come by the house instead to see the baby.

Learn From the Nurses

OB nurses are total experts in taking care of newborn babies and are happy to teach you basic skills, such as how to comfort, change, bathe and swaddle your baby. They love babies (they may even be a little reluctant to give them up) and will be very pleased to know "their baby" has a father who wants to take great care of them. Don't be shy about asking the nurse to show you how, and take advantage of any opportunity to learn.

Change Your Baby's First Diaper

Ask the OB nurse to walk you through changing your baby's first diaper. A confidence builder for you, this action lets everyone around know that you are serious about taking care of your child. Your partner will likely be exhausted and need some sleep, which provides an early opportunity to get involved on your own. When you get the chance, show mom how to do it. Seeing you already know how will build her confidence in you.

The Bonding Thing

Bonding is falling in love with your baby. If you fell head over heals in love the moment you saw her, great! Most dads, however, report feeling somewhat disconnected from their child weeks or even months after the birth, so if you don't feel close to your baby at first, you have lots of company.

Becoming a father involves many issues that need to be sorted out, and there is no reason to rush it. Trust that it will happen, and take advantage of opportunities to simply be with your baby, as this will help make it happen. Hold him in your arms and look in his eyes, check out his fingers and toes, snuggle her to your chest until she falls asleep and feels like she is part of you. The last thing you want to do if you are feeling uncomfortable is to shy away from the baby. Just give it time; it will happen eventually.

Welcome to Fatherhood

Congratulations, dad!

It may take some time, even years, to accept the full reality and magnitude of what you have done, but you are now the father of a little boy or girl, and you will be forever. Amidst all the uncertainty and commotion going on around you, you may have overlooked a fundamental fact about yourself– you are not just a father, you are a full-on dad who is doing his job for his family. In the toughest and most important role of a man's life, you are delivering.

If this notion does not fully register for you, carry your baby into the hospital bathroom and look at yourself in the mirror. As you look at a man with his child in his arms, tell yourself "good job, dad" or something equally appropriate, and as you look yourself in the eye, take pride in the fact that you have what it takes.

You may have noticed that becoming a father is mostly about learning to support and care for someone else. It is all about them. Our needs become secondary and there is a good deal of sacrifice involved. But ultimately, this personal commitment to our family defines who we are, gives full meaning to our lives, and becomes all about us.

Welcome to fatherhood and get some sleep. You are going to need it.

The birth was real long and the birth monitors were moving up and down like a roller coaster, everything worked out and after mom and little Isabella got settled for the night I went home to an empty house. I called up my buddy and got him to come over and proceeded to excitedly tell him every detail and he was good enough to listen to every word and be excited with me.

Veteran Dad

She delivered about midnight and both my girls were asleep several hours later, I walked outside to find a full moon and a sky full of stars on a beautiful silent night. I had been through the ringer and took a deep breath and the enormity of it all just overwhelmed me.

Veteran Dad

10

Taking Your New Family Home

Up until now you have mostly been sitting on the bench, perhaps serving as a tackling dummy. Mom carried and delivered the baby, and the hospital staff took over from there. Now its your turn to show what you can do.

The first few days at home are your best chance to impress everyone with your baby skills. Remember, your mate is still fatigued and may be in pain. Anything you can do to ease her burden will be appreciated now more than ever. Alternatively, if you lag at this crucial juncture, it will be remembered for a long time. Establish from the start that you are a capable and integral member of your child's parenting team. Take it one day at a time.

Leaving the Embrace of the Hospital

We came home to a full house of excited relatives who wanted to see the baby. Everybody wanted to talk at once, and after a while, I looked over at my tired and dazed wife, and my nod towards our upstairs bedroom was met with a look that said "please". I took the baby from someone's arms and together we went up alone. It was like we were in a cocoon, just the three of us, too tired for words, with this overwhelming feeling that we were a family.
Veteran Dad

The doctor has cleared mom and your newborn, and it is time to take your new family home. You gather your stuff, help mom into the wheelchair, put your baby into her arms, and walk them out of the hospital.

After the rush of the delivery and a day or two in the hospital, this moment seems surreal for many men, with feelings of pride, relief, excitement and trepidation. You and your wife are about to assume full responsibility for your infant. Don't be surprised if the feeling is a little overwhelming. It hits most of us as we walk through the lobby doors and realize are be on our own before we feel ready.

It's only natural to be anxious. It's true, there are a lot of unknowns, but keep in mind Benjamin Spock's timeless advice: "You know more than you think you do." When that fails, help is usually only a phone call away.

The Ride Home
Mom, tired and happy, may also be a little nervous. This may be the first time both of you are alone – really alone – with your new baby. Let

her know she can count on you. Make sure the car seat is good to go (see Appendix - *Protecting Your Baby & Family*) and you have plenty of gas to get home. As you drive home, be extra cautious. The little things are really important at times like these.

The first thing you're going to do is buckle your little bundle into the car seat, so make sure you know how. Your baby may not look very happy when he's strapped in, but under no circumstances should you or mom give in to the temptation to take him out and hold him during the drive home. Instead, mom should sit in the back to comfort and to care for him if needed.

If you are planning to take a taxi home, make sure you request an infant car seat when you make the reservation. When the taxi arrives, make sure the seat is in the rear facing backwards, and check the car seat straps to assure that it is hooked up properly.

Getting Settled at Home

Definitely, be prepared. Do everything possible ahead of time. Make sure that there is a supply of diapers, wipes, ointment, receiving blankets and spare baby clothes within a short reach wherever you change the baby.

Your life changes overnight. The baby is eight weeks old, and my life and my wife's life is still changing. We haven't totally figured it out yet. Sleep is always a concern. I'd do anything right now for eight hours of sleep.

Veteran Dad

- Keep a diaper bag stocked with baby items also, in case you need to go somewhere in a hurry.

- Eliminate unnecessary work during this period, as you will have plenty to do. This is a great time to take your relatives and friends up on their offers to cook and stock your refrigerator.

- You can also stock up on quick and easy meals, or prepare some meals ahead of time and freeze them.

- Use paper plates and plastic utensils for a while for easy cleanup.

- Be sure your baby's new environment is safe. (See *Protecting Your Baby & Family* in the Appendix.)

Setting Up Your Family's Support System
Make sure your family's support network is in place. Arrange for help from professionals, family and friends; keep a chart on the wall with

phone numbers, and call them in when needed. Your support network may include:

- Pediatrician, obstetrician, midwife
- Nurse answer line
- Lactation consultant if breastfeeding
- Hospital emergency number
- A friendly neighbor
- Mom's best friend
- Relatives who can help out
- Local take-out restaurants
- On-line grocery delivery service, if available

See *Learning More/Getting Help* in the Appendix. Your objective should be to assure that if mom or the baby needs something, they get it.

Taking Time Alone with Your New Family

Especially if you have family living nearby, your baby will be the focus of attention for the first few weeks, attracting a stream of visitors. This is natural and can be great. You may also have relatives staying with you to help out, or perhaps a nanny. This can be great as well. To a point.

The downside is that with other people around all the time, you may be foregoing a unique opportunity to bond as a family. You and your mate are going through dramatic changes, rapidly evolving into dad and mom. These first few weeks are when you get to know each other in a new way. Taking time to connect as a family will enable you to stay in sync as well as remind you what it is all about.

Making it easier does not necessarily make it better. Working through these tough times on your own, without lots of help, will bring you and mom together. You learn you can count on each other; that you are there for each other. You may have a rougher time, but the little mistakes will be the things you both remember and laugh about years later. You will also remember that you and mom got through it together.

This is a special issue for dads. Let's face it: how many of us will insist on diapering our babies when a nanny or mother-in-law is offering to take her off our hands? With a pro around all the time, we simply are not needed as much and have fewer opportunities to contribute.

The decision to have in-home help is often driven by the fear of the unknown, and appropriately by mom's concerns. Even if you decide on help prior to the birth, keep the option open to change course after your baby arrives. The best option may be to have help on call should you need it, or for a few hours a day. Just remember to carve out some time alone with your new family.

Visitors – the Good, the Bad and the Ugly

Everyone will want to come by to "see the new baby", and you and mom will naturally want to show him off. Word spreads quickly and next thing you know, you have a steady stream of people coming by. Moms are instinctively inclined to help entertain guests and she may even decide to clean up after them. What is wrong with this picture?

People trooping through continually to see the baby is the last thing your new family needs. You don't need the disruption and mom needs to save her energy for the baby. Probably both of you do.

Most visitors come with the best of intentions – they don't want you to feel ignored and they are inclined to help. Despite their good intentions, however, sometimes parents, siblings, in-laws, friends or neighbors can get a bit intrusive. They may get so excited about seeing the baby that they wake him up, pass him from one to another and basically handle him much too much. Others just can't resist the temptation to offer unsolicited opinions on everything from breastfeeding to starting a college savings account. They may bring their own children, adding to the chaos.

Remember that this time is about your wife, your baby and yourself – your new family – and not about anybody else. Talk about it with your partner and set some limits on visitors. Enforcing them is your job.

Your buddies also have to adjust to the fact that you have a new priority in your life, and they just took a big step lower in the pecking order. But they can become honorary uncles, if they so choose.

Set the Ground Rules and Don't be Shy
While help from friends and relatives may be welcome, it's up to you to enforce the ground rules.

Ask visitors gently to wash their hands if they are going to handle the baby. If they appear to be sick, or if they arrive with sniffling children,

We had a parade of people coming through and staying at our house and everyone wanted to hold her and feed her. It took about two weeks after they left to get her to go to sleep by herself, entertain herself, etc.
     Veteran Dad

If a neighbor or friend offers to help, don't say 'everything is okay'. Tell them you need help with the grocery shopping, meals, and cleaning the house. Take the help when you can get it.
     Veteran Dad

ask them to come another time. If your mate becomes tired during a visit, or if you both are just plain exhausted, it's okay to tell visitors that you need some quiet time.

Use tact, be sensitive to their feelings, but handle it. Remember what is important – your baby, mom and you, your new family. On the other hand, don't let your new authority or jangled nerves get out of hand. Assertive will do; no need to be obnoxious.

In addition to protecting mom and the baby, keep in mind that you may have to deal with friends and relatives who may inherently feel that you are less than capable of taking care of your own child. Stand your ground. If your mother-in-law reaches for the baby when he starts to cry, try saying "thanks, I'll take care of him now, but I will trade off with you later." Don't let anyone come between you and your baby, especially in these crucial first days.

Use the Answering Machine
Defend against unwanted intrusions. Consider turning the telephone ringer off and have your answering machine pick up calls. Record a new message announcing baby's name, size, time of birth, eye color, etc. Ask callers to understand that you are busy and settling in, and to leave a message, as it may be a while before you can get back to them.

Let them know that the baby is home and safe—but that you are busy.

Keep Your In-Laws from Becoming Outlaws
When relatives travel to see you, they often try to do too much, and it is difficult to ask for space when they are staying with you or in a hotel. Work out a policy for family regarding "help." If mom or mom-in-law comes to stay for a week, you and your partner should decide what you want her to do ahead of time. You may not want her to be holding the baby while you or your spouse cooks and cleans. On the other hand, you might be thrilled to hand off the baby for awhile and do some mundane tasks. Much depends on your relationship with your parents and in-laws and the type of people they are. Just remember that they are parents also and should understand that flexibility and cooperation are what's needed right now.

Boot Camp Veterans Have Their Say:
* *Family can really invade after birth, and the man might need to protect his wife and child from the onslaught.*

People started calling our house all the time right before the baby was born. It got to the point where I would look at the Caller ID number to see who it was. One time it was my mother-in-law and I told my wife 'We're not answering.' After a while we just turned the ringer off.

Veteran Dad

If family's nearby, use them. People always told me, "Make them clean the house not hold the baby while you clean the house."

Veteran Dad

- *My stepfather was dominating time with our baby, partly because he was enjoying the attention. To get through, I finally had to tell him to stop or he wasn't going to be seeing his granddaughter much. Pretty tough but it worked great.*

- *We had [my wife's] mother come the second week, which was really a blessing. My wife was really grateful that she came. [Her mother] was very careful not to step on our toes and it worked out to be very positive.*

- *Without asking, my mother insisted that she would stay with us the first three weeks to take care of the baby. Instead of saying no, I asked my brother, who had a bigger house, to ask her to stay with him. Everything worked out great, and I did not have to hurt her feelings.*

- *Instead of arguing with my mother-in-law, I asked her to teach me instead of telling me. Since then, we got along great.*

- *My father-in-law lives two doors down, which can be good and bad. We don't have to go far to visit grandpa (good), and he sometimes tries to step in where he shouldn't (bad).*

Again, stand your ground. Ultimately, your relatives will appreciate that you are just doing your best for your new family. Any ruffled feathers are easily smoothed out down the road, particularly by a dad who is doing the job for his new child.

Don't let your in-laws boss you around. Be polite, but have a backbone.

Veteran Dad

Sleep – Running on Empty

Fatigue is the most prevalent problem faced by new parents. It causes one to become irritable and even disoriented. A vicious cycle can develop in which you cannot relax and go to sleep, even when you have time.

Accept the fact that a full night of sleep is history for a while. Babies rarely "sleep like a baby" the first few months. Sleep deprivation will likely take its toll on both mom and dad. It can get very tough, especially when you are essentially exhausted and you have to go to work.

Grab a nap whenever you can, particularly when the baby is sleeping. Avoid relying on coffee to stay awake since it will keep you awake when you have the opportunity to sleep.

At fist the sleep deprivation seemed like a big deal. But I lived through it. It reminded me of my college days when I had to stay up late to cram for tests.

Veteran Dad

You'll both need as much rest as possible in order to get through the next few weeks. It's been estimated that new parents lose hundreds of hours of sleep during baby's first year.

A few comments on sleep:

- *Sleep is always a concern. I'd do anything right now for eight hours of [uninterrupted] sleep.*

- *Our first had colic and he seemed to cry all the time. Our second pretty much slept through the night her first night home. Both ends of the range, I guess.*

- *At first the sleep deprivation seemed like a big deal. But I lived through it. It reminded me of my college days when I had to stay up late to cram for tests.*

Common Issues

Some of the many issues you may encounter in the first weeks:

Caesarean Births and Moms
Cesarean births make it easier for dads to figure out how to help. Basically, you do everything. You have two people to take care of for a while, and both will need lots of it. Figure out how to get some help. Managing visitors is especially important for moms recovering from Caesareans.

Medical Concerns
It is normal for mom or even you to assume the worst over the little problems babies encounter because this is new territory for you both. If you are concerned about splotchy skin, a cough, sneezing, diarrhea, crossed eyes, not eating, etc., check with your nurse hotline or your pediatrician.

You may not be able to tell the big problems from little ones; hey, you are new at this. Just don't vacillate, and certainly don't argue with mom about it. Just call the doctor (that's what the doctors tell us). They will let you know if you are calling too much. (See Chapter 14, *Raising A Baby* for a list of symptoms requiring a 911 emergency call.)

What About Pets?

If you have a family pet, you'll need to take certain steps to assure a smooth introduction when you bring your newborn home. Cats, and especially dogs, may experience anxiety related to a baby's arrival. (See *Pet Safety* in *Protecting Your Baby & Family* in the Appendix.)

Preserve the Moments

If you get a little compulsive about videotaping and taking pictures, you can always cut back. But if you are on the opposite end of the spectrum, the moments may be lost. They may include a photo of you with baggy, bloodshot eyes, and a tired smile, with your baby daughter sleeping in your arms. (See *Recording Your New Family* in the Appendix.)

Strategies for Surviving

Boot Camp veterans offer lots of experienced advice for the first few days at home:

You are under more stress than you think and all incoming support is for mom and the baby.
Veteran Dad

- Watch your newborn while your spouse catches up on her rest. Now is the perfect time to get to know your infant by spending as much time as possible with her.

- Take care of meals, whether it means calling for home delivery, cooking from scratch, heating a frozen dinner, or reheating food that friends and family may bring.

- A little housework goes a long way in terms of morale. If there simply isn't time to clean it all, resolve not to stress out about a little clutter.

- Make a list with mom of the things that can be left undone for a while – vacuuming under the bed is not a priority task during this time.

- Take any opportunity to let your spouse know that you love her and that she is doing a great job as a mom.

- Be a hero.

First Weeks Learning Curve

The first three weeks or so are mostly trial and error, with plenty of both. Things to keep in mind:

- You and mom will need to work out your own routine for taking

After the baby was born I was running around like a chicken with its head cut off. I was going in so many directions… caring for the baby and my wife that I forgot to take care of myself.
Veteran Dad

care of the baby, including plenty of feeding, burping, changing, cuddling, and rocking. To go with the flow, you've got to develop the flow first.

•   Learning what works takes time, and you will learn as much from what doesn't work as what does.

•   After a few weeks, you and mom will likely be exhausted, and you may feel like you hit the wall. Doubts may emerge. You or mom may ask, "Am I being a good parent?" It will pass.

•   Your wife may feel overwhelmed and run the risk of depression; watch for the signs (See Chapter 12, *Caring For New Moms*).

Finally, remember there is no limit to the number of things that new parents can figure out how to worry about. If you and your mate don't add a few, you are not doing your share.

11

Caring For Your New Baby

Accepting responsibility for another human being, particularly one so small and helpless, is one of life's great challenges for men. It is also one of life's great rewards, as you will find out.

Learning to care for your new baby will take time, patience, and collaboration with your mate. For the first weeks you will be very tired; just figuring out what a crying baby wants can be intense and draining.

The best strategy is to just dive in and go for it, starting at the hospital. When it comes to babies, the best way to learn is by doing. Like fishing for trout or tuning an engine, there is no alternative to experience.

After the first few weeks, your new family's routine will start settling in and you and your baby will get to know each other. You will become confident and relaxed about caring for an infant and will also start enjoying your baby's responses to your voice and touch. They generally don't sleep through the night for a couple of months though, so you will be tired for a while.

Both the quality and quantity of the time you spend with your baby counts. The more you spend, the more you will understand why, as fathers, we come love them, enjoy caring for them, and would jump in front of a speeding truck to protect them.

There is a reason babies are made to be cute and cuddly, and develop smiles that can melt NFL linebackers. Babies are essentially designed to steal your heart, and you will want to give yours every opportunity to do so.

Let Them Know You are "Here to Play"

A decade ago a Boot Camp veteran said that he was not the most "domesticated" male around, and his relatives and friends, even his wife, expected him to shy away from caring for a baby. He wanted to prove them wrong when it came to his own baby, so he made sure he

At this point Katherine (2 weeks) is very healthy, happy, and pretty much a joy to be around, except for last night and a few other nights. Even at the difficult times, though they may be frustrating, I am always in awe that this little person I am holding in my arms I helped make and I will help guide for many years to come.

Veteran Dad

Before our son was born I figured it was mom's job to diaper, feed, and burp the baby. To be honest with you I wasn't sure I was capable of caring for my son. Now look at me. It's a piece of cake. I figure if I can do it any dad can... Sometimes my wife and I even argue about who gets to take care of the baby.

Veteran Dad

I learned that even when a baby isn't capable of interaction, the baby still needs the dads hold and touch to balance the woman's hold and touch. There's something there that brings a calmness to the baby. When it's just all mommy, the baby tends to fuss a lot more.

Veteran Dad

I learned that through working with my wife, we can make all the baby chores easy. Then everyone's happy.

Veteran Dad

My best move as a dad was getting involved with the baby from the beginning, including feeding, bathing and changing diapers. It built a strong foundation for the relationship with my child and helped strengthen the relationship with my wife.

Veteran Dad

was the one to change his baby's first diaper. He said he wanted to set the tone that he was "here to play."

It worked. The jokes and subtle criticisms about his attitude and skills regarding babies stopped, and those around him started taking him seriously. They looked up to him as a father fully committed to taking the best possible care of his child. It felt good, and he found their respect encouraged him to do more. Even his wife treated him differently; she was both relieved and proud of the father of her child.

Your attitude, right from the beginning, will mean a great deal, certainly to your mate, but most importantly to yourself and your child. It feels good to be respected as a father, and respect drives us to do our best.

When a father takes care of a child, the child is, of course, better off. But when that child grows up over two decades with a man who is proud to be his father and does his best for him, that child will have something very special indeed. So will dad.

Earning Your Stripes

Over the past decade, the bar has been raised considerably for new fathers. Good thing, since it used to be okay for a father to say that he found his baby boring and would wait until he could throw a ball to get involved with him.

On the other hand, expectations for new fathers have soared, making any sense of how you measure up as a father very elusive. To help you out, we have outlined bottom line standards for fathers during their baby's first three months:

- Get hands-on involved in caring for your baby, beginning at her birth. Any indication that you are reluctant to do so will automatically make you a third string player.

- Take advantage of early opportunities to learn the basics: holding, comforting, changing, burping, swaddling, bathing and putting your baby to sleep.

- Take on a share of nighttime duties.

- Select at least one activity with the baby – like bathing her – that you own. You become the designated bather, as well as the expert at bathing your daughter. Even mom defers to you on this issue. Swaddling, burping, and the big one - putting your crying baby to sleep – can also work.

- Make it just the two of you on a regular basis. Take your baby out for walks in a stroller or baby pouch, rock him in the rocking chair, show her the world starting with all the great stuff in your house (see Chapter 15 – *Your New Buddy*).

- The big test: 6-8 hours alone with your baby with mom out on her own. Before the end of the second month, you need to get this one under your belt, even if you have to boot mom out. Do it on your own (asking your own mother to come over and help does not count), and you will definitely earn your baby spurs.

Everything Was Fine

When mom comes home and asks how did it go with the baby, a few more standards apply. If the baby is screaming (about a 10% probability), explain that she just started crying, but she was happy all day. Otherwise, everything was fine; "no problems" works well. No matter how tough a time you had, unless there are paramedics parked out front, everything was fine.

World's Expert on Taking Care of Your Baby

It happens fast. After several weeks of taking care of him, you will become proficient at burping, swaddling, bathing, etc. Changing diapers will become second nature. Your baby also learns how you do it. With you and him in sync, nobody in the whole world, with the possible exception of mom, will do it better.

All Babies are Unique and Change Fast

Even at one day old, your baby can already do an amazing number of things. He can taste, smell, hear, suck, cry, sleep and probably dream. He will flinch at a bright light, although he won't really see details for about two weeks. He's got a powerful grip. If he needs something, he'll let you know about it, and if he's content he finds a way to communicate that as well.

Each baby is also unique; this will become more apparent over time. At birth, their weight varies and their individual features are apparent (mom's dimples, dad's nose). From day one, babies' sleep patterns differ widely. While all babies cry, those experiencing colic can seem to cry incessantly for the first three months. Some like to be cuddled all the time, some don't.

One time my wife left me with our baby, Madison, so she could run some errands and visit her parents. Madison had never been fussy before. But an hour after my wife left she wouldn't stop crying. I panicked and decided to call my wife and get her to come home and help me. I picked up the phone and started dialing her parent's phone number. Just before I punching in the last number I decided NO, I'm not going to call her. I'm going to stick it out. I hung up the phone and started finding ways to calm Madison down. A half-hour later she finally calmed down. It felt really good knowing that I could handle this situation by myself without mom around. It proved to be a real confidence builder for me.

Veteran Dad

Time is a precious commodity. When you're younger, you are invincible, and there are a million years left in your life. With kids, you realize how quickly time flies and that life it too short to miss even one minute of their life experiences.

Veteran Dad

Don't Compare

While you may be tempted, comparing your baby to others is counterproductive. Learning to notice and appreciate your baby's individuality is a major milestone to becoming a great parent, and is by far the most effective approach to bringing out the best in your child.

Babies are Fickle

Keep in mind that babies will change their preferences on a regular basis as they grow. One day they may prefer to be swaddled or carried in the Snuggli, but within days, they may prefer to ride in a swing. At one point they may not want to sit in a baby seat for more than a few minutes without fussing, and shortly thereafter they may prefer that position so they can look around.

Develop New Tactics and Strategies

As a father, you must continually develop new tactics and strategies for caring for your unique and ever changing child. Develop a mental list of ideas that may come in handy when your baby is crying, or when he wants to play, or needs to sleep, and be on the lookout for new ones. Refer to your list on a regular basis, and don't disregard items because at one point your baby did not prefer them. Victories in finding something your baby likes may often be short lived, so relish them while you can, and be prepared to move on to new ground.

She had a C-section and couldn't get out of bed the first week. I did everything except nurse the baby. It was tough but I quickly felt like a real dad.

Veteran Dad

Resources for Hands-on Baby Care

The following sections provide basic information on essential baby care skills. As a father, you need to be resourceful, so the more you know, the better. For more information, you can:

- Take a class on newborn care
  Your hospital will likely sponsor classes, and taking one together with mom gets you both up to speed and on the same page when caring for your baby.

- Ask your doctor or nurse
  They are always happy to help, so remember to bring up specific issues you are dealing with, whether or not they are of a medical nature.

- Read a book on caring for babies
  Ask to borrow the book other parents found most helpful, or visit the bookstore and buy one. Good baby care books are listed in *Learning More/Getting Help* in the Appendix.

- Ask experienced parents for ideas
  You may already be getting more advice than you want, but when you are dealing with a specific (non-medical) problem, parents who have experience with the same issue are your best bet.

- Visit parenting websites
  While they sometimes take a "compulsive mom" approach, for additional information on baby care skills visit www.babycenter.com or www.baby-place.com. See *Learning More/Getting Help* in the Appendix for more websites.

Holding Your Baby

You are going to hold your baby a lot and will ultimately develop several intuitive methods.

Five Minutes to Get Comfortable
You weigh 180, she weighs 7. You are 6 feet tall, she's 21 inches. She can almost fit in your hand. You might feel awkward, like a clumsy giant, afraid of dropping her. It's natural to have the jitters about handling a newborn, especially if you've never held a baby before.

This is a familiar scene at Boot Camp where most of the rookies hold a baby for the first time. Some of the men are downright nervous as they rigidly position themselves to receive the baby being handed to them by a veteran father. Once the baby is in their arms, they look down and start to check him out. And then they start to relax and that warm and soft baby just seems to mold into their arms. About five minutes is all it takes them to get comfortable.

Your First Time
Sit down, if you can, and have the nurse or doctor place your baby in your arms. Remember, he has a heavy head and weak neck muscles. As the baby is handed to you, make sure that one of your hands is supporting his body and the other is under the back of his head. Then gradually settle him in so that his head is resting in the crook of your arm and you are holding him. Other pointers include:

- If you're picking your baby up, slide your hands under her head and her rear and lift her whole body at once.

- A gentle rocking motion of a few inches side-to-side or up and down will often comfort a baby that starts whimpering.

- Change her position carefully, maintaining support of her head and neck while protecting the soft spots on her head.

- When you hand her back, go slowly and get close to the person you are handing her to. It is even better if this person is sitting down.

Suggested Baby Holds

There are a variety of ways to hold a baby, and a few of the best for men include:

- Carry your baby so his chest is against yours and his head is resting on your shoulder. A very good position for burping, and babies like it because they can look at things over your shoulder.

- Sit her on your lap with her back resting against you and your hand holding her chest. Then rock back and forth. If you have a rocking chair, all the better.

- The forearm lift will often calm a fussy baby. Bend one arm and place your baby, tummy down, along the length of your forearm, with his head resting in your open hand and his legs straddling your arm. Bring your arm close to your body for security and then stroke or gently pat his back with your other hand.

- Laying him tummy down across your knees will also often calm a fussy baby. Stroke or gently pat his back.

The best hold is laying your baby across your chest so he can fall asleep listening to and feeling your heartbeat.

Long Time Standing

Babies generally like and need to be held a lot, for long periods. This is an acquired taste for busy fathers who have difficulty finding the time. Part of the solution is to just accept the fact that babies take time. The other part is to integrate holding a baby with your other activities, particularly relaxing ones like watching TV, talking with friends, reading the newspaper, taking a walk, or even taking a nap.

For some reason, many babies like to be held while you are standing up and in motion, and they can tell the difference. So you may find yourself, for hours a night sometimes, with your baby in your arms, walking or standing while you sway side-to-side. That is why many new fathers will find themselves unconsciously swaying while at work, or elsewhere.

I came home ready to relax for the weekend after a stressful day at the office. Saturday I told my wife to take off and enjoy some time to herself. I put a pizza in the oven and was going to relax in front of the TV with my baby. She started crying, the dog needed out, the phone started ringing and someone was knocking on the door. After all that it took a while for me to settle her down and she started to fall asleep until the burnt offering in the oven set off the smoke detector and scared her. I actually wished Monday was here.

Veteran Dad

Feeding Your Baby

When feeding your baby, you will be holding him in one arm and using your other hand to hold the bottle. The typical duration of a meal is 10-15 minutes, so you will want to develop a routine which includes a comfortable place to sit. There is no rushing it, so you may as well use the opportunity to relax.

First Few Days
Babies don't really eat much for the first few days, since a mother's milk does not normally come in right away. The baby does get colostrum from her, which is a thin yellow substance with antibodies and protein. Most newborns have plenty of fat, sugar and fluids to tide them over. They like to suck though, and it is this action that will help mom's milk come in.

When Mom is Breastfeeding
While the first days of breastfeeding are often frustrating, when they do start nursing, babies are little eating machines. Relative to their body weight, they eat two to three times more than an obese adult, which places a major responsibility on mom. When she is breastfeeding, you can help out tremendously by bringing her the baby and/or burping him.

Introducing the Bottle
After a few weeks of breastfeeding, you can start using a bottle (if you try too soon, your baby might get frustrated with mom's breast since it is harder to suck on). Your mate can express milk during the day so you can help out with feeding, particularly at night or when she needs some time for herself (otherwise her outings or sleep are limited to the times between nursing). Breast milk should be stored in bottles in the refrigerator with the date marked on a label.

Believe it or not, 2:00am feedings when I can be alone with my daughter are the best times.

Veteran Dad

You can store breast milk at room temperature for 6–10 hours and in the refrigerator for 5 days. You can also freeze it for up to 6 months, and after you thaw it, you can keep it refrigerated for 24 hours. Never re-freeze breast milk.

To use, heat the milk in the bottle (see note below), get your baby positioned in your arm or on your lap, and bring the bottle's nipple to her lips. Once she feels the nipple and tastes the milk, she should start sucking. Move the nipple into her mouth so she can latch on and fill up on mom's milk.

Since this is different from breastfeeding, it may take her a little practice to get it down. If she does not start sucking, push the nipple into her mouth and gently rub the top of the nipple on the roof of her mouth just behind her gum. This should trigger her sucking instinct.

If she gags a little, it is because the milk flows easier out of the bottle, and she'll get a lot more milk than she is used to. To cut down the flow, move the nipple out of her mouth so she can only suck on the tip. As she gets used to it, gradually move the nipple in further. Make sure you are buying "newborn" size nipples.

Formula in a Bottle

If you are bottle feeding your baby, you'll notice that he might not be very hungry for the first few days, and might even gag on the formula. Don't worry; he's just not ready to eat yet. Let him practice on the tip of the nipple, using the approach described above.

Bottles generally come with one hole. What I did was take a needle and put about five more holes in the nipple. It's helped our son get his food quicker. My wife really appreciated that.
Veteran Dad

Bottle feeding involves a system that includes stocking formula and bottles, heating formula, and cleaning bottles, along with a comfortable chair. Get the system down because you do not want to deal with a hungry, screaming baby with no formula or clean bottles around.

Warming Milk or Formula in a Bottle

Expressed breast milk and formula need to be warmed to body temperature before feeding the baby with a bottle. There are several products for this purpose, or an alternative is to set the bottle in a pan of hot water. The microwave is not recommended since it does not heat the milk evenly and your baby may get a mouthful of hot milk. Check the milk's temperature by shaking the bottle a little and squirting a few drops on the inside of your wrist, which is sensitive to temperature.

Teaching Your Baby to Burp

Babies swallow air when they're feeding, which causes discomfort that can keep them awake when they need to be sleeping. It's up to you to help your little one expel the air after each feeding until he can do it on his own, perhaps to the tune of the Star Spangled Banner.

Basic Burping Techniques

You and your baby will essentially work together to get burping down, as it is a learned skill for both of you and there are a variety of alternatives. Try them out to see what works best. Basic burping techniques include:

- Over Your Shoulder
  Hold your baby to your chest with one hand on her bottom and her head on your shoulder. Make sure her tummy is in solid contact with your chest because the pressure will help get the air out. Gently pat or rub her back.

- Over Your Lap
  Lie your baby face down across your lap with his tummy over one leg and his chest and head over the other. Gently rub or pat his back with a motion that works the air up from his tummy.

- Sitting Up on Your Lap
  With your baby sitting upright on one of your legs facing sideways and leaning slightly forward, place your hand high on her chest where you can also support her head. Pat her on the back.

Sometimes just holding him up with your hands around his upper chest (with him looking at you) will do the trick. If your baby doesn't burp, don't worry. He may not need to.

Top Off the Tank
While feeding your baby, if you notice she is starting to fidget, take a break. Try burping her, and then continue. If you burp her after mom nurses her before bedtime and she lets out a big one, suggest that mom "top off her tank" so she will sleep longer. A very tired mom will think you are a genius.

Be Prepared for Spitting Up
Always assume your baby will spit up when he burps. That's what burp cloths are for, so keep one handy and use it. If he does spit up, wipe it up and clear his mouth.

Changing Diapers

Hopefully you were able to get the nurse in the hospital to walk you through changing your baby's diaper before you need to do it at home alone. Not a real problem, though, as no matter how you start, you will get to a point where you can do it with one hand, blindfolded, in under 60 seconds. (We don't recommend you try it blindfolded).

"I'm the champion burper in the family!"
Veteran Dad

The only advice I have to give is to be patient and carry an extra shirt with you wherever you go.
Veteran Dad

Setting the Stage

It is important to remember when handling a baby is that you only have two arms, and one of them is usually required to hold him, leaving only one arm to reach for things. Make sure you have everything you need close by before placing your baby on the changing table. This includes baby wipes or warm water and a cloth, a clean diaper, and ointment.

Place your baby on a towel or changing pad on a flat surface (a bed, floor, table or changing table). Especially when using a changing table or any high surface, never turn away, even for a few seconds, without holding her.

Step by Step

Essential steps for changing diapers (disposable) include:

- Undo the sticky tabs and close them so they don't stick on the baby and you can reuse them to wrap up the dirty diaper when finished.

- With boys, place the clean diaper low on his tummy and over his penis to minimize the risk that boys present.

- As you undo the dirty diaper and pull it down, use it to wipe off as much poop as you can. Grab your baby by the ankles, firmly but gently, and lift his bottom up so you have full access to his backside.

- Either set the dirty diaper aside or fold it under him with the clean side up. With his bottom still in the air, grab a baby wipe and wipe him down.

- Clean your baby's bottom area thoroughly, using multiple wipes if necessary. If you have a baby girl, be sure to wipe from front to back to avoid wiping poop into her genitals.

- Pat her dry and dab ointment on any areas that are red.

- Place the new diaper tab side first under your baby's bottom. Bring it up between his legs and fasten it on either side with the tape tabs. The diaper should be snug, but not tight.

- For new infants, fold the front of the diaper down so it does not cover his umbilical cord.

- Roll up the used diaper, refasten the tabs, and stick it in a Diaper Genie (highly recommended by Boot Camp vets).

I like diaper changes. I use it as an opportunity to talk to her, but I like to make her laugh.
Veteran Dad

Don't worry about all the mechanical things like changing diapers. It's actually easier than changing a tire.
Veteran Dad

I was ready for work and offered to change his diaper before I left. When I removed the diaper he peed. I thought I dodged his bullet until my coworker said "what's on your back?" He got me! Never underestimate the power of the stream!
Veteran Dad

Changing diapers has been a fun thing for me. It's like play time for both of us. We have this thing where I stick out my tongue and he sticks up his tongue. We mimic each other. It's a cool bonding thing.

Veteran Dad

Swaddling Your Baby

At Boot Camp we call it "burrito wrapping." During the last months of pregnancy babies are stuffed tight, secure and warm in mom's womb. Swaddling and wrapping a baby tightly in a blanket replicates that secure feeling, and also makes sure they stay warm while their bodies adjust to life outside.

Babies are swaddled right after birth in the hospital, and the nurse will be happy to give you a lesson. Do it a few times yourself and you will be a pro. Trying it with a squirming, kicking baby, though, might feel like you are roping a calf for the first time.

The main purpose once you are home is to comfort and keep your baby calm. Babies can scare themselves with their own kicking and flailing, and wrapping them snuggly in a blanket prevents this. Most babies like the security of swaddling; some do not like to be so confined. Look for signs of distress or discomfort. If you think she might not like being swaddled, try loosening the blanket or freeing her arms. Babies that do like it, will change their minds at a month or two and let you know by kicking and struggling to get loose. Time to stop, but they may still like to sleep swaddled for a while (make sure they don't get too hot).

Step by Step Baby Burrito Wrap
You will need a small flannel blanket called a receiving blanket. If you don't have one, a light towel will also do the job. Essential steps include:

- Spread the receiving blanket on a bed, couch or the rug.

- Place your baby on the blanket diagonally with her head on one corner of the blanket.

- With one hand, bring the bottom corner up to her chin, so her legs are tucked in.

- With the other, pull one side corner snuggly over her and tuck it between her back and the blanket.

- Pull the other corner over her and tuck it under her back.

Now you have one calm, bundled little package with just her face showing. Pick her up, kiss her forehead, tell her you love her, and rock her for a while to take full advantage of swaddling.

Bathing Your Baby

She may not like bathing at first, and you may find handling a squirming, wet and slippery infant a little unnerving as well. But a little experience goes a long way for both of you, as most babies find their bath soothing, and many new dads report it becomes the highlight of their day. When your baby discovers the joy of splashing and kicking like a frog (both are apparently instinctual), you may want to get in and join him (you can).

Bath time is great. She will just lay there and smile and watch as you pour the water on her.
Veteran Dad

For the first couple of weeks, sponge baths are all that are required. You can begin giving your baby a full bath as soon as the stump of the umbilical cord falls off – usually during the second or third week. If your baby has been circumcised, follow your doctor's instructions about when to begin bathing him. Pre-crawlers only need a bath 1-2 times a week, as long as they are cleaned well during diapering, but many mom's believe otherwise.

The Problem with Men in Charge of Babies
My wife and I waited 8 years to adopt our baby. When we finally got a baby, he was 2 ½ months old, and I took the first 3 months off work to take care of him. At the end of the first week, my wife came home from work and walked in and picked up the baby. She held the baby for a minute, and then said "What's that smell?" After sniffing around for a minute, she realized the smell was the baby. She said 'When's the last time this baby had a bath?' I looked at her, and said 'Bath?' I had been so enthralled with this baby, playing with him all week long, that it never occurred to me to give him a bath! This 'baby' is now 6'4", and a San Francisco policeman.

Veteran Dad

Setting the Stage

A small plastic baby tub with a sponge base designed for a baby is your best bet. Fill it with 3 inches of warm (90-95 degrees), not hot water. Keep the room warm if you can. Any time you plan to do something with your newborn, you want to make sure you are as prepared as a NASCAR pit crew. Everything should be ready and within reach, including:

- Soft washcloth
- Baby soap
- Towel
- A cup for rinsing him off
- New diaper
- Ointment
- Change of clothing

Safety First

Always check the temperature of the water with the back of your hand, wrist or elbow. Your fingers and palm may be callused and you won't feel the temperature accurately. Water should feel slightly warm to touch. Make sure you never leave your baby unattended; not for a second. If you have to leave the room for any reason, bundle him in a towel and take him with you.

Step by Step

Essential steps include:

- Undress him, dip his feet in the water, and then lay him in the sponge insert. Hold his head up with one hand while you wash with the other. The water should be deep enough to keep him warm, but not so deep that he will start floating and become difficult to hold onto.

- Using a soft washcloth and a small amount of baby soap, bathe him from the feet up.

- Dip the washcloth in the warm water repeatedly and let it flow over him to keep him warm.

- Be careful to not get soap in his eyes; wipe them from the inside out after you squeeze excess soapy water out of the washcloth.

- Do his scalp last, and using the cup, make sure the water flows off the back of his head and does not get in his eyes.

- Rinse him off with cups of warm water, then carefully lift your slippery baby out of the tub, bundle him in a towel to dry, and diaper and dress him.

Enjoy the moment and then show mom her happy, clean, sweet smelling baby.

Bicycling Your Baby

For some time now Hunter enjoys the diaper changes. Maybe he feels the difference between being "messy" and "clean!" Or, maybe he just enjoys the birthday suit. Giving him a bath is enjoyable as well as taking him to the grocery store. Also, just holding him and feeling his little body molded to mine, smelling his hair and breath.

Veteran Dad

Boot Camp vets regularly report excellent success with this obscure maneuver. Place him face up on your lap with his head at your knees. Grab his lower legs with your thumbs next to his feet. Gently move his legs back and forth like he is running in place. If he stiffens his legs, wait until he relaxes them.

While there is no medical documentation of this technique, our veterans swear by it. Our theory is that babies can get constipated or develop gas and you can help him relax and move things along by bicycling his legs and loosening up his lower abdominal area. Signs of gas and constipation include a belly tight as a balloon, and crying along with vigorous kicking of his legs.

Babies like it whether or not they have gas, and with your baby looking up at you, it is a good position to talk or sing to him. And if your want to raise an Olympic sprinter, well, it can't hurt.

Dressing Your Baby

Babies need to be dressed so they stay warm. More importantly, they need to look cute.

A good way to assert yourself as your baby's father is to pick out something interesting for him to wear, or for the truly brave, actually go to a baby store and buy her an outfit you choose. Matching sport team shirts are a safe bet, and putting her in a dress and headband will score big points. The baby grunge look - diaper and dirty t-shirt – won't cut it.

With so many mothers around, your sense of fashion may be questioned. If so, calmly explain that your baby likes the outfit, and won't wear anything else.

Dressing a baby can be more challenging than it would seem. Clothing goes on easiest when a baby is dry and relaxed and comfortable and warm. If you've just given him a bath, try applying a little baby powder or cornstarch. Put some on your hand and pat it gently on his skin. He will love it, and it will make it easier to slide his clothes on.

As with most baby rituals, if you take your time, getting your baby dressed can become an enjoyable experience. If he starts fussing, distract him by singing a song to him, kissing his fingers, letting him push his legs out against you. Calm him with your voice and let him know he's doing great.

Putting Her Socks On
Hands down the trickiest task in caring for a baby. When you put a sock on, you point your toe. When you put a sock on a baby, she curls her toes. Stick both thumbs deep into the sock so you can snug it up against her toes and then pull it the rest of the way up.

Putting On a Shirt
Since a baby won't stick his hand and arm down a shirt sleeve, it is best to reach through and pull his hand through. Most babies hate having clothing pulled down over their heads, and will let you know it. The first few times can be rough, especially until you get the hang of it. You have to support the baby's head while gently easing the shirt down. Stretch it as far as you can before attempting to put it on. Once it's down over his head, then put his arms into the armholes.

Getting the Snaps Aligned
Baby sleepers and jump suits often have snaps, and lots of them, and they often end up one or two snaps off as you finish closing them. The trick is to start at the very bottom; get the first one aligned properly and the last one will line up too.

Dressing Your Baby for Bed
Keeping your baby from being too hot or too cold can be a challenge. Newborns have little ability to regulate their own temperature and can chill easily. You may be tempted to bundle up your baby at bed time, but overheating can be a serious problem. To keep her comfortable:

- Keep the room temperature between 68 and 72 degrees.

- Dress her in a diaper, an undershirt and a one-piece sleeper.

- Only use a thin knit blanket to cover her, and tuck it in at the edges of the mattress so it doesn't come loose and get wrapped around her.

If She is Too hot

A baby who is too hot will feel sweaty or clammy and may have a heat rash, especially around the neck. He might look red in the face and may cry. Removing a layer of clothing (or a blanket) will help cool him down.

If She is Too Cold

A baby who's too cold may shiver and cry. Her hands, nose and feet will feel cold. If your baby is too cold, hold her next to your body to warm her up and then add a layer of clothing or a blanket.

Baby Massage

You thought before you had the baby you couldn't do anything right, but after the baby, sometimes, you feel you are not doing anything right either.

Veteran Dad

Your touch is sometimes the best communication of all. Touching and talking are the same to a baby. A loving touch can actually decrease the production of stress hormones, reduce crying and fussing, and help your baby into a sound sleep. Mostly it builds the bond between you, and helps you relax and have fun in the process. Massage is but one way to accentuate the touch that helps you bond with your baby. It's a soothing action that can bring relief to stressed babies who are irritated, colicky, and crying.

The way you touch is important. Avoid poking, rubbing or pressing too hard. If your hands are rough, use a little baby oil or pure olive oil. Make sure to rub your hands together to warm up the oil. And then stroke him lightly (you might only need to use one finger) in a downward direction. Talk gently to him as you put your warm hands on his chest or back, then move them slowly and lightly up and out as if you are smoothing the pages of a book. Try placing him face down on a Boppy Pillow or across your lap and rub his back in slow, light, downward strokes.

There are several ways to massage your infant. The main thing is to be gentle and hold your baby in a way that is comfortable to him. Stroke in circular, smooth motions on the stomach, head, legs, and arms. This is a way to help you both unwind at the end of a hard day.

Don't forget, while you're at it, that you and your mate can enjoy each other's massages, as well, and it will help you reestablish your relationship after the changes a new baby brings. For links to information about baby massage, see *Learning More, Getting Help* in the Appendix.

Sleeping Like a Baby

Newborns sleep a lot, up to 80 percent of the time, but rarely for more than a few hours at a stretch. Some babies start sleeping through the night after a few weeks, but others don't get there until they are six months old or more.

Night is for Sleeping

Some infants are night owls and will be wide awake just when you want to go to sleep. For the first few days you won't be able to do much about this. But once your baby is about two weeks old, you can start teaching him to distinguish night from day. When he's alert and awake during the day, play with him as much as you can, keep the house and his room light and bright, and don't worry about minimizing regular daytime noises like the phone, TV, or dishwasher. If he tends to sleep through feedings, wake him up by wiping his face with a damp, cool cloth.

At night, don't play with him when you go into his room for a feeding, and keep the lights and noise low. Before too long he should begin to figure out that nighttime is for sleeping.

Putting Your Baby to Sleep

Since it was established that there is a link between babies who sleep on their stomachs and SIDS (Sudden Infant Death Syndrome), parents have been careful to put their babies to sleep only on their backs. The number of SIDS deaths has been cut by 40 percent. So put him to sleep on his back.

Putting a crying baby to sleep is like finding the Holy Grail for new parents. A variety of techniques are available. Some of the most effective techniques reported by veteran fathers at Boot Camp include:

- Walk him in the stroller around the block or through the house. After you finish walking, rock the stroller side-to-side for a while to make sure he stays asleep, and gradually reduce the movement to zero.

- Carry her in a pouch (e.g., Snuggli) around the house or the block, or rock her in a glider or rocking chair. The warmth of your body will help lull her to sleep.

- Music designed for babies, or even white noise, like a vacuum, often does the trick. One dad found static from an untuned radio worked.

- Some babies will wake up continually as you try to put them to sleep at night; dads say they seem to "fight it" like they want to stay up and party. Stay with whatever technique you are using for awhile after they close their eyes to make sure they are fully asleep.

- If you are away from her normal bed and need to put her to sleep, bring her regular blanket along to make the environment smell and feel familiar.

A creative approach will help you come up with more techniques that work for your baby. One father, frustrated when his sleeping initiatives failed as soon as he placed his sleeping baby on the cold sheets in the crib, started using a heating pad set on low to warm them up. He removed the pad right before he put his baby to bed.

After struggling to put your crying baby to sleep, you might look at your quiet, very peaceful little angel and suddenly feel the urge to check if he is breathing. This is a standard reaction among new parents; go ahead and check to confirm that he is, in fact, just sleeping like a baby.

Keep in mind that success in getting him to sleep more during the day likely means he will sleep less at night.

Putting Your Baby to Sleep in Your Bed
The American Academy of Pediatrics says the best place for a baby to sleep is in his own crib due to the dangers associated with babies sleeping in their parent's bed (they can get caught up in loose bedding, a parent might roll over the baby, or the baby might get caught between the bed and a wall). But many parents feel that the "family bed," which has existed for millenniums in many cultures, provides the baby the warmth and nurturing he needs. It also relieves the parents of getting out of bed for feedings. Ultimately, the decision belongs to you and your mate.

Putting Your Baby on a Schedule
Babies typically sleep, wake up, are wide awake and happy, get fussy and start crying all during a cycle that repeats every 3-4 hours. While tempting, trying to alter the natural schedule of a fussy baby to fit in with yours usually just leads to frustration. There are constructive steps you can take to develop a more compatible schedule, however. These include:

There are times when I talk to my son and tell him to just go to sleep. I like to think that he understands what I'm saying. And sometimes I think he does by the look on his face. If anything, I talk to him for my peace of mind. For example, when I know he's tired and he doesn't want to go to sleep, I'll say you can sit there and cry or go to sleep while I take a shower. You decide. And after I walk over to the shower he's cool. My wife and mother-in-law, however, will try to talk and sing him to sleep.

Veteran Dad

Hit The Ground Crawling

- Develop a routine that enables her to learn to put herself to sleep. Lay her down while groggy but not fully asleep, allowing her to fuss a little. She will eventually get the idea that it's sleep time.

- After 2-3 months, stretch out the time between feedings so mom can get more done during the day and he sleeps longer at night. Time the last feeding to take place just before you'd like him to go to sleep at night.

Resources for Sleeping

If your baby is having problems with sleeping or you want to learn about the tradeoffs of "putting your baby on a schedule," check out *Healthy Sleep Habits, Happy Child* by Bryan Weissbluth. Excellent review and great suggestions for dealing with your baby's sleep issues so you can get some too. See also Chapter 13, *Troubleshooting Crying Babies* for more tips.

Basic Health Issues

A good reference manual for baby care on hand will provide solid information on health issues presented by babies. A brief review of basic issues is as follows:

Colic

Colic is a term generally applied to babies who cry a lot, as in "she is colicky" or "he has colic." Its cause may be due to an immature digestive system, or an immature nervous system, or perhaps something else. New theories develop and every now and then someone claims to have a cure.

There is little you can do other than have your doctor check him out, try to make him comfortable and endure it. The good news is that colic typically goes away by three months. The bad news is that it can seem like an eternity, as your baby, obviously in pain, will cry and scream for hours on end.

Umbilical Cord

The remains of the umbilical cord usually fall off within two weeks after birth. The best way to help it heal is to keep the area clean and dry. Give your baby sponge baths and generally avoid getting the cord stump wet. Don't cover the area with a diaper that will rub against it and irritate. The more you can expose the stump to the air, the faster it will heal.

The stump can get pretty awful looking, and may even bleed a little just before it falls off. This is normal. Let it fall off by itself, and afterwards keep the area clean and dry. You can begin to give tub baths, but make sure to gently and carefully pat dry the belly button afterward. Consult with your doctor if the skin around the cord becomes red or swollen.

Diaper Rash

Almost all babies will develop some irritation or rash during their first months. It's not a serious problem, and the best way to treat it is to change your baby's diaper as soon as it gets wet. Clean him carefully with baby wipes or warm water, making sure not to rub or scrub which will make the irritation worse. Exposing the area to air for awhile will help, and then apply a soothing ointment to the spot before putting on the diaper. If the rash doesn't clear up, or if it seems to have definite edges, ask your doctor about it.

Baby Sun Burn

Their skin is delicate and easily subject to sunburn. Even if it's a cloudy day, protect your baby from the elements. Cover him up with light clothing, and keep him out of direct sunlight and wind. Use sunscreen; a complete sun block is best. Most baby sunscreens have a UV factor of at least 30 (be careful when applying around eye areas). Use a sunhat and make sure your stroller has a good sunshade.

I found that 1st, you need to be very patient - with your baby, your wife and yourself. 2nd, you have to be tough. 3rd, you have to be flexible
Veteran Dad

Getting Connected

The bonding thing; whether it hits you at birth or sneaks up on you down the road, is a deep, warm, satisfying feeling. It doesn't go away, and it is what keeps you going as a father. This is an important issue, for if you are going to sustain your commitment to your child, you need to get something serious in return. Fatherhood needs to be much more than changing dirty diapers and getting up three times a night.

Getting to Know Her

The more time you spend with your baby, the better you will know her and the more she will respond to you. These are the fundamental building blocks of your developing relationship, and simply spending time is the best thing you can do.

The next best thing is to take a practical, constructive approach to his care. When he is crying, instead of becoming frustrated or even aggravated, focus on the 100+ ideas that you can use to calm your baby down. In any given situation, there's always something that you haven't tried that may work, and the more you try, the better you will get. Your ability to maintain a positive attitude will be tied to your competence, and that comes from knowing that there is always something that can be tried to quiet your crying baby or put your tired baby to sleep.

Courting Your Baby

The notion of courtship between a father and his baby is a good analogy, because it's a relationship that needs to be developed, and this will take time. Seek out the opportunities early on to take her out with you, tell her about your world, and defend her from all threats. These actions create true love, and if the opportunities are consistently pursued, a very deep and enduring relationship is the result.

If somebody else fills the gap, your baby won't be as responsive to your touch and voice. You won't feel as confident about her love for you, or your love for her, and you will not be as important as you could be in her life. Like any relationship, you can expect some ups and downs, but there is nothing like getting off on the right foot.

A man should take every opportunity to be a part of the nighttime experience. Not just because it's the right thing to do. The night time is a magical time. Until you've sat up with your child at night while the child nurses and comes in and out of sleep, you're missing something. If you're sleeping through all that…you're missing something. Not to mention that your wife could use the help. Don't deny yourself a great experience. You've got the rest of your life to sleep.

Veteran Dad

One Veteran's Love Story

"It took me three or four days to really develop a strong attraction (to my baby), and it happened by taking care of her. This included calming her when she was crying, feeding her when she was hungry, changing her diaper, burping her, working her legs to help relieve gas. In return, I had this lovely young thing gazing into my eyes (sometimes cross-eyed), responding to my touch, snuggling into my chest, and rewarding me in only a way that a baby can. In fact, I'll swear that I've even gotten some genuine smiles out of her at this impossibly early date. She is too young to know what love is, but she is already making it clear that I am the one big guy in the whole world that she looks for when she needs something. I know that one day I will be teaching her how to play catch, and another day I will be walking her down the aisle.

How to Love Your Baby

As her father, you will have moments when you will really know that this baby is truly yours. Those that are recommended by veteran dads include:

Check Out His Fingers and Toes

And don't forget his nose. Babies are exquisitely, intricately detailed miniature human beings, with all the parts and potential. Amazing creatures, and if you look close, yours will surely become the first wonder of your world.

Use Your Finger as a Pacifier

Babies love to suck. A clean finger works just as well as a pacifier, and it is a surreal feeling as you actually feel instinct at work. You can also get an idea of what it is like when he latches on to mom's breast.

Hug Your Baby

They make a very huggable bundle when swaddled, or when wrapped in a blanket after a bath, or really at about any time. Hold her close to keep her warm, and give her the secure feeling that you will protect her at all times.

Carry Her in a Pouch

Many veteran dads report that carrying a baby in a pouch (e.g., Baby Bjorn, Snuggli) is the ticket. Either snuggled in, warm and asleep, or looking out at all of the new wonders of her world that continually pass by.

Get in Contact

Remember that when taking care of a baby, physical contact makes a lot of sense. Your body will provide warmth to your baby, which helps comfort her and puts her to sleep. Skin-to-skin contact with your soft, sweet, freshly bathed baby on your chest is a piece of heaven.

Just the Two of You

Get out for some time together, just the two of you, where no one else in the world can intrude. Go for a long walk, or take her to the hardware store, or to the beach where you can show her where you will be teaching her how to surf.

Introduce Him to Your Father

Grandfathers are last in line, and often shy, so make it special when it is time to introduce your baby to your own father. Take your baby and ask your dad to follow you into another room, show him how your baby likes to be held, and ask your dad – father to father – what he remembers about his newborns.

Take Her to See Your Friends

You can stay cooped up at home, or you can go visit your friends. Park your baby in the stroller near the basketball court while you shoot

We use the pouch. She likes the movement and noise of the vacuum. It just calms her down so you can put her in the pouch and get all your chores done and be close to her too.

Veteran Dad

I've learned from just being here that I'm building a relationship with my child just like I did when I first met my wife...I've got to learn to find out what my child does and doesn't like. Basically, I'm building a new relationship with my child.

Veteran Dad

Hit The Ground Crawling

some hoops with the guys. You will interrupt your game when you check on her, but by taking your baby, you are scoring points all around.

Talk to Your Baby

Babies love to hear you talk to them. Tell him what you are doing, describe yourself, or describe him, sing songs, "you're wonderful" and "who's the best baby in the world? Take a walk around the house with him and point out colorful things, describe everything around you – the birds chirping or a dog barking outside.

Get Him Started Early

"Infants can remember the sounds of words almost a year before realizing their meanings. The experiments suggest that infants learn language by first storing familiar sound patterns and then attaching meanings at around 18 months, when language skills start to blossom."
"Babies Don't Forget What They Hear," *Science Magazine's Academic Press Daily Insight,* September 26, 1997

Babies are great listeners as well and will see it your way every time. So if you have anything on your mind that you want to get off your chest, your baby is all ears.

Start a Lifelong Love Affair

The regular expression of love and encouragement to your child is the most important practice you can develop. We tend to be more critical of ourselves than others, and we extend this to our children, especially our firstborn. While at times negative feedback may be appropriate with her, the rule should be regular expressions that are very positive. Your child's self esteem, motivation, and zest for life to a large extent will correlate with how positive you are in his upbringing. Saying "I love you" often will also become a self fulfilling prophecy on both ends.

This practice ultimately becomes a habit, and is one that should start on day one of your child's life. With your child in your arms, looking into his eyes and gently murmur how beautiful he is. When he grabs your finger, tell him how strong he is. If he burps, tell him what a good burper he is. Crying indicates healthy lungs, and potential as a singer. Crying at night indicates a partier. You get the idea - your child can do no wrong.

In addition to developing an exceptionally good habit at a very early stage, this practice will also help you cope with the frustrating times of

I've discovered that it's okay to talk to your baby. I just hope nobody is recording me while I'm calling her dumpling, snuggle bunny...and all that other stuff. You'll get real creative with the name calling but that's what she'll be to you.

Veteran Dad

your child's infancy. While it may be difficult after a nighttime of crying to think in terms of what a healthy set of lungs he has, you will be much more likely to hang in there with him.

Even After a Rocky Start

Let's consider the worst of scenarios. You didn't feel much for your baby at the beginning, or maybe you were just bewildered. You bring the baby home and his cries grate on you like somebody scraping their fingernails on a chalkboard. You're typically a deep sleeper who doesn't like to be disturbed, and here you are with a baby that doesn't care. You try to be supportive of your wife and she takes it as a threat to her role as the lead parent, the mother.

You know she has been a lot of work and there have been a lot of sleepless nights with the colic and all. But I wouldn't trade her for the world.

Veteran Dad

Just as you get frustrated in trying to cope with the new baby, you have to refocus on your job to make up for the time you spent away. You try to juggle your many responsibilities, while at the same time making time for this new addition. Lets say at the end of one month things haven't gone very well and you're wondering whether it's all worth it.

Well, trust all us veteran dads, it will all be worth it provided you keep the faith, don't give up. You may be frustrated but your baby doesn't know the difference. The real key is that if you keep after it, things work out just fine. Keep in mind that daddies can do no wrong as far as babies are concerned, and that over time, even the most frustrated of fathers will figure out how to do things right. At about one month, babies start learning how to smile. Maybe it's just gas, but it doesn't really matter; a smile is a smile.

How to Love Your Baby II

(By a Boot Camp Coach, with his third child, a one month old baby girl, on his lap).

Sit down with your baby after she's well fed, burp her and lay her on your lap so she's looking right up at you and then take your finger and just run it around her face. Tickle her cheeks real lightly, tickle her nose, run it all around her head, sort of lightly messaging her head a little bit. Sometimes, she will smile - mine's smiling right now - rub your finger around and just play with her. I'm not sure why, but they like it. They like the closeness they feel as they respond to you. You will feel closer too.

Now try the other end. Grab her feet and rub them. You can do this a little more firmly. They seem to like that too. Nobody seems to think about massaging a baby's feet, but if you notice, babies tend to move them quite a bit. They're very flexible and she's very expressive with them - most babies are. So just rub them.

Now, try another thing - her hands. She's been able to grasp your finger for awhile, so let her grab one in each hand and just pull her up a little bit and play with her like she is doing little baby pull ups. Tell her how strong she is and how she will drop kick any boy who gives her trouble. She'll hold onto your fingers, and look up at you every now and then like you must be pretty special.

Spend some time looking at her, at all the little exquisite features, like her hair, or bald head as the case may be, her ears, double chins, and tell her how cute she is. Enjoy all her cooing and babbling and all the little sounds he makes, and respond in kind. Carry on a conversation about something important to you, and let him know what a bright child he is, and not just because he agrees with your every thought.

Take a tape recorder and place it so she can babble away into the microphone, and then play it back to her. She will be fascinated and will think you are a genius. Keep the tape, and make sure you label it, because this will be special for you in the future. You'll always remember that moment when you made the recording and played it with your little baby.

There is nothing like coming home and seeing a smiling face come running toward you, yelling "Daddy, daddy, I want you to hold me." To this day it still brings a tear of happiness to my eyes, and I know in my heart that it always will.
Veteran Dad

12

Caring for New Moms

Motherhood is beautiful, but it can really mess with a woman's body, mind and life.

Keep in mind the incredible transformation your partner is going through. She is brand new at being a mother and is coping with major physical, emotional and lifestyle changes. She is recovering from birth and maybe a C-section, riding a hormone roller-coaster and perhaps trying to breastfeed a screaming infant. She may also have lots of "expert" advisors, but little experienced help.

In the short run, mom may be inundated by the baby's needs as well as her own. You may find yourself trying to learn to care for a demanding baby and an overwhelmed mother at the same time. You will need to help her get through it.

Motherhood truly is beautiful, especially when the woman you love, confident and comfortable as a mother at last, smiles at your son asleep in her arms, whispers a few sweet nothings and gently kisses him on the forehead. Becoming a mom brings out a new side of your partner that warrants your deep respect. Her unconditional love and commitment enables your child to thrive.

About New Mothers

All new mothers are different, even though they may share many experiences, and your partner may react in ways that surprise you.

Some new mothers embrace motherhood immediately and totally thrive, as if they were born to be a mom. Some babies sleep almost through the night within weeks and rarely cry. If so, count your lucky stars, but keep in mind that a new mother and baby who don't need you very much can seriously reduce your opportunities to be involved. Contribute any chance you get.

Most new mothers struggle, as life as they knew it has evaporated. She may feel trapped and virtually chained to the baby, and under most circumstances gets no more than a few hours rest at a time. Exhausted and overwhelmed, she is also expected to inherently know what to do with a crying infant and be as happy as a little girl playing with her favorite doll. Talk about a setup!

Her New Life Began at Birth
Remember that your mate's life started again at the birth of her baby, and to a large extent so does her relationship with you. Your performance as a father and a husband in the first months of your new family will have a great impact. She will form a new perspective of you – as the father of her child and her partner as a parent – and this new perspective will substantially determine your future fortunes both in romance and fatherhood. You have the opportunity, by your attitude and your actions, to take a permanent place as a partner that she can count on.

Ultimate Responsibility
Your mate may be a real "go getter," the one everyone turns to when they need to get something done. But as a first time mother, this paragon of organization and energy might feel completely overwhelmed at the realization that it is she who has ultimate responsibility for the very life of her fragile infant. She feels it is up to her, literally, to keep her baby alive and thriving physically while feeling safe emotionally. Even hiccups from the little one can be a frightening episode that sends her thumbing through her baby books and keeps her from sleeping. The first few weeks after birth can be especially trying for a new mom until she is able to balance her uncertainties about her ability to care for her newborn with the reality that the baby is growing and becoming stronger every day.

Everyone's Expectations
No matter how she is feeling, a new mother typically believes that she must live up to everyone's expectations of her, that she should do what she imagines the people around her expect her to do. She must always gaze lovingly at her baby; she must handle him with expert ease and grace, whether breastfeeding or diapering or strapping him into a car seat. She must fulfill that eternal symbol of beauty and strength – a Mother. Sometimes the most intense expectations come from those closest to her, and the feeling of being watched and scrutinized can be a shock.

Maternal Instincts
Maternal instincts are real. They include intuitive ways of holding, touching and communicating that build the bond between a mother

and her baby. They also include a strong emotional pull to care for her baby, which is often extended to other babies as part of a universal motherhood that bonds moms together. As these instincts surface and she realizes she has an untapped reservoir of innate capability as a mother, it boosts her confidence, which in turn allows her to relax and rely more upon her instincts.

Chronic, Intense Fatigue

Dads get tired, even exhausted at times during their babies first weeks. But moms get more than tired; they can suffer from extreme fatigue. It's caused not only by the unpredictability of the baby waking to nurse or to be changed every few hours, but also by the constant pressure a new mother feels of being responsible for her baby's survival. Very young babies require a constant vigilance that makes getting any rest elusive. Even if she has help, a mom is still on the job, delegating, being watchful, ready to take over at the first sign of distress.

A New Mindset

She was extremely upset & touchy after the baby was born. I attribute it to hormones, but like they said in class - if your temper is out of control, you should just walk out the door. Fortunately, it didn't happen much.

Veteran Dad

Your mate has to come to terms with the demands of motherhood, and ultimately develops a new mindset or sense of being a mother. After the birth, a process of self discovery ensues as she struggles to adjust to the life changes and intense responsibility thrust upon her. As she watches her baby grow and flourish, she learns to trust her instincts and steadily develops confidence as a mother. As she finds she is able to give her baby everything he needs, a profound sense of validation, a feeling that she is a real mom sets in. She will take on the aura of one who has been tested and has proven herself, and in a sense, is reborn as a mother in her own mind.

A Note to Dad

Writing this section was interesting, in that after 15 years of conducting Boot Camp For New Dads, it is clear that becoming fathers profoundly changes us men as well. As expectations of fathers rise and we respond, similar dynamics are developing within us. While they occur earlier and more intensely in mothers due to the nature of pregnancy, birth and breastfeeding, the more engaged we become, the more we will enjoy a profound sense of validation as fathers. In a sense, we men are reborn as fathers as well.

How to Help Her

Basic suggestions from veteran dads for helping mom in the first few weeks include:

- Quickly learn to change diapers, burp, and calm your crying baby. Show mom she can count on you.

- Coordinate any help. Obtain what you need from family, friends or neighbors, and make sure it is actually helpful.

- Keep necessary resources available, including phone numbers of doctors, the hospital, resource books, etc., and use them.

- Help her get some sleep, and try to get some yourself.

- Let her know that you don't expect her to be a fairy tale mom.

Looking back over the first two weeks, the most important factors for me as a father were a positive attitude and understanding my role compared with that of my wife.

Veteran Dad

Pitch In

Pitch in as much as you can. In the middle of the night when the baby is crying, and both of you are dead tired, reach deep and find the strength to get up and handle the baby. The long term potential of your actions during the intense, demanding first weeks home will easily justify any effort you can muster, and then some. And in a short time it will pass.

Little Things Count

It is often the little things that count the most:

- "Nice job, mom," on a regular basis.
- The impromptu backrub that feels good and leaves mom feeling loved and appreciated.
- An encouraging afternoon call home when your baby is fussy and mom is frustrated.
- Taking your baby for a walk after work (even if it's just around your house).
- Handling intrusive in-laws and acquaintances.
- Taking a little time each day to talk about something other than the baby.

No matter how hard you work, when you get home don't expect your wife to make your dinner or sit down to watch Monday Night Football and expect your wife to appreciate you. Ask your wife first what you can do for her and then go do that. You'll have a much better relationship.

Veteran Dad

Talk to Her

While your partner may talk a lot, her most troublesome thoughts are often private. It's difficult to talk about anxiety and insecurity, especially when you're supposed to be a happy new mom. The incredible shifts and changes are unnerving, and she can feel like she's lost her moorings and is being carried along by a tide. Encourage her to talk, even if it doesn't make much sense to either of you. It will help her understand what is happening to her and will help her feel less isolated.

Give Mom a Kiss

For years the Boot Camp standard for dads arriving home, no matter how tough the day at work, was to walk in, take your baby and give mom a break. Then a veteran said, "First kiss mom to let her know you love her, and then take your baby." We had a new standard. Moms not only need a break, they also need to be reminded that they are special to us.

On occasion, when your child is calm, remind her of the miracle that she brought into your world. Together, check out your baby's exquisite fingers, toes and nose, and talk of the future – your child's first date, first day at school, and of course, the first time he sleeps through the night.

Keep the big picture in mind. Think long term. It will help get you to where you want to go with your new family.

Helping Her Breastfeed

It is important that you get educated on breastfeeding because while it is an issue most dads leave entirely up to mom, your attitude and assistance can make a big difference in whether she and your baby are successful in making it work. Breastfeeding offers a broad array of benefits to your child and wife, so anything you can do to help make it happen is worth the effort.

Breastfeeding Will Benefit Your Child

Breast milk is a complex substance perfectly tailored to provide everything your baby needs for nutrition and healthy development. It also provides natural defenses against bacteria and viruses, and adjusts to a baby's needs depending on the time of day and stage of development. Because it is better digested by infants' immature gastrointestinal systems, they are less likely to spit up, develop colic, or suffer from uncomfortable gas.

Remember your wife has gone through a lot of changes. Before and after the birth. You'll find that she'll start crying and she won't know why. When she does just hold her and tell her everything is going to be okay. She's going to be sore, tired and overwhelmed. She's going to think she's ugly. That she's a bad mom. And you're going to think you're a bad dad sometimes too! So, just be patient and keep communication open about everything.
Veteran Dad

I was behind her with a hand massaging her breast to help the milk flow and the other hand on the baby's head, trying to position him on the breast. It took us a week to get him hooked up.
Veteran Dad

Several studies have also indicated that breast milk offers long-term health benefits to your child, including improved intelligence, lower risk of obesity as a teenager, lower blood pressure and reduced heart attacks and strokes as adults.

Breastfeeding Benefits Moms

For moms, the benefits are also numerous; perhaps the most important is how a new mother typically feels once she and her baby get breastfeeding down. Nothing can boost her confidence as a mom more and make her feel more connected to her baby than breastfeeding.

A nursing mother normally recovers from pregnancy and delivery sooner as lactation (milk production) helps her lose excess weight more rapidly, releases hormones that help shrink her uterus back to its normal size, and delays resumption of her periods. Hormones released during lactation often promote a pleasant feeling of drowsiness and peace.

There is also an obvious benefit in terms of convenience and cost. Breast milk is always at the perfect temperature, it's sterile, it's readily available, and the price is right.

Getting Hooked Up Can be Very Challenging

Moms have tremendous pressure on them to breastfeed successfully, which can be counterproductive. It usually takes some time for the baby to learn how to latch on and begin nursing, and moms often encounter problems. A common one is feeling she is starving her baby because actual milk production doesn't really start for a few days. The baby is fine during that period even if he loses a little weight.

Like driving a car, it mostly takes experience to get the hang of it. If mom gets frustrated over initial problems, she will not be in a frame of mind to learn, and her milk may simply not "let down" (mom and her breasts need to be relaxed for the milk to flow). In these situations babies get frustrated and cry since they are hungry and are not getting much; this in turn further frustrates mom. Her nipples may also go through a painful process of getting broken in.

How You Can Help

Anticipate the challenges she will face and be encouraging and involved from the beginning. Start by rubbing her shoulders to relax her. Let her get positioned, and then hand the baby to her. Reassure her, and ask her how you can help.

It was tough for her at first, but once she had it down, she felt like she was in a warm, cozy cocoon with her baby when breastfeeding at night.

Veteran Dad

I was helping her try different positions and it just wasn't working. The baby was crying because he was hungry and she was crying out of frustration. At one point the baby ended up upside down, and it was funny and she laughed. It relaxed her, which helped. It still took a while though.

Veteran Dad

If problems develop, take your crying baby and calm him prior to another attempt by mom. This will be tough because babies cry when they are hungry, so try to stay relaxed yourself. Music may help calm him, or something with bright, contrasting colors to temporarily take his mind off the fact he is hungry. Do what you can to make sure mom is rested when she is trying to breastfeed as otherwise she will frustrate easily.

My husband got our son onto my breast initially by dripping some sterile water onto my breast. He was so proud that it worked and that he thought of it, and not me, an OB nurse. I was proud of him too, and our son was delighted!
Veteran OB Nurse

An engineer participating in Boot Camp broke down the functions of breastfeeding into components, which makes problem solving easier. Is mom relaxed? Is her breast milk letting down? Is the baby getting anything? Is the baby too upset to suck? Is he positioned wrong?

If it is not working, try another position, as this is a major factor according to breastfeeding experts. And if the new one doesn't work, try another. Get her a "boppy pillow" to help get the baby positioned comfortably. A variety of positions can be tried, and you can also take the baby and hold him to her breast yourself.

Refrain from giving him a bottle with formula because he is not getting enough milk from her breast. Babies find the milk flows much easier from a bottle, and will then become even more frustrated when trying to latch on to the breast.

Even if it doesn't work at first, mom will appreciate that it's not her up against it alone, and that you are there with her.

Call in the Reinforcements
If problems persist, keep encouraging her. Ninety percent of moms who quit breastfeeding early don't really want to give up. Look to your hospital, physician or breastfeeding organizations for resources, and the sooner the better. They can include lactation (breastfeeding) consultants who can stop by your home or give advice over the phone.

Your wife may feel embarrassed because she's supposed to know how to nurse a baby, and may be reluctant to call on these resources. It's a simple matter for dad to pick up the phone, give a call, come up with a few ideas and suggest them. You need to help her make her best effort. If it works, it will be well worth it—and if not, you will both want to know you tried everything possible. Check for breastfeeding resources in *Learning More/Getting Help* in the Appendix.

If It Just Won't Work

Given all the benefits of breastfeeding, why would anyone choose not to breastfeed? As it turns out, there are several compelling reasons. The fact is that some mothers are unable to breastfeed, despite their desire to do so. Some need to take medications that prohibit breastfeeding, or they might have problems with adequate milk production, or with letdown. Others have trouble with inverted nipples that a baby can't latch on to. Still other women find breastfeeding too painful, or demanding, especially if they feel pressure to return to work quickly.

If breastfeeding is simply not going to work, reassure your mate of your love and respect, and be the first to tell her it's no big deal. New mothers tend to beat themselves up over their inability to breastfeed, and your partner will need your support now more than ever. Even if you are disappointed that your baby will not be breastfed, the bottom line at this point is helping your partner overcome her disappointment and getting on with becoming the best mom possible to your child.

Formula is Not So Bad

While formula will never fully match breast milk's benefits, it is certainly adequate. Virtually an entire generation of more or less healthy adults attests to the suitability of formula. Formula-fed infants are also more likely to go longer between feedings, due to the increased time it takes for babies to digest it. Also, a new mother who doesn't breast feed doesn't have to contend with the annoyance of leaking breasts. And formula allows new dads to get involved with feeding.

Help Her Get a Little Privacy

Many moms find breastfeeding in public with people watching to be awkward. You might feel the same, especially if it is one of your friends watching. You can help by finding her some privacy or shielding her from view by draping a blanket loosely over her shoulders. If some lout feels it necessary to express disapproval, you should feel free to suggest that if his mother had breastfed him, he might be smarter (or perhaps something a little more eloquent).

How Do You Really Feel About Breastfeeding?

Hopefully you feel that your breastfeeding wife is the epitome of motherhood and is beautiful to see. However, at first, some men get queasy at the sight of the baby feeding at mom's breast. You may also find yourself somewhat resentful about the closeness she has with her nursing newborn. This is all very normal, especially if you set your sights on being highly involved with your baby, and particularly when

Breastfeeding makes mom feel good but in some cases at some times it's not going to work out. We tried and then decided to stop, after we stopped things were actually worse because my wife felt like such a failure and that she should still breastfeed. Obviously we had wanted to breastfeed and she did make it for about 3 weeks. I tried to support her as much as possible but it was a little too much for her. I didn't say to her "you have to do it." I just encouraged her and then together we made the decision to stop.
Veteran Dad

Day one was great. She latched on but then my wife's milk would not come in for days. The baby was dropping weight and my wife was also saying "good mothers breastfeed." Finally, I said "breastfeeding and bottle feeding are both good answers you just try to choose the better of the two." We switched to bottle feeding and within a couple of days she was the happiest woman in the world, she had more freedom, she could drink whatever she wanted to and so it actually worked out real well for her.
Veteran Dad

your baby is crying with hunger and only mom will do. Try being the bath specialist, because babies learn to love that too.

Get Dad in On the Act

Once the baby is used to breastfeeding (3-4 weeks), encourage mom to use a breast pump and introduce a bottle so that she is not tied to the baby at all times and you get a chance to "play." Giving her a chance to take several hours away from home and the baby, doing something she enjoys, can also work wonders for a new mom.

> **Who Gets Up With the Baby at Night?**
> If your baby is going to be breastfed, your mate is going to have to do it. You can share the load, however, by getting up when you hear the baby cry and bringing him to her in bed. You then go back to sleep while she cuddles the baby to her and nurses him. By the time she is finished, she is awake and can put junior back to bed. Either one of you can do the diaper duty, or you can share it. Try variations of this theme to figure out what works best for you and mom. If you are a heavy sleeper and are worthless at work due to disrupted sleep, figure out some other way to seriously pitch in.

Helping Her Bond

Don't be surprised or disappointed if your mate does not mimic the stereotypical mother who falls in love with her baby at first sight. While moms tend to bond faster than dads, many experience difficulties developing a deep emotional attachment with their babies. It is critical that she ultimately does so, because to a large extent, the way a mom loves her child will eventually permit him to love and be loved as an adult.

Since her strong connection with the baby is essential, you may need to help her. Just as you might be battling with your own doubts about the love you may or may not be feeling, she may be going through a similar experience. If so, you and mom will have the opportunity to get to know your baby - and bond – together. While challenging, this can also be a powerful prescription for a strong parenting team.

Early Bonding

Magazine ads, TV commercials and recent celebrity new mothers make it seem like every new mom should expect to fall madly, head-over-heels in love with their babies at birth. Bonding is a process of growing close that lasts a lifetime. Mothers who get a late start due to health problems, adoption, or confused feelings move on to develop strong relationships with their babies just as those who get an early start.

In spite of everything you have heard or read about the magic of maternal bonding, many great mothers will tell you that they did not feel an immediate and overwhelming love for their babies. In fact, women sometimes experience weeks of tortured insecurity and doubt about their ability to love this needy, crying, demanding and incomprehensible child.

How fast mom gets to first base is not particularly important. Getting there and moving forward is, and anxiety over bonding can become an obstacle along her path. Worrying about bonding is a good way to block it, and this is often the fundamental problem. Especially for the mother of an infant who is taken immediately to a neonatal care unit, there can be severe feelings of guilt or failure or even fear that the future relationship with her child has been compromised.

Bonding Takes Time
Maternal bonding is both an emotional and innate biological process, and it takes time. As with all relationships, each one develops differently. There is no magic formula and it cannot be forced. This is a classic version of a problem that if ignored, will usually go away on its own. The same goes for dads. Babies born prematurely or with special needs can present bigger bonding challenges, so use your resources to get the best information and guidance you can.

I found that it was harder to maintain my wife's needs than the baby's.

Veteran Dad

How You Can Help
Sometimes it only takes a sympathetic ear or even a good laugh to dispel the myths of automatic bonding and unqualified love. Let her know that her feelings are more normal than society's unrealistic expectations of her to be some kind of saint. To help her connect and develop confidence in her capabilities as a mother, point out all the things she does right for the baby. Encourage her to do the following:

- Touch, cuddle and engage in regular skin-to skin contact with the baby. Touch is an early form of communication that your baby will understand and respond to.
- Eye-to-eye contact with your baby. Another form of communication, and when he starts moving his head so he can see her as she moves around the room, it is like he is saying "hi mom."
- Babies also enjoy human voices and cooing and babbling back themselves, so talk, sing, even read the newspaper aloud.

- Babies can learn to imitate your facial expressions, so smile away. Whether it's gas or the real thing, a baby that smiles at you is much easier to love. In fact, a cooing, smiling baby is perfectly designed to steal both mom's and dad's hearts.

If her first post-partum doctor's appointment arrives and she has concerns over her feelings for the baby, suggest that she talk it over with her doctor. If the feelings persist or worsen, it may be related to postpartum depression, in which case you will want to take appropriate action (see below).

Helping Her Succeed As a Mom

Moms struggling to cope with a new baby get frustrated. She may feel she is not a good mother, which rattles her confidence. It can be about anything – nursing problems, the baby crying, health issues or even diaper changing or swaddling. They can also feel very alone, with no one to talk to who understands their plight. Even when surrounded by their families, new moms can feel isolated and trapped in a life over which they have no control.

Reassure and Encourage Her
A mom can feel incompetent or even guilty when she cannot calm her crying baby because her "maternal instinct" is supposed to tell her exactly why the baby is crying and how to comfort him. Being dead tired, feeling fat and unattractive, having little control over her own emotions, and seeing no end in sight can make her plight seem hopeless.

Encouragement and support by dad is essential. Point out what a great job she is doing, what a wonderful baby she produced, and how much you appreciate her. The more support, the better the mom. Assure her that you are in it together and you will get through it together. Be positive, constructive, and help build her confidence. Keep in mind she is in a process, and that you can't nag her into motherhood. Build her up instead.

Help Her Deal With Isolation
After a month or so, the excitement over the baby's birth winds down, the calls and visits taper off, and mom no longer attracts much attention. Our friends, especially if we are the first in our group to have a baby, grow weary of constantly hearing about "the baby." Although

Do anything you can to help your wife go through the process of being a mother. Even though it's more natural for her, it also requires an adjustment that's much greater for a woman because they're demands being put on her body that you don't experience. So the best thing to do is swallow your own point of view for a while and just be there.

Veteran Dad

babies tend to be portable, going out with a newborn can be so much work that it may not happen often.

A sense of isolation can start to develop. If mom is staying home, she goes without the daily contact with colleagues. She may also see less of her spouse, who is picking up the financial slack by working more, leading to further isolation. After several months, she can hit the wall, confused as to why she is so unhappy being a stay-at-home mom.

Develop a Support Network
Some new parents, bleary-eyed and on auto pilot, forget that there is a support network out there that they should be calling on often. This includes family, friends, and especially other new parents; a circle of people you trust and can depend on. Reaching out and using this network is crucial for you and your mate.

Encourage Contact with Other Mothers
New moms seem to automatically gravitate towards other experienced mothers, including their own. New mothers often have issues with their own moms, but they still tend to have very close relationships during the first months of motherhood. Her mother can provide guidance that she trusts and a strong sense of security. You should also encourage her to have a high level of contact with other mothers who can do the same. New moms who become isolated without a support network are more likely to have problems with the baby and with postpartum depression.

Encourage Her to Join a New Moms Group
Your partner will find other moms who totally understand her situation and are highly sympathetic, who have lots of advice she can trust, and who serve as a readily available support system. She can blow off steam about an insensitive husband who does not understand her (that would be you) at a group meeting, as well as hear about another husband who is much worse (priceless).

The first few times out, offer to drive mom and baby to a group if she is feeling overwhelmed at the idea of getting out.

Recognize Her "Gatekeeping" for What It Is
A mother has an intense relationship with her baby, and it's not always easy, even if she is exhausted, for her to share him with you. There you are, primed and ready to do your part, and she's hovering over you, scrutinizing everything you try to do. What do you do if your wife wants to do everything herself?

My wife had complications afterwards and was bedridden. I got to jump in very solidly with both feet...so don't plan on doing anything if you have complications for two to four weeks.

Veteran Dad

If she automatically tries to take over, remind her that you need the practice. Let her know how important being close to your son or daughter is to you, right from the beginning. Stand your ground gently, and suggest she'll be glad for your involvement in the long run.

If she's constantly looking over your shoulder and correcting you, take the baby into another room. Try to get her out of the house alone so you can prove to her that you are fully capable of taking care of your own child. Don't be afraid to make a few mistakes as you find your own way of doing things.

Understand that her life is wrapped around the baby, and her "control freak" behavior is tied directly to her desire to do a good job as a mother.

Baby Blues and Postpartum Depression

After the baby arrived, her life was a mess. Her job stressed her out and she quit her exercise class and going out with her friends because she felt guilty about being away from the baby. I told her that taking time for herself would make her a better mom. It took her a few months to get her sense of balance back.

Veteran Dad

Most new mothers feel seriously down at times, which can be confusing to new dads who figured that having a baby would make them happy. This can also be very frustrating when it occurs after the baby gets settled into a routine and life has started returning to normal.

There are many factors that drive "baby blues", including being tired over interrupted sleep, going back to work and a reversal of the hormonal changes that occurred in pregnancy. There is also the more serious forms of postpartum depression, which can threaten the well being of mom and your baby, as well as your marriage. Understanding this common occurrence will provide a basis for helping your mate through it, as well as enduring it yourself.

What are the Baby Blues?

Despite the happiness a new baby brings, many new mothers find themselves subject to the "baby blues," a mild form of postpartum depression. Common symptoms include mood swings, crying, feelings of anxiety, a general sense of unhappiness, irritability, nervousness and/or insomnia. These feelings are confusing to mom as well, and may be compounded by guilt, since most new mothers believe that they should be nothing but happy and content.

Post-partum depression got severe for my wife. I wish we had more information ahead of time.

Veteran Dad

The baby blues generally occur between birth and six weeks after, and about 80% of new moms experience them. A drop in estrogen and progesterone levels following delivery provides a chemical trigger, and contributing factors include:

- Feeling inadequate as a mom
- Guilt about returning to work and having to leave her baby at day care
- Staying home and feeling trapped and isolated
- Problems in bonding with her baby

While disturbing, the baby blues usually disappear after several weeks, as mom and the baby settle into a routine and her hormone levels stabilize. She will begin to seem her "old self" again and her energy and outlook will improve. Later on, weaning the baby from breastfeeding may trigger a new bout of mild depression, due again to changes in hormone levels, but it too will pass.

What You Can Do

Your first take on the baby blues, after helping your mate through pregnancy, birth, and the first weeks at home with a baby, may be "now what's the problem?" It is easy to get irritated and even angry, which of course doesn't help, as well as worried about both mom and the baby.

My wife went through a bit of postpartum [depression]…Sometimes you have to have some intervention.
Veteran dad.

Consider this as one of the final hurdles she faces in getting her own body back under control and her life back into balance. Remind yourself that she doesn't want to act this way, and that the hormones are at it again. Also take comfort from the knowledge that it will probably soon be over.

Your job during this new trial by fire is to remain supportive and understanding. You may well find yourself serving as a punching bag again. Continue what you are already doing to help, including reassuring her of your love and what a great job she is doing.

- Encourage her to talk about what is going on.
- Remind her it is normal and will pass.
- Lighten her load. Women who don't have adequate help and support have a harder time snapping back.
- Insist she get out of the house and away from the baby.

Just feeling appreciated helps. A change of scenery, perhaps some free time at the mall, helps even more. Many new moms feel trapped at home with the baby, but at the same time they may also feel that good moms don't turn their infant's care over to a babysitter. Handle it; a few hours out can work wonders.

For new moms who cannot pull themselves out of depression, some professional help may be in order. Talk to your physician. It's paramount to take care of emotional problems quickly, so that you and your wife can continue to have a healthy relationship and be good parents.

What is Postpartum Depression?

Up to 20 percent of new mothers develop full blown postpartum depression, which typically occurs between six weeks and one year after childbirth. This is a medical problem, and women with a family or personal history of depression are more likely to suffer from it. In addition to being very tough on mom and you, unmanaged postpartum depression is linked to poorer cognitive skills and behavioral and emotional problems in children.

If some of the following symptoms persist for more than a week, notify your spouse's obstetrician or a helpline at the hospital immediately and discuss your concerns:

- Inability to sleep, or sleeping too much
- Loss of appetite, or overeating
- A lack of interest in any of the activities that normally interest her
- An inability to concentrate on simple tasks
- Persistent feelings of helplessness, hopelessness or lack of control
- Noticeable lethargy, or obvious hyperactivity
- An abnormal preoccupation with the baby's health
- Disorientation and confusion
- Loss of touch with reality
- Panic attacks
- Extreme mood swings and crying
- Not able to care for herself or the baby

A very small percentage of women suffering postpartum depression may develop a still more serious condition known as postpartum psychosis. This illness may lead a woman to consider harming herself or her child. This condition requires immediate medical intervention.

What You Can Do
As a new father, it is extremely important to know the signs of depression and take action on your mate's behalf if you suspect that she is slipping beyond ordinary baby blues into true postpartum depression. Due to mom's isolation at home, you may be the only one who is around to even notice these symptoms, much less help. For the sake of your family, you need to take matters into your own hands.

As with "ordinary" baby blues, your understanding and compassion are of paramount importance to your partner's recovery. She isn't a bad mother, wife or person for acting this way, any more than a diabetic is a bad person for going into shock without insulin. She is ill and requires medical attention. Essential steps for you to take are as follows:

- <u>Take care of your baby</u>
  Make sure your baby is getting appropriate care, and consider asking for help from friends and relatives.

- <u>Get professional help for your wife</u>
  Talk immediately to an experienced counselor or to your physician about your partner's symptoms and circumstances.

- <u>Get educated</u>
  Review materials on postpartum depression from the doctor or hospital as well as online information (see *Learning More/Getting Help* in the appendix).

- <u>Talk to her</u>
  Talk to her about postpartum depression, about how she feels, as well as about how you feel. Talking will help you maintain your relationship.

- <u>Get involved in her treatment</u>
  Go with her to visit the doctor and/or her therapist, and volunteer to sit in on a therapy session.

- <u>Call in the reinforcements</u>
  Reach out to her mother, father, sisters and friends, and ask for their support and involvement as necessary. Call on support groups as well.

- <u>Reassure her</u>
  Consistently remind her that you will be there for her, that you will get through it together, and that it will pass. Hold her close when she is upset.

Take it seriously, take action, and you will get through it together.

Special Challenges for New Moms

Surgical Births

If your mate had a Cesarean or other type of surgical delivery, she will probably have stayed in the hospital for a few days. By the time she gets home, her staples or sutures may have been removed, but she is still in pain and will probably be taking pain medication. She will be restricted from lifting and will need extra help caring for the baby and for herself for a few weeks. If you can afford it, get her professional help. Otherwise, try to have a friend or relative assist if you need to go to work.

Women often feel disappointed in themselves when they "fail" at a successful vaginal birth. Your mate will depend on you to remind her that the only important thing is your beautiful and healthy baby and her good health. Most women who try a vaginal birth after having had a C-section are successful, so chances are she'll be able to have a "normal" birth next time. Within six-eight weeks, she can start exercising moderately once her doctor gives the go-ahead.

Premature Baby

A premature baby can cause a great deal of anxiety and confusion for both you and your partner. For your wife, the feelings can be intense, as the pregnancy is suddenly interrupted and her hormones go into disequilibrium. She may be frantically worried about her baby, and after the birth, may not be able to be with him. When the baby is bundled off to the neonatal unit for care, she is left in a strange and lonely place of helplessness and fear. While all of her instincts are pushing her to care for and nurture her newborn, all she can do is wait and hope.

If your mate wants to breastfeed, she'll have to begin expressing milk right away, without the benefit of help from the baby. This may be the last thing she wants to do, but it will be a way that she can still care for her baby.

This is when the love and support between you is most important. Don't let your fear overwhelm your relationship at this time. Do whatever you can to stay connected to your mate and baby until he comes home. Arrange for the two of you to visit him often, hold him and feed him if you are allowed to.

Make sure your partner does not "give up" if she becomes overwhelmed by it all, but instead remains involved in the care of the baby as much as possible. Fortunately, neonatal intensive care units are now offering support programs to help moms cope.

Injuries or Illness

As you know by now, childbirth makes huge demands on a woman's body, and in a small number of women, injuries or health problems result. These can include a bruised or broken tailbone, postpartum hemorrhage or infection, or a ruptured uterus. Women who give birth to unusually large babies (over 10 pounds) may damage their tailbones. There isn't much you can do medically except take pain medication and take it easy until it heals. Lying on her side will be more comfortable, and when sitting, she actually may find a hard chair most comfortable. Holding an ice pack on sore spots also brings relief.

A small percentage of births will result in an infection. Symptoms to look out for are fever, lower abdominal pain, difficulty urinating, and pain and tenderness at the site of the infection. Other infections cause redness, discharge around the site, and a foul-smelling vaginal discharge. Make sure she reports unusual symptoms or any postpartum fever, to her doctor. If your mate needs to take antibiotics, make sure she takes them all. If she's breastfeeding, make sure that she consults a medical specialist before taking any pre-pregnancy prescription drugs or over-the-counter medications. Drinking extra fluids and resting are the tried and true methods of recovery from most postpartum injuries.

The Gift of Balance

Over the past decade working with Boot Camp For New Dads, I thought that fathers would close the gap between their level of involvement and that of mothers, and that as a result, mothers would become happier. I was often wrong on both counts.

While fathers are much more involved, increasing expectations have pushed mothers to become even busier, and a large gap still remains. In addition to their natural responsibilities, mothers today are expected to resume their careers while breastfeeding. They are also cautioned against subjecting their babies to daycare, and they feel compelled to get back to a size 6 like the celebrity moms. They feel their babies must show signs of genius by six months, while they remain happy and serene.

The best thing you can do to be a better father is to be a good husband at the same time. If you can give your wife back some of her sanity that will make it easier in the long run.

Veteran Dad

While stress levels drop for fathers after the first months, stress due to new demands on moms builds throughout the first year. Mothers are very vulnerable to new expectations, especially those that suggest her baby will be better off in any way. They come through the media and are often reinforced by well meaning friends and relatives as well as competitive mothering. These messages target a woman's most intense feelings for her baby, and suggest that she is a poor mother if she does not meet expectations.

The bottom line is that more than anything else, moms today need to get the balance back in their lives. They need some relief from constant vigilance and response regarding her baby's needs. Your partner also needs time to herself, and something else in her life beyond family and work. She also needs a little adult conversation.

Pull Her Out of the Deep End
New fathers are continually admonished to do everything moms want. Moms, especially due to all the demands they face, can want a great deal. They often feel like they were thrown into the deep end of the pool and are drowning, and they want dad to jump in too. Don't. Stand on the edge and pull her out. Help her regain her footing on firm ground by balancing out her myopic, consuming focus on all things baby related. Be firm that she have a life beyond the baby.

Get Her Out on Her Own
A mom who cannot think of much other than her baby will find it hard to leave him, even in your care or that of a babysitter. A change of scenery is essential for her to enjoy a little guiltless freedom, so you may have to boot her out of the house while you handle the baby. Perhaps she'd like to go to a movie, the hairdresser, or the mall, or visit with friends. The fresh perspective she gets from some rejuvenating personal time will make your efforts totally worth it.

Insist She Do Something for Herself
Insist that she do something for herself, and help make it happen. An exercise or art class, or girl's night out, in addition to a regular date with you, is essential. Remind her that she needs balance in her life to be able to do her best as a mother. She needs her old friends, too, and not just other mothers, so she can be more than a mom at times.

Remember This is the Time that Counts Most
More than any other issue, veteran dads stress the importance of taking care of new moms. When you're dog tired too, and perhaps taking heat for not being perfect, being magnanimous with mom can

Take care of each other. Talk to each other. Don't try to be the Superdad… Be aware of all the changes going on and communicate with your wife.

Veteran Dad

be trying. But down the road, when you look back, you will want to know that no matter how tough it was, you were up to it. You will want her to know it too.

If you help bring out the best in her as a mother, she will do the same for you as a father.

13

Troubleshooting Crying Babies

Her first cry after she was born may have been music to your ears, but as time with a crying baby wears on, the more you hear it, the more it can feel like fingernails scraping on a blackboard. Particularly if you don't know what to do to sooth her.

While all babies cry, yours may be calm and cry relatively little. At the other end of the range is the 20 percent of babies who develop the continual screaming associated with colic. If this is the hand you were dealt, you and mom may be in for the most aggravating and frustrating experience of your lives. Even dealing with normal fussiness and crying can be very trying, so while you can hope for the best in the form of a really calm baby, you will want to be prepared for anything.

To take a proactive, constructive approach to comforting a crying baby, learn the basics so you will be ready to go, and then get hands on right from the beginning. Be prepared to be overwhelmed with aggravation at times, as it happens to the best of us. Remember the best option, when all else fails, will be to place your crying baby in his crib, close the door, walk away for a while and let him safely get it out of his system.

Dad's Challenge and Opportunity

If there is any challenge new fathers need to take head on, it is a crying baby. This is the role that separates the men from the boys; diapers, baths and feeding are easy compared to trying to calm an inconsolable infant.

While this notion may be hard to grasp, a fussy, crying baby also presents you an opportunity. Not only will mom welcome all the help you have to offer, you can score huge points with her if you become skilled at quieting those screams and putting your fussy baby to sleep. You will find that you will also score points with yourself, building your confidence as a dad, as well as with your baby, who will respond with a feeling that "help has arrived" when she sees you.

While a few months with a crying baby may seem like a lifetime, it passes, and the bad times become a distant memory. The points you score last a long time.

Crying Babies are Hard to Take
Especially if you feel incompetent to help. Trying to cope with persistent crying, with a limited ability to make your baby feel better, can be profoundly demoralizing. It can play tricks on your mind, like dredging up bad memories from your past, making you feel like a failure, or even driving you to ignore your baby's needs. This is not where the joy of fatherhood kicks in.

Crying Babies are Tougher on Moms
The shock to our emotional and nervous systems from our babies' screams is muted compared to that of our hardwired mates. This cuts both ways; it certainly makes it easier for you to blow off your baby's needs, as some new fathers do. But it also makes it easier for you to deal with the crying, since dads do not react as intensely as moms. Your mate may quickly feel like she is a terrible mother since she cannot even tell what is wrong with her baby, let alone fix it. We generally don't get these feelings, which allows us to focus on solutions.

It Will Strengthen Your Connection With Your Baby
Colic definitely makes it tougher to bond. But there is an upside for the father who hangs in there and does his best. Even limited success in calming a crying baby is rewarding, and you will always know that you were there when your baby needed you the most. This will cement and strengthen your bond with your child for a long time to come.

I learned a few things. Now when she cries, it's like "dad to the rescue!"
Veteran Dad

It Will Strengthen Your Relationship With Mom
High maintenance babies typically strain a relationship long after the crying dissipates because mom is left feeling bitter when she believes dad did not do his part. Parents who are not in sync and working together can really stress out, even reaching the point of a marital crisis. The opposite can also be true, especially if she feels that you developed a special talent for making the baby feel better.

You Can Get Good at It
Dads who work at it can become very good in soothing upset babies, and in some respects are better equipped than moms to take on the challenge of crying. Many babies seem to respond best to their fathers when they need comforting, and if you step into the role of "Dad to the Rescue," your baby will feel better just hearing your voice, something that will last a lifetime.

Regularly turning a baby who is "howling like a Banshee" into one who is "sleeping like an angel" will get you into your neighborhood's new father hall of fame. Good luck.

Troubleshooter's Guide to Crying Babies

Our baby's cry flips on a switch in our nervous systems, and we instinctively respond to her calls for help and attempt to fix the problem. First we must determine the reason; she has many possibilities but she can't tell you what is wrong. Maybe she's hungry, maybe her diaper is irritating her, or maybe it's just a bout of "unexplained crying." If you knew what the cause was, you could fix it. Therein lies the problem. If only you knew.

The Troubleshooter's Guide
It's the middle of the night, one hour after his last feeding, and he has been crying for ten minutes. For no apparent reason. Mom is exhausted and close to losing it. You have to go to work early. While tempted, acting like you are asleep is not an option. What do you do?

A logical, proactive approach is in order. The Troubleshooter's Guide To Crying Babies employs the same practical approach used when troubleshooting cars, computers or other mechanical items. It is one of the most popular lessons at Boot Camp and has been proven as an effective tool for over 15 years.

It works because infants are logical. When they cry, there is a reason, and men tend to be logically, mechanically oriented as well. It also works because having a plan minimizes your frustration level and enables you to remain cool, rational and focused on a solution. So allow your natural problem-solving instincts to take over and treat it like you would any other problem – as a fixable one.

1. Develop a Checklist for Your Baby
To determine the cause, develop a mental list of why your baby cries. Hungry will be at the top of most lists, followed by tired. Your list will be unique to your baby, but think gas, wet diaper, rash, constipation, hot, cold, just wants to be held, burped, etc. - and add new causes as they develop: too much light coming in window at night, loud noises or too quiet might be among them.

A typical list, starting with the most prevalent causes of crying, is as follows:

The best thing that I picked up from this class was the checklist. Sometimes babies cry for no apparent reason, but if you've gone down the checklist and haven't found anything wrong, you can at least keep yourself sane by saying "I've checked the diaper and it's not dirty, he just ate so he's not hungry, he doesn't have any visible injuries, etc. And, of course, sometimes you go down the checklist and find exactly what the problem is.

Veteran Dad

Using the troubleshooters guide was a confidence builder. I continue to be the trouble shooting champion and I am never afraid to try new ways to calm upset babies.

Veteran Dad

- Hungry
- Tired
- Needs burping
- Gas/constipated
- Dirty or wet diaper
- Diaper rash
- Too hot/too cold
- Clothes rubbing
- Diaper pinching skin
- Frustrated
- Needs to be held
- Too much noise
- Room too quiet
- Other

Always keep in mind the "you never know" category, which may include:

- Finger bent back in sleeve
- Hair wrapped around toe
- No hole in bottle nipple
- Many other possibilities

After an hour of trying everything, I undressed him and found a hair wrapped tightly and painfully around his toe.
Veteran Dad

2.   Check Each Item in Sequence
From the top of the list, check each of the causes, much like you would with your car if it didn't start (check the gas, battery, starter, and so on). Start by ruling out hungry (fed in last two hours; no rooting around or sucking reflex on your finger), and then continue down your list.

3.   Rule Out Problems by Trying Solutions
Try different solutions like burping or swaddling him to rule out problems on your list. Be careful to not over stimulate him and make the problem worse. Remember that your own anxiety can become a problem as well.

4.   Check for New Problems
When you finish your baby's regular list, check for "you never know" problems. The new nipple on her bottle may not have a hole (this happened at Boot Camp), the edge of the tape on her diaper may be rubbing her, etc. Of course, if at any point you suspect your baby may need medical attention, call your doctor's office.

Babies cry. Once you check all the possible reasons a baby cries, sometimes holding them (or walking away) is the only thing you can do. Remain calm. Take it slow.
Veteran Dad

5.   Move on to Advanced Crying Strategies
When you have tried everything and nothing has worked, go back to "tired." After 30 minutes of crying, your baby is likely to be overtired, and putting her to sleep will be challenging. Refer to strategies for dealing with crying and colic later in this chapter.

Babies and Crying

There's going to be a point when you're going to run into the end of your check list and the baby is still crying. It happens. Sometimes a baby just cries. If anything, working my way through my baby's crying has been a real test of patience for me as a father. The worst feeling is hearing your baby cry. But sometimes you also need the patience to just put the baby down and let it cry.
Veteran Dad

An overview of crying baby issues will help provide you an understanding of what you may be dealing with:

Getting Over the Three Month Hump
While there is considerable variation among babies in terms of their amount of crying, they tend to follow the same pattern. As newborns, they generally do not cry very much. Really. But then their crying increases steadily for several weeks and tends to plateau at 4-6 weeks. They can carry on for weeks, and then taper back down, with crying largely over by 3-4 months. For serious criers, it is definitely a "get over the three month hump" situation for mom and dad.

Fussing Peaks at Six Weeks
Fussing may be a very benign term for the screaming a seriously colicky baby can engage in, but whatever its intensity, it typically occurs like clockwork in the late afternoon and evening (just when you might get home from work). It is referred to as unexplained crying, because the cause is not apparent; she is full, diapered, and warm, as well as cranky, hard to please and maybe downright inconsolable. Unexplained crying indeed.

Parent's Learning Curve
The more experience you have with your baby, the better you will get at diagnosing the cause of his crying (whether explainable or not) and determining a workable course of action. The 4-6 week buildup period gives you a chance to develop skills and strategies that will put you ahead of her crying curve; while you won't know how bad it will get until it does, anticipating colic's progression will make it easier to cope (many parents are surprised and confused that it worsens over a 6 week period even though this is the universal pattern for babies).

You'll sense degrees of urgencies in cries. Sometimes it's not too loud; other times it's blood curdling.
Veteran Dad

Crying Does Not Reflect on You
It is easy (and very common) for a father to take it personally when his baby continues to cry, no matter how hard he tries to help her. If you find yourself doing this, remember that the length and intensity of your baby's cries reflects her nature as a baby, and is no indication of your quality as a dad or your wife's capability as a mother. Doing your best is all that can be done.

Baby's Learning Curve
Over several months, your baby will actually start learning to sooth himself, often by sucking on his fist (eventually perhaps finding his

thumb), cooing, moving around, or focusing on the colors and movement of a mobile. Like learning to read or throw a ball later, some will be better at it than others, and you can do things that help them learn. Provide a calm environment, work towards a normal routine of care that makes him comfortable and secure, watch for cues that your baby is trying, and hang a NASCAR mobile over his crib.

Can You Tell What is Wrong by Your Baby's Cry?
New baby literature is full of suggestions that you can decipher what your baby is crying about from the tone, intensity and duration of his cry. This gives new parents the notion that if they just learned the lingo, they would know what to do. This faddish theory falls apart in practice. While crying may be a baby's way of communicating, new parents don't know the language.

While you will get used to a certain cry signaling feeding time and another when she is just fussing, that is the easy part. It is all the other times, and especially the "unexplained crying" times that are the problem. You will also find that the type of cry is just one of a variety of cues that will help you determine his needs, such as his feeding schedule, yawning when he is tired, a check of his diaper, etc.

Baby's cry is designed to get your attention. And they don't have a lot of modulation. They also don't know how to speak. So when they cry because they have wet diapers, they're hungry, or cold, it sounds the same as though someone set you on fire.
Veteran Dad

Pacifiers, Thumbs & Your Finger
Any debate over pacifiers in your home quickly concludes when you first cork your screaming baby with one and she immediately quiets down. The sucking reflex comes standard on all babies and sucking on something – breast, bottle, your finger - is very soothing to them. While not all go for it, babies who learn to use their thumbs are going to be even happier, as they can calm themselves anytime they want. This is definitely a good thing; you can even help her find her thumb by popping it into her mouth occasionally.

You Can't Spoil a Baby
Not only is it not possible for the first year, it is essential that you respond to your baby's cries and needs so she develops a sense of security and wellbeing over the first months. She will learn to cry for your attention, a serious development step, as well as your invitation to cuddle, entertain, play and elicit a smile that will light up your day.

You Can Develop an Effective Routine
Your baby will develop a pattern of sleeping and feeding that you will both count on and need to work around for the first months. After this you can start modifying his pattern to better fit mom's and your needs – like more feedings during the day so he sleeps more at night. Trying

Instead of feeding him on the cry, we wake Brayden up to feed him. It's really helped my wife out a lot because it put Brayden on a consistent feeding schedule.
Veteran Dad

to get him to adhere to a rigid schedule will likely be frustrating for everyone, but gradual adjustments that bring your family's routine into sync are very possible. Be sure to not do the opposite; getting him to sleep more during the day may result in him sleeping less at night.

Calming Crying Babies

It's cool when you are fresh and aware. But when you're really tired - and you will be - that's when you need more patience. Baby's can be very fussy. At first it was like what do I do with this baby. And you pass it back and forth with your wife. We both had to learn sometimes to try this and this and if it doesn't work you just hold him, talk to him, sing to him, and let him be fussy. There's nothing you can do sometimes but let him be fussy. Some days the baby is fussier than others. Even though this is my first baby I still feel like a rookie. I'm learning every day.
Veteran Dad

Firemen, drag racers and poker players know that there is both a science and an art for getting the job done, and the same goes for calming crying babies. You go with a standard approach, but you also want to be ready with alternatives, so if something doesn't work, you can immediately try something else. They know that if they ignore the science, they will get into trouble, but if they rely on it all the time, they will sometimes be left without answers.

The basic rules of the trade:

*   Your evolving troubleshooters list should guide your selection of methods.
*   There are many methods to try, and always another that you can develop.
*   Try something, and if it works, do it again; If not, try something else.
*   Don't be surprised if what has been successful stops working; babies develop and change rapidly.
*   Stay calm yourself; your baby will quickly pick up on your tension and anxiety.

It can be like learning to dance together, with you learning to pick up her cues, and she learning to respond to your lead. And the more you do it, the better you both will get.

When she fires up her pipes, fundamental fixes, depending on your initial diagnosis, are as follows:

Feeding
If it fits her normal schedule, hand her to mom or get the bottle with pumped breast milk or formula, and go for it. If she is not on schedule, but you think she might be hungry, go for it. If she gulps it down; you have the solution; if not, move on down your list.

Mom as Pacifier

A breastfeeding mom will often bring her crying baby to her breast to see if he is hungry. Even if not, he finds her breast to be the ultimate pacifier, and he will use it as one. Dads pick up the habit as well, routinely handing mom a baby who has started crying, with "pop her on to see if she is hungry." The problem is that being used for a pacifier can get really old for mom, as can having a baby constantly hanging on her.

Changing

Check his diaper. Make sure you treat any redness with ointment, because a clean diaper alone won't fix a diaper rash.

Burping

Burp her after she feeds of course, but also do so with her over your shoulder when she is crying because she may have swallowed air. Feel free to do it often, because burping is essentially patting her on the back, which is soothing whether she needs to burp or not.

Swaddling

Swaddling a crying, flailing baby can be tough, but it is a proven method for calming a baby and keeping him calm. Even if he doesn't seem to like it at first, keep at it to give it a chance to work. Make sure you check his diaper first; otherwise you have to do it all over again.

Sucking

Put your knuckle to his lips to see if he wants to suck; if he starts going at it, you can pop in a pacifier or use your finger soft side up. If he gets used to the pacifier, keep a spare handy; you will also find that sterilizing it every time he drops it is not practical; just wipe it off with a clean cloth. If he sucks away vigorously for awhile and then starts crying again, he may be hungry.

Bicycle Her Legs

A taut tummy or kicking legs may indicate gas pain or constipation, so put her on your lap face up and gently work her legs up and down. Many babies like it regardless of whether they have to get anything out, as it appears to relax them. It is a great position to talk and play once she has calmed down, so try it out for a while so she can get used to it.

Hold, Walk & Rock Her

Sometimes all you can do is hold them, walk around or rock them in a rocking chair. Try holding him over your shoulder, face down over your

My biggest frustration is that when he is crying and you can't figure out what to do for him, there is just no consoling him and you just walk him through it. There is really nothing else that you can do for him. Usually if he does this I'll just say to my wife who is nursing him, "here, he is hungry" but that always isn't it. I guess that is sort of my out.

Veteran Dad

My son likes movement when I need to calm him down or get him to sleep. But I don't always pick him up when he cries. I don't walk him much but I do put him on the motorized swing. And when I do hold him and I am moving he will fall asleep. My wife however, feeds him to sleep.

Veteran Dad

arm (football hold), or face down across your lap. This puts a little pressure on his stomach, which is often soothing. You can pat his back or his bottom in these positions as well.

Fussing and Crying Prevention

Infant Swing
A battery-powered infant swing, borrowed or new, is considered essential by many parents. Just strap your baby in and switch it on for soothing back-and-forth motion that buys you time to get things done. Some babies like to sit in it while stopped where they can watch what is going on.

Frontpack, Backpack Or Sling
The historical method in many cultures is to carry your baby a lot, snuggled warm and comfortable and calmed by your natural movements. Today's baby carriers provide great alternatives that allow you to care for your baby while you work around the house or take a walk.

Stroller or Jogger
Getting out for a stroll or jog around the block is great for you and your baby. The movement transmitted from the wheels traveling over the bumps and rough surface of the pavement relaxes your little one, and the fresh air helps as well. Bundle her up if it is cool outside, and make sure there is no direct sunlight hitting her face.

Bouncy Seat
Place her into this seat, propped at a 45-degree angle, and position it so she can see the world. It's built to gently bounce with her movements, and may have toys, music and lights to occupy your baby's developing mind.

White Noise
This can be amazingly effective for calming and lulling cranky babies to sleep. Try the vacuum cleaner, dishwasher, washer or dryer. Sometimes a radio turned down low putting out static between channels will work. Some dads will hum or generate some noise themselves (often confused with singing).

It is cool when you learn how to calm them down, my wife doesn't know about it but I have a little competition going on with her when he is crying. I try to figure out what he is crying for, she will say he is hungry and I will say no he has a dirty diaper so after she does her routine of checking for 4 or 5 different things then she checks out and finds I guessed right! It is just a cool little game we play.
Veteran Dad

Singing

Actually, no matter how you sound to mom, your baby will think you are the greatest. Slow tunes and lullabies are best around bedtime, but most anything you like works well for fuss prevention. He will be fascinated by your rock star antics and expressions as well, and may end up supporting you in old age as a rock star himself.

Music

Music to a fussy baby is, well, music to their ears. Anything you like, in moderation, can work; if you like classical, great, but rock & roll with heavy bass on low volume can work great as well. Try one of the many CD's made for babies.

Distraction

Introduce a new toy, make a funny face, massage her ears, or blow on her forehead or neck. One veteran could always calm his crying son by taking him to see the family pets. Distraction is often the key to interrupting a cycle of crying.

More Things to Try

There is always something you can do:

*   Try a bath or massage routinely before bedtime to sooth and relax her.

*   If you get her to sleep and then need to put her to bed in her crib, use a hair dryer to warm her bedding a little so the shock of cold sheets doesn't wake her up.

*   Going for a ride in the car is a classic technique used by dads when their babies are crying, as the vibration and noise will put most babies to sleep within the first mile or so.

*   A heated bottle wrapped in a towel and placed against her body may help – put it against your body first to make sure it's not too hot.

*   Put her baby-seat on top of a running dryer for both the vibration and white noise. Stand there with her, of course, as the dryer's movement can walk her seat over the edge or shake her too vigorously.

Do not get flustered when your baby cries. I learned that my baby cries for five reasons. Either because he needs a diaper change, is hungry, is tired, is in pain, or he just wants to be held. Anyone who thinks that a baby can manipulate you at this age needs their head examined. My baby needs to be held, loved and know that I'm going to be there for him.

Veteran Dad

Imagination and Even Genius: Dads' Finest Hours

Men who use their natural creativity to quiet a crying baby are the elite among new dads:

Modified Rocking Stroller
"Walking him around the house in the stroller calmed him and rocking it side to side put him to sleep, but the moment I stopped, his eyes popped open along with his mouth. To keep him asleep I rigged up a motorized contraption using my son's Construx toys that I hung on the stroller's handle to keep the rocking motion going."

Multitask Mowing
"I like my old manual mower (my lawn is small), and I found that carrying my son in a Snuggli on my back put him right out. Since I leaned over to push the mower, it was a better sleeping position for him, and from their comments, it must have looked good to the neighbors too. With him warm and sacked out on my back, it felt great, and I also got the lawn mowed."

Fancy Footwork
"We liked to go out to eat, but a fussy baby puts a real damper on such events. I found that if I parked him under the table in his umbrella stroller or plastic carrier (with a curved bottom), I could easily rock him with my foot for an hour. Sometimes it didn't work, but most times it did."

Working At Home
"It was great being at home, but I had a job to do, and it seemed every time I sat down at the computer, he started crying. I found that if I laid him across my legs I could get counter pressure on his belly, and if he started fussing I could gently bounce him on my legs. If necessary, I could also pat him on the back with one hand, while I kept working away with the other."

Use your imagination. Often times it's the simplest things that work. Experiment with whatever works for you as long as it doesn't hurt the baby.

Veteran Dad

> **Dr. Harvey Karp's 5 "S's"**
>
> We are highly selective in recommending books, and *The Happiest Baby on the Block* (A Bantam Book, 2002) immediately struck us as right on target based upon years of experience with babies at Boot Camp. It focuses on crying in the first months, especially colic, and provides a solid framework for understanding crying babies as well as a broad range of tactics you can employ. It will strengthen your capabilities and reinforce your feeling that there is always something you can do.
>
> Dr. Karp's basic approach, summarized as "the Five S's," is grounded in a deep understanding of babies, parenting in other cultures, and what he has found to work over decades as a pediatrician:
>
> *Swaddling:* The wrap that we like to call the "burrito."
> *Side/Stomach:* Holding your baby side or stomach-down is soothing.
> *Shhhhing:* Words with the shhhh sound are soothing to your baby.
> *Swinging:* Being in her mother's stomach was like nine months at sea for your baby, and she's in no mood to dock at the shore now. Try an electric swing or rocker.
> *Sucking:* On a pacifier or your finger triggers calming chemicals to your baby's brain.
>
> If you find your crying baby to be a challenge, or want to be prepared should it become one, *The Happiest Baby On The Block* is a book you should check out. You may find the video or CD, where you can actually see what works for calming a baby, better than the book.

Living With Colic

Colic is among the most difficult challenges a father will ever face. It comes early as well, just as your strong attachment with your child is beginning to develop. When these crying jags occur about the time you walk in the door from a long day at work, it can be particularly hard to take.

A screaming colicky baby appears to be clearly in pain with legs crunched, tummy tightened, red faced, and fists clinched. Try to keep in mind that after 3-4 months, it will disappear as inexplicably as it arrived, with no significant health effects on your baby.

While physicians cannot settle on what causes colic, most agree that it likely has to do with either an immature digestive or nervous system, with the nervous system theory currently gaining favor. Once your physician has eliminated any specific (and treatable) cause of your baby's pain and crying, you are left with a vague notion of what is wrong and what to do about it.

Colic: Supercharged Crying

With theories about its causes abounding, the term colic has also evolved into a general description of extreme, unexplained, intense crying that can carry on for hours during a baby's initial 3-4 months. Current theories include an immature nervous and/or digestive system; an evaluation by your pediatrician to rule out treatable problems will be essential. While there are specific criteria that define colic (crying for 3 hours straight at least 3 days a week), they won't matter if your baby cries a lot, you will consider it colic. Once it's over, though, it's over; there are no aftereffects of colic beyond mom's and dad's jangled nerves.

Since vague explanations for why your baby is screaming and in pain are very frustrating in themselves, it may help to define the problem in your own mind, or together with mom. Ask your doctor for an explanation, and if it is still vague, try: "Babies' systems develop rapidly in the first months, some get out of sync for awhile, and they just lose it for hours. We do what we can to keep him comfortable, but often there is nothing we can do beyond listening to him cry."

A Rational Approach to Colic

Remember to run through your Troubleshooter's checklist to be sure there is no specific explanation for his crying. Try out your various methods to see what, if anything, might help. Feed, burp, change, hold, cuddle, rock, walk and perhaps come up with something new.

Then let him be for a while, because generally there will be little you can do to make your baby happy. As harsh as this might seem at the time, his crying is his way of getting his system back in sync. Certainly vigorous crying is physically exhausting for a baby, which should help him sleep better at night.

This will happen day after day for months on end, so developing a routine for dealing with the nightly trauma of colic will be essential for your and your partner's piece of mind. Remember that a colicky baby can make you, and especially mom, feel like failures as a new parents. Not only is this not your fault, you and mom should take pride in the fact that you are experiencing a trial by fire and you are surviving.

T. Berry Brazelton's Theory: Don't Overdo It

The widely respected pediatrician, T. Berry Brazelton, M.D., has a theory for dealing with colicky babies that makes a great deal of sense. His believes that colic is caused by the overloading of a baby's immature nervous system, and that anxious parents can add to the problem by trying too hard to fix it. The normal period of crying and fussing can be extended with too much handling and stimulation of an already overloaded nervous system.

He advises that after trying everything you think might help, put your baby down for ten or fifteen minutes to 'let off steam' and help her to get it over with. After this period you can pick her up to care for and calm her again, after which you can put her down again. Your baby may need a few cycles of caring and fussing. Afterwards, she should seem calmer and better prepared to sleep or feed.

For more information, see *Touchpoints: The Essential Reference,* by T. Berry Brazelton, M.D.

Sometimes Nothing Works

Sometimes there is nothing you can do for your baby. Sometimes the frustration of trying to make an inconsolable baby calm, and the crying itself, can be too much. It happens to most of us who were not dealt an "easy baby."

Critical issues to keep in mind:

Extreme and Intense Emotions

No parent likes to admit it, but screeching infants can generate ugly feelings, especially when frustration and sleep deprivation enter into the mix. Understand that you are not a bad person for occasionally having unpleasant thoughts and emotions. Babies' cries trigger an involuntary elevation in your blood pressure. Stress hormones are released and your pulse goes into overdrive. It is as normal as it is automatic (and thus unavoidable), and it helps ensures our babies' survival by demanding that we attend to their needs.

A squalling infant who refuses to stop crying, despite increasingly desperate attempts to calm him, tests the patience of even the most tolerant parent. He may even seem to be screaming right at you. So don't be surprised if you experience feelings ranging from frustration to outright rage. Or even hatred.

When to Walk Away

Although they may be fleeting, episodes of extreme emotion are exceptionally dangerous. If you feel yourself losing control, put the baby down in the safety of his crib and walk away. Never react in anger. Given enough provocation, it may seem almost natural to want to shake a baby who won't stop crying. But doing so can permanently damage an infant's brain. It may even lead to death.

Walk away before incessant crying pushes you to that point. Call a friend, your spouse, your doctor, a neighbor, a family member, your clergyman, or anyone at all who can offer some relief. Look up the child abuse hotline in the classified section of your phone book. Trained counselors will talk you through the crisis. But whatever you do, put the baby down gently and walk away.

> ### Don't Shake Your Baby!
> Shaken Baby Syndrome is the suite of symptoms associated with head, neck, neurological, and body injuries from the violent shaking of infants and young children by parents, babysitters, and other caregivers. According to the Inter-Agency on Child Abuse and Neglect, Shaken Baby Syndrome is responsible for about 40% of child-abuse deaths. The major triggering event for this shaking is the seemingly unstoppable crying of a baby. According to the U.S. Department of Health and Human Services, crying is the number-one cause of infant abuse.
>
> For more information: National Center on Shaken Baby Syndrome (www.dontshake.com)

Boot Camp For New Dad's Approach

Attend a Boot Camp workshop and you'll witness a simple demonstration that illustrates the fragility of a baby's brain. Coaches discuss how frustration over crying can build, and using an ordinary egg inside a plastic container, demonstrate the shocking ease with which a grown man can damage a newborn's brain by simple shaking. The veteran's report of having that image of the splattered egg seared into their minds helped them remember to keep the frustration factor in mind during the worst of times.

At first, when I got home at night, it seemed like he was yelling and taking all his frustrations out on me.

Veteran Dad

PART THREE: HITTING YOUR STRIDE

14

Raising Your New Baby

Once you get the basics of baby care down, you can relax a little and start focusing on raising your child. No golf lessons yet (best to wait until she is at least nine months old), but babies are like sponges when it comes to soaking up new experiences, so there is plenty you can do. No reason to rush it, but it is a lot more fun and interesting than changing diapers.

Your skill set will expand steadily as your baby develops new capabilities. You will move down the learning curve from novice to expert as your child grows from infant to crawler, toddler to talker, big wheeler to t-baller to reader. Like the karate system of belt colors, if you stick with it you will ultimately earn your black belt, which will prove essential for the teenage years.

You may find that the more time you spend with your baby, the more you like him. But periodic feelings of burn out, or even regrets about having a baby are common. So the good stuff may come further down the road. Like climbing a tall mountain, the trip to base camp is heavy on work and short on rewards.

If you keep at it though, at around 3–4 months, you'll notice that she is becoming enthralled with you. She will look for you when she hears your voice, flash a smile when she sees you, and then gaze at you adoringly. She'll get excited when you hold her and may start cooing, by far the sweetest sound on the planet. She may even grab your nose or lip and see if she can tear it off, a native baby ritual signaling that she is yours forever.

I have a wonderful daughter - when I come home she is doing something new or different every day. She crawls a little better every day, she pulls up on things. At this age you see an improvement every day, always something to look forward to. Starting about 3-4 months, you will really start to notice that.

Veteran Dad

Your Baby's Personality

All babies are different, and understanding your child's unique characteristics will help you determine the best approach to caring for him. The differences include how he responds to you, to a wet diaper, to hunger, and how he likes to be soothed and played with. Some babies thrive on interaction, while others seem more self-contained.

Some babies relax and fall asleep when you gently massage them, others become rigid and seem to be uncomfortable with a lot of touching.

Temperament: Your Baby's Personality

The technical term is temperament, and it refers to a baby's nature: how she sleeps, gets upset, calms down, moves, interacts with you and mom, absorbs new information and learns. Understanding your baby's temperament relative to other babies will provide a framework for understanding her.

Checking His Temperament

When your baby is at least four months old, visit www.preventiveoz.org, where you can get a profile of your child relative to all other participants in terms of energy, adjustability, frustration tolerance, sensitivity, regularity in sleep and eating, and distractibility. Getting a handle on these factors will help guide your care strategies and interactions with your baby, as well as strengthen your sense of confidence as a capable parent.

Tough Babies

A highly sensitive baby might get upset when you try to play with him. While this is frustrating, your touchy baby is letting you know he is overloaded. For this type of baby, a quiet environment is necessary, along with a very gentle, "baby step" approach to play. Start by just making eye contact for a while, then talk softly, and wait some more before you add in some gentle rocking. This incremental approach allows your baby to get used to each stimulus before adding the next.

A very quiet baby who turns away or frowns when you pick her up can be worrisome as well as make you feel rejected. Again, go gently. Don't even make eye contact; just hold her first for a while and then gently massage her legs. Then let her grab your finger, and after a while whisper softly to her. If she gets tense, go back to massaging her leg. After a while look into her face and whisper sweet nothings.

Different From Us

We celebrate the similarities (mostly) between our babies and ourselves, but there are also differences. It can be confusing at first when you first realize she does not react the same as you; if you are generally a happy-go-lucky person and she would rather be left alone, or if he bears hardly any resemblance to you or even your side of the family. We almost expect them to be a piece of us and are surprised, sometimes frustrated, and even delighted that they are not.

It wasn't very long before the baby began to display an individual will; a like and dislike for certain things. This began as a very small infant. These likes and dislikes didn't and don't always parallel mine. I am learning that give and take is important, even with very little ones.

Veteran Dad

Baby Brain Development

Babies learn by reacting to the sights, sounds, smells and shapes around them. They also learn by meeting challenges put before them – reaching, grabbing, getting you to pay attention. As a father, you are more likely than your mate to initiate these learning experiences between your baby and his surroundings, so go for it.

From outward appearances, a typical infant spends two-thirds of his day sleeping, and about three hours eating, one hour pooping and wetting, two hours crying and two hours staring into space. All very basic functions. However, the world's most sophisticated computer could not keep pace with the activity and development going on inside her brain.

Incredible Brain Development

At birth a baby's brain contains 100 billion nerve cells (or neurons), all she will ever have, but not the programming of those cells. The circuitry is all laid out but the switches have not been turned on. The sensory experiences she receives are what connects those circuits into that which is necessary for language, vision, understanding, physical coordination and loving.

You get into an upward spiral - he gets to know you, you feel great - play more, he smiles more, etc. You have bad days but it always keeps getting better.
Veteran Dad

Just after birth, her brain produces trillions of connections between neurons than it can use. It then begins the process of stimulating those that she will use, and eliminating those that she will not. Each stimulation the baby encounters helps forge a path, or circuit, between her brain cells, like building roads or an electrical grid that connects neighborhoods, communities and cities.

Stimulation Is Critical

Rich experiences produce rich brains. What turns the mass of brain power into a functioning human being is stimulation. Like a muscle, a baby's brain increases its function according to how much it's used. You stimulate your baby by talking to her, touching her, being affectionate, showing her the world around her, and introducing objects for her to see, feel, taste, and experience. Think of it this way – every time you put something new within your baby's field of vision, thousands of new connections are being made among her brain cells.

They Grow Fast, Don't Blink

By eight weeks old your baby will be much more alert and will become entranced with a mobile over his crib. At around 12 weeks, he'll catch sight of his hands and for awhile you'll notice him staring at them as if they were aliens from another planet. Other development milestones and the general timeframe when they can occur are as follows (remember that all babies are different and may reach various milestones before or after this timeframe):

Month	Activity
1	Sees at close range. Smiles, but not in response to anything. Lifts head while laying down. Tightly grasps an object.
2	Controls neck and extremities better. Smiles in response to a stimulus. Raises head higher when lying on stomach. Sees greater distances and sees color.
3	Responds to an object coming toward her. Reaches for objects. Starts cooing in long, musical sounds.
4	Begins to roll from her front to her back. Transfers objects from one hand to the other. Laughs more.
5	Sits with support. Rolls from back to the front.
6	Sits up without support. Is able to retrieve objects. Your baby may start to creep along the floor.
7 - 12	Walks while holding onto things like furniture. Begins understanding "NO"
7	Feeds himself with his fingers. Inspects objects with detail.
8 - 9	Crawling. May start to say "mama" and "dada". Starts to understand names for things .
10	Starts to imitate. Shows improvement in motor skills such as placing objects into a cup. May be able to say a couple of words.
11	Able to stand-alone and drink from a cup.
12	Begins to walk. Stoops and stands back up. Marks on paper with a crayon. Becomes more cooperative when getting dressed.

How to Help Your Baby Grow

A stimulating environment doesn't mean flash cards, videos, or the many other commercial products being foisted on naturally naïve new parents who want to give their child the best possible start in life. What it does mean is deceptively simple:

Be Warm and Caring

Babies who are cared for, held, soothed and smiled at feel secure in their new world, and learn to calm themselves. Later on, when they go to school, they perform better and make friends more easily.

Communicate with Your Baby

Your baby will learn to communicate continually through her body movements, her voice, and her expressions in response to yours (give her lots of different facial expressions). She will learn to connect and effectively interact with other people this way, and will go after what she needs in life with confidence.

Talk, Sing and Read to Your Baby

You'll notice that your voice can soothe and delight. Babies begin to pick up inflections and gestures and start to understand storytelling at a young age. Some will utter nonsensical sounds mimicking you. Talk to her about daily events, sports news, your job; anything at all will do. Sing and read as well. Use a variety of high and low pitches, loud and soft tones.

Play With Your Baby

Start early, as having fun is the best brain developer of all. This includes letting her grasp your finger, showing your baby her refection in a mirror, and making new sounds for her to figure out. Play improves her senses and muscle development and control, and builds her sense of inner excitement.

When your baby smiles at you and you smile back, or coos and you respond, his face lights up, he gets excited and wiggles with glee. You can tell your bright little prince is very pleased with himself, as he knows he has accomplished something! It doesn't get much better.

Babies Need Downtime

Remember that babies need a lot of downtime. Their minds are furiously active much of the time they are awake, and sometimes they just need to slow down and recharge. When they have had enough, they tend to look away, arch their back, and get cranky.

When we dads come home from work, we often try to squeeze in a lot of interaction with our babies. But sometimes he has been stimulated all day and is in need of down time more than play time. Follow his lead and don't feel bad if he's not responding to you much.

Beware of Mozart

Information about the electrical wiring of the human brain surfaced in the late 1990's and led to a frenzy among anxious parents to do everything they could to "stimulate" their babies' brains, sometimes even before they were born. From playing music through speakers into the womb during pregnancy, to teaching sign language to infants,

We both almost decided not to become parents because of our ages and careers. To have kept that thought would have been the biggest mistake of our lives. I love my wife and son, and now I feel my life is complete, and I would not trade my life with my family for anything in the universe.
Veteran Dad

many parents want to give their children their best, but end up overdoing it.

The Mozart Myth or, "Babies Learn Just as Much From Rock n' Roll"
The Governor of Georgia went so far as to send every baby born in the state a classical music CD because "listening to music at a very early age affects the spatial, temporal reasoning that underlies math and engineering." Turns out that the "Mozart effect" was based on overblown press reports on a study that found college students who listened to Mozart for ten minutes performed better on a spatial relations test conducted immediately after. The lead researcher finally clarified the results: "There is no scientific research on the effect listening to music has on a baby's intelligence. Our Mozart effect research was blown way out of proportion." Whole companies are based on this myth, so be forewarned.

Tempted by the Boob Tube

The television is an alluring and very available babysitter. It captivates your baby with an intense stream of audio/visual stimulation, keeping him occupied and quiet for long periods. When you are tired, or want to read a book, it is very tempting. Therein lies the problem. New research and common sense indicates that a significant amount of TV is bad for your baby, especially since his brain is developing very rapidly during this time. Even in TV shows and videos supposedly created for young babies, the rapid movements and pacing have been shown to have negative effects on their brain development. Moderation is key.

Keep in mind that there is a distinct difference between holding your baby on your lap while you're watching a football game together and plunking him down in front of the TV while you talk to your friends.

Your Baby's Health

When it comes to your baby's health, always err on the side of calling the doctor too often, rather than not enough. Get to know your baby's doctor by going to his well-baby checks. Go with mom or take turns with her.

Don't give your baby any medicine without checking first. A small dose of an adult pain reliever or decongestant may seem reasonable, but babies present special issues that you are unlikely to be aware of. Better to be safe than sorry.

My previously busy working life schedule was not really all that important. Time with my daughter was.
Veteran Dad

I guess the most surprising thing was that none of the 200 terrible things I thought may happen did happen.
Veteran Dad

Keep Your Resources Handy
In addition to keeping the doctor's number readily available (next to the phone), essential resources to keep on hand include:

Nurse Hot Line
Experienced pediatric nurses are readily available 24 hours a day by phone and will spend all the time you need talking about any issue related to your baby's health. They will also tell you if you need to contact your doctor. Find out which hotline your doctor recommends.

Emergency Phone Numbers
This includes the local hospital's emergency room, your regional poison center, a neighbor you can rely on, etc.

Medical Guide
They are thick with useful information. Get one and skim it to get a feel for how you can use it. Popular ones include:

- *The American Academy of Pediatrics Guide to Your Child's Symptoms*, by Donald Schiff, MD and Steven P. Shelov, MD (1997)

- *American Medical Association Family Medical Guide, 4th Edition* by American Medical Association (August 20, 2004)

- *Mayo Clinic Family Health Book*, Third Edition by Mayo Clinic (May 1, 2003)

First Aid Kit & Guide
When you need a bandage, antiseptic, or cream for a minor burn, you need it readily available, so keep a well stocked kit handy. Take a first aid class also and your family will have a dad who knows what he is doing in an emergency. A comprehensive family first aid guide is also prudent to have on hand. Check out how to handle emergencies at the Red Cross website: www.redcross.org.

How to Tell If He's Not Well
Babies give signals when they aren't feeling well. The most obvious are a fever, runny nose, cough or rash. There are also less obvious signals: he seems lethargic or very cranky, not interested in anything or anyone around him, he has little or no appetite, he is spitting up more than usual, or his stools are either very hard or runny. The intensity and duration of such symptoms are also factors that will help you, a nurse or a doctor determine how to treat them.

I have really been amazed at the lack of time for everything. I never knew babies required so much attention. That should be discussed. Also, I really went through an "I don't want to work anymore" phase that lasted close to 6 months, and looking back, I never expected that.
Veteran Dad

Fevers and Colds

Fever is how a baby responds to an infection. If his temperature is over 101 degrees, he has a fever. If he's less than two months old and his temperature is higher than 100 degrees, call your pediatrician. Make sure to also call if the fever has lasted longer than a few days, or if there is a rash along with the fever.

Sniffles and respiratory congestion can make your baby miserable. Make sure her airway is clear and that she is not having difficulty breathing. Call the doctor if your baby's cough comes from deep in her chest, if her breathing is labored, or if she is wheezing.

The Dreaded Nose Bulb

A baby cannot blow his nose, so you will need to do it for him using a nose bulb (looks like a small turkey baster that sucks the mucus out). He will hate having it stuck up his nose and will thrash around, making this a very difficult maneuver. To get the job done, wrap your arm around his head (i.e., put him in a gentle but firm headlock) with your hand on his chest to immobilize him. Squeeze the air out of the bulb with your other hand, place it gently but snuggly in his nostril, and let the bulb expand. Repeat in the other nostril.

Teething

Most babies get their first teeth starting between 4-6 months. They grow and push through their gums, which is painful for them. Drooling is the first sign of teething, and there may be a slight fever. Most babies will let you know loudly that they are uncomfortable. Give him a teething ring that has been cooled in the refrigerator to chew on. Your knuckle will also work. Rubbing Oragel™ (a topical pain reliever) on his gums is the standard treatment; keep some in the diaper bag and handy at home.

Falls and Bumps On the Head

No matter how careful you are, babies can take spills, and the older they get the more likely they will be to fall and hurt themselves. If he tumbles off a couch, falls out of his high chair or slips out of your arms after a bath, you should do a thorough check for injuries and watch him closely for awhile afterwards. If he cries after he falls, it is a good sign that he's not seriously injured. If he has fallen on his head or back, be even more careful in your observations. Watch him carefully for 24 hours, and take him to the doctor or emergency room if he:

- Seems weak or confused.
- Is having trouble moving any part of his body or there seems to be a deformity of an arm or leg.
- There is blood in the whites of his eyes or pink fluid coming out of his nose or ears.
- Shows signs of a concussion, such as crossed eyes or pupils that are unequal in size, or if he vomits.
- If he cries loudly when you move any part of his body.
- If he is sleeping more than normal.

When to Take Him to the Emergency Room

Common emergencies can be confusing and the signs of injury can be subtle. Also, pediatricians can be difficult to reach after hours. Get to know where your local emergency room is; injuries to your baby that indicate a trip to the ER include:

- A cut that may require stitches
- Vomiting for several hours, especially if she is vomiting forcefully.
- If she is difficult to arouse or wake up, especially if she has a high fever or if she's had a fall.

When to Call 911

There are obvious emergencies that require a call to 911 immediately, and some not so obvious:

- Severe burns, serious bleeding, or unconsciousness.
- Seizures or other uncontrollable or unusual body movements.
- Difficulty breathing, or taking more than 60 breaths a minute.
- Has swallowed a poisonous substance or a foreign object and is choking.

If He is Not Breathing

Even if you have not taken a baby CPR class, if your baby is not breathing, you can try to save his life. First, yell for someone to call 911. Cover his mouth and nose with your mouth and breath lightly into his lungs, just enough to see his chest rise. Don't breath in too much air, since his lungs are small and you could damage them. A newborn baby will take only about a mouthful of air. Give him one breath every three seconds. Stop after 20 breaths to take his pulse. 911 will provide you additional instructions.

The first two months I was trying to get my son to show me the same kind of affections he was showing to his mother. I could never get it, so I started doing more things and tried to be with him more often. I actually found myself getting jealous. He seemed to respond to mom but not to me even though I was feeding and doing everything else. But what I found eventually over time is that with me I had to make an extra effort to try to get to know him. Now when I come home from work, he smiles and reaches out for me.

Veteran Dad

Day Care Essentials

About half of new parents do not have the luxury of mom or dad staying home to care for their babies. Day care may be the only option that works for your family. While leaving your new baby with a stranger is not an easy thing to do, don't feel that you're a bad parent because of the choice you and your wife have made. Focus on making it work.

What to Look For
There are different day care options, including day care centers, day care at your place of work, relatives, live-in help, and perhaps friends or neighbors. Check them all out to make sure you find the best possible arrangement for your new family.

Suggestions for choosing day care include:

- If possible, find day care by getting references from family or friends. Ask around yourself; don't leave this to just mom.

- If it's a day care center, make sure you inspect it thoroughly, including making an unannounced visit. If they have a problem with your thoroughness, consider it a red flag.

- If you choose an individual, make sure you do a background check, including calling 2-3 previous work references.

- Trust your instincts. If it doesn't feel right, keep looking.

How to Protect Your Baby
Don't hesitate to take precautionary measures to ensure that your baby is in good hands and is well taken care of. If you have a babysitter and you are not happy, or for some instinctive reason you don't feel comfortable with this person, listen to your feelings.

- Drop in unexpectedly during the day.
- Pick up your baby early on occasion.
- Talk to other parents.

Settling In for the Long Term

At three-four months, the fun really starts. Your baby is no longer a fragile, demanding stranger; you've weathered the initial storm and now he is a part of your life. Bonds and affection are interlacing your

"My wife and I just bought a new house and there was no way we could afford to keep our home on one income. Yeah, it was hard to leave Jessica with a stranger, especially for my wife. We both felt terrible about it but we got over it."

Veteran Dad

My wife and I decided on a live-in. After interviewing several people we finally chose one. But after two weeks I didn't feel right about this person. So, we got rid of her and went through the inter-viewing process again. The one we hired the second time around is still with us.

Veteran Dad

new family together. You may wake up to his smiles, miss him at work and can't wait to see him when you get home. You're starting to see the amazing growth he is going through during this first year. Soon he will start babbling, a big step towards talking, and then he will reach for and try to use objects, especially the remote control.

Remember your boring friends from your previous life who could only talk about their babies? Actually, your baby is brighter, cuter, and much smarter than all those other babies. Just in case you have to talk to someone who does not appreciate the most wonderful creation on the planet, periodically glance at the newspaper to see what sports are in season.

Your Baby Returns the Favor
You have been taking care of her, and now it's time she returned the favor. And she will if you let her.

We live a fast paced life, one that seems to get faster every day. Multi-tasking, doing and thinking of everything all at once. Our minds and bodies are racing constantly just to keep up with our jobs and responsibilities, and it's difficult to slow down. It's called the rat race.

Babies demand that we take another look at this imposed frenzy of activity. They bring us back to a more simple way of living, to a life where long minutes are spent staring at a brightly colored toy, or delighting in the repetition of a sound or a song, or lingering before a flower bush, or having a lazy walk without any special place to go, stopping to have a chat with a neighbor.

Savor the time, talk to him, get down on the floor with him and see what he sees. When you relax, think of things to do with him. Your child is asking you to really be there with him, to see the world unfolding through his tiny eyes and to be as fascinated by it as he is. In some ways it is like you get to do childhood all over again. Sure beats the rat race.

Tuning in to Your Child
The greatest rewards, both for dads and their children, come from tuning in, even at this young age, and getting to know them. This acquired skill, accompanied by increased patience, essentially requires paying attention. Start by getting to know your baby's moods, likes and dislikes. This is how the real connection between a father and child is built. Start the habit now and you'll always be glad you did.

I find myself laughing at more stuff that my baby does than be bothered by it. Even if she pooped on the wall, I'd find humor in it. I try to enjoy every phase and aspect of her growing up.

Veteran Dad

Creative Solutions

"Adversity is the mother of invention." Whoever said this was likely a father of a cranky baby. A creative approach might be to tape record the vacuum cleaner and play it to put your baby to sleep. Arrange for a portable bed or jerry-rig one so you can go to an afternoon barbeque at the park without messing up his sleep schedule. Spending five minutes in your car listening to rock 'n roll before you walk into the house might be an efficient way to de-stress after work.

When You Spend a Lot of Time Away From Home

Spending time away from your little one can be tough, especially when you're talking a week or even a month at a time. Travel for long periods, as for military personnel, can be depressing. It's important to stay focused on why we work in the first place – to provide for our families. It is also important to remain as involved with your child as possible, even if it has to be in a minimal way. Suggestions:

- With little time at home, play with your baby before you leave in the morning and just after you get home. Many dads report that their babies sleep longer if they play with them at night.
- Keep his picture where you see it often, and keep him in mind while you're on the road.
- Call mom often and get the lowdown on junior's antics and accomplishments for the day.
- Enlist mom, who can send you pictures and recordings and hold the phone to your baby's ear so you can talk to him, or show him his daddy on the cell phone picture.

Recently a young father deployed to Iraq tape recorded a dozen nursery rhymes that his wife plays for their baby so that he will recognize dad's voice when he gets back home.

15

Your New Buddy

Of all the powerful and complex dynamics in the circle of life, a father's critical role in teaching his baby to play has got to be one of the coolest.

Apart from basic bodily functions like eating, playing is your baby's main job. Playing teaches him how to laugh and take risks. It develops his motor skills and speeds the development of his brain and nervous system. Very serious stuff.

As a father, you are designed to be her perfect playmate. Tickling, flight lessons, peek-a-boo and wrestling all come naturally. Babies become ecstatic over beer drinking songs (a very effective speech and tone development technique).

As an added bonus, playing is bonding at its finest. Dads elicit the most radiant smiles and infectious belly laughs, sometimes with just a wink.

You can pretend to be anything, and he can be anybody you choose as you carry out incredible exciting adventures together. Playing encourages your flights of imagination about what he will be when he grows up, so let it soar.

Finally, it is never too early to start her on a career in sports (these days, kids turn pro in elementary school). She will love the bench press (with you using her as the weight). And she will reward your demonstration of wrestling moves by pulling a fistful of hair out of your chest (babies have amazing upper body strength).

It's a Dirty Job and Dad Has to Do It

Research has found that you're destined to become your baby's primary playmate. Despite the obvious advantages moms enjoy in terms of baby appeal, two-thirds of six-month old babies choose dad when it comes to playtime. (The other one-third was just hungry.)

The "Raiders" Gene
Babies are genetically predisposed to favor their dad's favorite sports teams. The "Raiders" gene is passed down from father to child, but lies dormant unless activated, usually by the visual stimulation and tactile feel of official team apparel.
Veteran Dad

Why He Picks You for Playing

It starts right after birth when your bright little bundle notices that you look, smell, feel and sound different than mom. While mom is soft, warm, comforting, beautiful and smells good, you are, well, different. Your baby won't know what to think of you right off, which is why she stares at you so much, just taking you in.

As far as finding time, that's easy! You just have to want to make time. I make sure I leave work early enough so I have plenty of time to spend with my son when I get home.

Veteran Dad

As the weeks go by, a baby notices that while mom tends to be protective and calming, dad is more playful and physical, and sometimes very surprising. Your baby soon learns that mom will pick him up when he is fussy, but dad tends to tickle him or lift him into the air. When even a very young baby hears her father's voice, she's likely to raise her shoulders and eyebrows, or begin kicking her legs, anticipating something exciting.

As the months go by, mom might ask dad to not get the baby worked up before bedtime, but all dad has to do is walk into her room and she's thinking, "play time!" A mother's natural reaction might be to put out her hand to steady a set of blocks that are about to fall near the baby, while a father is likely to let them fall or even push them over, usually to squeals of delight.

Mom and Dad: Complementary Roles for Raising Babies

While they can come into conflict, a father's adventurous role complements that of a mother's, and the combination is what turns out well rounded children. Dads introduce new challenges to their babies and encourage them to explore their worlds. Bottom line, playtime with dad contributes to your baby's physical, intellectual, and social development and leads to great qualities later in life: good relationships with peers, a knowledge of limits, a spirit of adventure.

Babies Grow By Playing

Never underestimate the power of play. For example, the skills a three-month old baby learns by playing a simple game of "peek-a-boo!" includes, observation, language, coordination, communication, exploration, problem solving, socialization, rhythm, creativity and humor. Other games work on things like dexterity, balance, trust, strength and timing.

So remember when you are crawling on the floor, perhaps barking like a dog as you chase him around, it is a dirty job, and dad has to do it.

Toys for Babies and Dads

Babies and fathers have a natural affinity for toys, and sharing this special bond from the beginning will strengthen your connection for decades. Equipment to consider includes:

Baby Boom Box

Music is a must for babies and a portable CD or tape player will make it easy to keep the tunes flowing. Play what you want and see what she likes; dancing with her multiplies the fun. Don't blast the music (babies have sensitive ears and are easily frightened), but you can crank the bass up so she can get her rhythm down.

Tape Recorder

When he starts cooing and babbling away, grab a cheap (usually around $35) little tape recorder and hit the button. Then play it back to him and watch the fascination grow in his eyes along with the smile on his face. Record and then play back his fussing as well, and he will stop and take in this new but familiar sounding distraction. (If you go on business trips, take along the cooing/babbling tape along with his pictures.)

Bike With Baby Seat, Trailer, Jogging Stroller or Back Pack

Taking her along for a ride, run or hike is great for both of you. Doing so on a regular basis will make her a serious part of your life early on. Safety comes first, of course, and beyond that enjoy the exercise and the company.

Lifted, Supercharged Chevy Suburban

While a high performance, high capacity offroad vehicle may at first seem incongruent with caring for babies, in reality it represents a long term commitment to your child's welfare. Every time you drive the carpool to work over curbs and small cars, you will be focused on planning fun for the next weekend. Before long, you will have established family traditions of camping out under the stars, and when a good storm comes through, goin' mudbogging!

Playing With Your Baby

While playing with babies comes naturally to men, there are a few things to keep in mind:

In Memoriam

She was a beauty in Midnight Blue with a 4" Rancho lift and in-cab adjustable shocks, 35" Duelers, her third 4:10 rear end, and a Gibson exhaust which made her sound great despite her stock, never supercharged engine. She had 153,962 very hard miles, significant air time, and smelled like a decade old clubhouse on wheels for kids of all ages. One of our favorite road trips was to get up at 5 AM before school and go off road to a local trout stream. I once got detention from the 6th grade teacher who apparently didn't like kids being late (we limited out), or trout. Due to multiple, simultaneous breakdowns of major components, she recently expired. We will all miss her deeply, except my wife, who found her perpetually muddy and juvenile presence in our driveway embarrassing.

Head Coach

Short Field of Vision at First

For the first couple of weeks, a baby's vision is fuzzy and he'll fixate on things that are about a foot from his eyes. Place a picture or toy with highly contrasting colors in his line of sight to catch his attention, and then move it back and forth slowly so he can track it.

Her Favorite Mug

She will also fixate on your face and can recognize it at about one month. She might be able to imitate you sticking out your tongue, so give it a try. If it works, make sure you treat your buddies to a show.

Just You and Him

There's no one else around. It's time for ELVIS! Or Bruce Springstein, Radiohead or whatever you like. Got a comedy act buried deep? Time to drag it out. No matter how bad you are, he'll think you are the best. And when he starts rocking out, you'll be taking him on tour to whomever you can get to watch.

If He Is Easily Upset

Start gently, perhaps with massage and music, and then ramp it up over time while making sure to stay in tune with his temperament.

Stop When She Has Had Enough

She may be finished before you are, and it is important to recognize the signs before you irritate her. If she turns her face away, arches her back, or whimpers when you expect her to be having fun, there is a good chance she is getting worn out or overstimulated and it is time to quit.

Don't Scare Him

Inadvertently scaring your baby might elicit a funny response, but it is not good. And not just because it will trigger crying. Remember all those neurons firing for the first time? You want him wired to trust you and his new environment, and not grow up anxious. Be gentle and careful about situations – sudden loud noises, people getting too close or picking him up roughly - that may frighten him.

Nurture an Adventurous Spirit

Notice when he's reaching out for something and encourage his exploration. Let him take his time. Let him try for something just beyond his reach. Before you do something for him, let him try to do it himself. Encourage, don't frustrate.

Improvise

Put your own creative stamp on playing with your baby; build your repertoire of games that only she (and you) know. Opportunities abound; make your sock into a puppet and make it "sing" to him. Dip her toe in ice cream and give her a taste. Start to blow raspberries on his tummy and then stop a couple of times until he is bouncing with anticipation. Then cut loose with a big one.

Show Him the World

As chief adventure officer in your new family, this is your job. Babies are incredibly curious and will become quickly mesmerized with anything new to check out, so walking around the garage can be exploration at its finest. If he is fussy, it is also distraction at its best.

When I work around the house or go to Home Depot I take my son and let him play with tools.
Veteran Dad

Start by carrying her against your chest facing out, with one hand under her bottom and the other over her chest, with her head resting against you. Just walk around slowly, positioning her so new things come into her field of vision. It doesn't really matter what it is; just watch her face to see what captures her attention. Describe it to her in a soft voice and just let her take it in.

Around the House
Start with wallpaper, the light switch and move on to pictures, mirrors (always interesting) and windows. The kitchen is full of interesting stuff, so take your time and open the cupboards one at a time. A garden with flowers is great; let her check them out and touch them (careful she doesn't try to eat them). Bugs are very cool as they crawl around; ditto on the eating. Check out the grass; anything new, colorful or moving will do.

Away From Home
Every new place presents a new set of opportunities. Not just someone else's house, but their neighborhood, local parks, the mall, and the local truck dealer. Getting fussy at a restaurant? Show her the menu and the pictures in the hall leading to the restrooms, or take a walk around outside where you can introduce her to cool cars. Make showing him the world a habit. A soft baby carrier that allows you to carry her around on your chest facing out may become essential.

The Home Depot Baby Tour
Hard to imagine a place with more interesting stuff for a baby to check out than Home Depot. Aisle after aisle with lots of colors, tools and

materials that you can tell her about, and chances are you will always find something you need at home. Careful she doesn't get close enough to grab things that might hurt her; letting her get the feel of a hammer while you firmly hold the hammer's head in your hand is fine.

Keep in mind that as you show him the world, you are continually adding information to his data banks and building his curiosity about what's out there.

Games for 0 to 2 Months

Getting in just five minutes each day playing with your baby is a great start. Favorite games for 0-2 month-olds include:

Monkey See, Monkey Do
Get close to her face and smile, and around four to six weeks she will start smiling back. Many babies will imitate your facial gestures, so open your mouth, widen your eyes, and of course, stick out your tongue. Even if she doesn't, keep trying, because this game can hold her attention for a long time.

Airplane
Hold your baby with both hands—one under her bottom and the other cupped on the back of her head and neck. Hold her up in the air and let her fly around slowly and gently. Always firmly support her head and keep it higher than her bottom.

Pull-ups
Put him on your lap facing up, place one finger in his hand so he grabs on, and pull it up a little. Then put another finger in his other hand so he grabs on with both hands. Pull him up just a little (Keep his unsupported head on your lap), and then let him down and repeat.

Baby Calisthenics
Games involving limb movement are possible at this age, but you'll have to do most of the work. With your baby on her back, gently pull her legs up toward you and then side to side, talking to her the whole time. Do the same with her arms.

Jumping Jacks
With your baby on her back, raise her arms over her head and then put them down. Then take one arm and gently cross it over towards

the opposite shoulder. Repeat with the other arm. While you're doing it, count off the moves (a one and a two and a three and a four).

Walking at One Month
Their walking reflex is very cool. Using both hands to hold him, stand him on the bed and lean him forward. He will slowly raise one foot as if to take a step, and if you move him forward, he will take another. Another amazing feat to show the guys.

Lots of Belly Time
Now that doctors insist we put our babies to sleep on their backs, not only do they tend to get flat heads, but they have few opportunities to develop their upper body strength by lifting their heads and pushing themselves up with their hands. So give him plenty of belly time while playing and he will be the first and fastest crawler in his Mommy & Me group.

Your Response is Her Reward
Kiss her hand and then give her a chance to touch you in return. If she knows that you delight in her attempts, she will do it more and more. Be demonstrative and let her know how wonderful she is. And how all her moves are amazing. Tone it down when she turns ten; you don't want to embarrass her.

Playing at 2 to 4 Months

Your baby will become more active from two to four months, smiling and starting to coo and babble away, and responding more during playtime. Your baby will love having fun with you, especially if you smile and talk to her. The possibilities for games increases; examples include:

Mattress Trampoline
Lay your baby on her back on the bed. Push down on the mattress so that she bounces a little bit. Go slow and be gentle so she enjoys it and doesn't get anxious or upset.

She Needs to Learn to Trust You
As a father, you may be inclined to ramp up the action by bouncing her higher, especially if she is enjoying it. That's cool, as long as she is having fun, but if you push it too much, she can quickly decide she doesn't like the game at all. The trick is to be very patient and go

slowly; let her get used to the action the first few times you play the game, then take it up a notch the next time, and slow down the moment her face tells you she is no longer having fun. If she is going to let you push her as a father, she needs to learn to trust you first.

Kick Boxing

With your baby lying on his back, put the palms of your hands up so they are nearly touching the soles of his feet. Gently push his foot with your hand, switching back and forth between right and left. Soon, you'll do nothing but hold your hands there and your baby will kick them in the same right to left pattern you initiated.

I would never have predicted this but it is extraordinarily satisfying and relaxing so far.
Veteran Dad

Essential Benefits For Babies of Football

Boot Camp For New Dads conducts research on men's interactions with babies to foster their full development as fathers. An intriguing issue is the importance of cognitive and spatial factors to a new baby's ability to see, focus, and learn. Scientists have known for years that infants are able to focus better on contrasting colors, and that they are also attracted to movement. When the movement of contrasting colors occurs in rational patterns, ideal learning conditions for infants are presented.

Anecdotal evidence from Boot Camp workshops indicated that babies are attracted to football on TV (movement of contrasting colors in rational patterns), and we decided to explore this matter. We asked 250 Boot Camp veterans to watch a football game with their babies at four, eight and twelve weeks to determine their enthusiasm for the game using a scale of 0 to 10 with 10 being best.

The results were conclusive; 98% of the babies scored 8-10, clearly proving that watching football on TV with dad is highly beneficial for babies as well as an essential bonding opportunity with dad. This "quality time" is also essential for dad to teach his baby important life lessons regarding commitment, passion, and the West Coast offense.

Due to an infant's poor vision in the critical first weeks, a big screen TV is considered essential to a baby's optimum development. Veteran dads recommend the largest screen you can afford; a 50" plasma or a 60" projection with HDTV produce the most benefits.

Author's note: It is important to maintain an authoritative tone when describing the benefits of football and big screen TV's for babies to new moms as they tend to be skeptical.

Sit on Your Chest

Lie down on your back with your baby sitting on your chest facing you. Let him explore your face. Enjoy his intense concentration as he checks everything out. Be careful because he may grab your nose and try to remove it.

Baby Acrobatics
Sit on the ground, facing your baby. Get a firm grip around her midsection and roll back, holding her up in the air while you say "wheee!" If she loves it—and, there's a good chance she will—you'll be priming her for Olympic tumbling down the road.

Balloon Game
Attach a ribbon to a helium filled balloon and then tie the end of the ribbon around your baby's ankle, so when she moves her ankle, the balloon will move. She will entertain herself while she's figuring out that she can control the movement of the balloon. Change to the other ankle, and then tie it to her wrist. Stay with her, of course, and then remove the balloon and string from her room when you leave.

Flip Over
Place your baby on his back and sit behind him. Hold a colorful toy over his face and then slowly move it to one side, encouraging him to grab for it. If he turns over, or starts to, cheer him on, and then repeat it with the other side. If he's almost there, give him a little push. If he gets all the way over, give him the toy (some babies will learn to roll across an entire room before they can crawl).

For me, I can't wait to come home and see Francesca. That is my free time.

Veteran Dad

Serious Games at 4 to 6 Months

At 4-6 months he is significantly bigger, stronger, more active and responsive, which opens up a whole new range of possibilities. Babies love to be cheered on at this age, so don't hold back.

Peek-a-Boo
Always a favorite. Put your hands in front of your face for a few moments, then jerk them away and say "peek-a-boo!" Repeat about five times, and then put her hands over her eyes and show her how to do it. Over time she will catch on and after a month or so you'll be peek-a-booing back and forth with her giggling away.

Her First Song
When she is cooing or babbling, take her hand and place the back of it over her mouth to cork her briefly, then lift it and repeat. The result will be bah-bah-bah, which she will find fascinating as well as a new trick to enthrall her adoring audience (mom, grandma).

Rock 'n' Roll

He will love this one, although mom may not. Raid the kitchen for wooden spoons and a few pots. Use the wooden spoons to make some music, and then put a spoon in his fat little hand and show him how to do it. Cut him loose to bang away on his own. As he flails away, try to make sure he doesn't inadvertently bang his head (hence no metal utensils), or yours.

Bucking Bronco

Sit your baby on your knee as if it were a horse, hold him firmly, and bounce him rhythmically. Every once in a while bounce your knee a little higher, and he will soon anticipate it coming.

Hide and Seek

Take something your baby is playing with and hide it inside or underneath something bigger. If it's a cloth book, put it underneath a light blanket. If it's a block, then put it inside a plastic bowl. Show him where it is and then hide it again, until he starts to find it himself.

Crawler in Training

Put him on his belly over a towel. Grab both ends of the towel in one hand and lift him up a few inches, supporting him with your other hand. Get him on his hands and knees, and then start moving his arms and legs one at a time in a crawling motion. While this maneuver is probably useless in actually teaching him to crawl, he will find it interesting and maybe fun, and it can't hurt.

Raising a Road Warrior

With babies, there is always a reason to be stuck at home. "Don't interrupt the baby's schedule… It might rain…" Just loading all the stuff your baby might need into the car can be a chore. Few fathers have the confidence to take their babies out on their own in the first six months. As a result, most new families end up cooped up at home, isolated from their former lives and friends and often getting on each other's nerves.

You Need to Get Out

Clearly, getting out of the house is in order. If you go out on your own, leaving mom stuck at home with the baby, you are tagged a laggard. Take your baby with you, and you are a fine example of the male species. Start by taking him along on an errand, like a run to the hardware store. Not only will you quickly get used to taking care of him on the road, you will find yourself using him as an excuse to get out of the house.

Turn Your Buddies Into Uncles
After being tied up at home in the months before and after the birth, your friends get the idea that you are out of circulation and joining them to watch a game, or to just hang out, is no longer an option. Jump back in by showing up with junior. After a few times asking, "can you hold her for a minute," they'll be reaching for her all the time. Show them how to feed her with the bottle, rock her to sleep, and of course how to do the tricks you have taught her. If she learns to stick out her tongue when they do, they will be calling you up to ask if you can bring her over to play.

Trust me on this: After 15 years of having guys work together to take care of babies in Boot Camp, it is clear that most men are fascinated by babies and will readily pitch in to help you out. After growing up with the message that babies were essentially off limits to men, the guys are amazed by what they have been missing.

What to Bring
While you want to be careful in the first six weeks when their immune systems are just cranking up, there is no reason to keep a healthy baby at home. Make sure the diaper bag is fully stocked for an outing that will last more than several hours; if all day, add a daypack with extra diapers, undershirts, footed pajamas, an extra blanket, bottles and a few of his favorite toys. Include a plastic bag for disposing of diapers.

If the temperature is over 75°, a diaper and t-shirt underneath a pair of footed pajamas is usually good enough. If it's breezy, add a light jacket and a hat to keep the sun off his face and his head warm. Add layers as the temperature gets lower.

> **Protecting Her from the Sun**
> Because your baby has sensitive skin, it's important to avoid using sunscreen until she's six-months old. Use other methods of keeping her out of the sun, like a baby-seat canopy. If you're taking a stroller walk, and the sun is in her face, just hang a light blanket over the stroller's canopy to shield her.

Sleeping Schedule
It's a good idea to stick close to your baby's sleeping schedule, but it won't hurt if you deviate a little. Some babies are distracted from

sleeping by the new sounds and excitement around them and putting them down can be a real challenge. Try replicating his normal sleeping environment, or wrap him up in a familiar blanket from his crib and hold him so he gets warm and falls asleep.

Girls Can Do Anything Boys Can Do

We often relate to our babies by imagining them growing up to do the things we like. So there are a lot of great athletes about 2' tall. Picturing our sons playing in the NFL comes naturally, but girls, well, they do girl things and then fall in love with some guy with questionable motives. In fact, our instincts tell us to roughhouse with our sons, but to hug and protect our daughters. So you can see it is easy to shortchange our baby girls in terms of opportunity right from the start (same with our baby boys when it comes to hugs).

The great news is that girls today are showing they can do anything boys can do. (Powder puff football leagues are organizing in our neighborhood). Times have changed, and while most girls still like playing with dolls, more and more grow up to like softball, soccer, basketball, water polo, and lots of other athletic and adventurous activities. Someday your daughter could be teeing off as a golf pro, racing a car, or climbing mountains (perhaps with you).

So start her early. She definitely benefits from roughhousing with you—probably more than a baby boy does because his whole environment growing up features rough and tumble play. And keep it going, as research clearly shows that girls whose fathers engage them in sports grow up to enjoy better fitness, stronger self images, and healthier, lasting relationships later on in life with men. (On that note, teach her a martial art.)

Most Surprising
That I would enjoy pacing the living room floor at two in the morning. That a burp, etc. could be so rewarding. That I thought I was busy before Katie was born.
Veteran Dad

Words of Wisdom

When my first child was on the way, our OB told us guys "you think that a baby means that you will no longer be able to do the things you like to do. Actually, a child will provide you the opportunity to do what you always wanted to do."

That OB turned out to be right. My son (now 24) and I went to an island off Thailand to learn to scuba dive when he was 14. I could never have justified going on my own. I learned to play softball with my daughters, who also enjoyed backpacking, paintball and offroading in my truck together with my sons. My 16 year old son and I just bought an old Porsche to work on.

With kids, my life turned into an ongoing adventure. Turns out having them along is the very best part. It all started with playing with them when they were babies. Nothing is more important for a dad.

16

New Dad Six-Week Checkup

It's the most frustrating but rewarding experience.

Veteran Dad

As you know by now, the first weeks can be a trial by fire for both you and mom. You may be enjoying a strong sense of fulfillment, or you may have major doubts about where your life is going. Perhaps both, depending on the time of day. Be advised that these temporary circumstances can play some serious mind games on you.

At around 6-8 weeks old your baby will be due for a checkup. Consider this event a milestone for you as well, for you will have survived one of the roughest parts of your own metamorphosis into a dad.

Take the opportunity of your baby's checkup to do one on yourself. The list of questions under Orient Yourself (page 231) will help you put things in perspective. If you are having a tough time at this point, you may be in danger of getting in a rut as a father. It is helpful to remind yourself that you are far from alone, and that becoming a father is one of the most difficult and important challenges any man can face.

One of the most difficult struggles you will have to face after the birth is your fear of losing your freedom. It isn't so much change we fear, but rather that we will lose ourselves; our individuality, our free spirit. If we knew that the changes were positive, our fears would be constantly reduced.

Veteran Dad

Hang in there, as the worst part is over. Maintain your hands-on approach with your baby and you will continue to build your confidence and skills. As you and your child get to know each other, you'll relax and enjoy the ride. At around 3-4 months, when he is past the fussy stage and his smiles are lighting up your days, you will understand why 50 million men across America feel that being a father is the most important part of their lives.

You're Transforming

You are in the midst of a personal transformation that is profoundly changing you. Like new moms, we also go through a process of self-discovery as we struggle to adjust to our new responsibilities. While fathers may have a smoother transition to parenthood than mothers, ultimately we become different people as well.

Think back to the guy you were before you heard "I'm pregnant!" Or even the day before you drove your partner to the hospital. Your life and priorities have changed significantly since you watched your baby's birth, and they will continue to do so.

Don't dwell on your pre-baby life, as you may find it very tempting to want to go back. Like military boot camp, the process of becoming a father tends to break you down and then build you up, and at this point, you are only getting past the break-you-down part.

Developing a Dad's Outlook

Over time, we gradually develop a new, stronger sense of ourselves as fathers (a cross between a pack horse and a lion.) As we learn to meet our babies' needs, we come to trust our instincts, just as moms do. And as we become comfortable in raising our children and helping them learn new things, we develop a deep awareness and sense of validation as dads.

While this transformation into a father clearly occurs in the circumstances of our lives, it ultimately takes place in the depths of our own minds. This is where we develop the extraordinary commitment and drive necessary to not only do the job, but to excel.

You get a lot of messages that women have maternal instincts and you kinda get the message that they're the only ones that do...But the fact is that dads have instincts too, and I think that as long as you follow that I don't think you make too many bad choices.

Veteran Dad

A Taste of What's to Come

Over the past 15 years at Boot Camp For New Dads, over 30,000 "veterans" have returned to orient the "rookie" dads-to-be. They bring their new babies, typically 2-4 months old, and take care of them for the duration of the three-hour workshop. They hold, feed, rock, change and play with their babies while showing the rookies how it is done. The babies sleep, smile, fuss, cry, poop, and take in this unusual scene of men and babies with no women in sight.

It's also an unusual scene for the rookies. While the babies are interesting, the rookies focus on the veterans, men just like them except they are now fathers with babies on their laps.

This is what the rookies see in these men:

First thing he does in the morning when I get him up is smile at me...or when he gets me up actually.

Veteran Dad

- **Confidence** - While this may be their first trip out alone with their babies, these fathers know how to handle any need their children present.

- **Pride** - Not only are they happy to tell you all about their babies, these men have the calm air of those who have been tested and have proven themselves.

- **Sense of Purpose** - Whether truck drivers or corporate CEO's, these men feel needed, important, and they know that no one else can replace them in the lives of their children.

- **Excitement** - Ask them, "Do you like her? Is it worth it?" and they just come alive. They might struggle to explain it, but their smiles come straight from their hearts.

Veterans are remarkably different than they were five or six months earlier when they attended Boot Camp as rookies. Even though they may be looking through bleary eyes, these men feel very good about what they see in the mirror, and especially about what they are holding in their arms. These are upbeat men, on a mission, with a future full of potential.

Status Check on Common Challenges to Bonding

Keeping up the front that, Gee! This was swell, I'm going to be a father was like the hardest job of all. Because no one would come up to me and tell me that it was okay to admit that I didn't really feel anything for this new baby. But that all changed 5 months later when my child knew who I was. In fact, what happens is, it's the one thing that lives up to it's billing.

Veteran Dad

New fathers find that many things can get in the way of their bonding and attachment to their children. If problems, such as those mentioned below, persist and continue to impede your relationship to your baby or your partner, they can become ingrained and undermine your lifelong experience as a father.

Overcoming these challenges requires that you understand what is happening. If you do not, you are likely to have an angry or equally unconstructive reaction that only makes things worse.

It is crucial to understand that you are not alone, that you are not the cause, and that these problems will pass in time. While this "dark side" of fatherhood is rarely discussed, these issues are very common. The cause is not your mate or your baby either, but a new, demanding set of circumstances that requires time for all involved to adapt.

Review this list of common challenges to see if one or more is preventing you from connecting with your child:

Being Left Out By Mom?
You were prepared to be an involved father, only to have a mate so absorbed with "her" baby that she does not trust you to care for him. Her wonderful, exclusive relationship with her baby is essentially excluding you (she's being a "gate keeper"). Or perhaps she is

restricting your access due to her anger over (add in any reason). Instead of encouraging your involvement, she is pushing you away from your baby.

Pushed Out By Grandma
When she was a new mom, dads were not supposed to be involved with their babies. And she may not have a clear understanding that you want to be. She loves that baby so, is such a big help to your wife, and knows so much more than you do, that it is okay, right? No. The bottom line is that grandma has come between you and your baby, and it is definitely time to stand your ground and set her straight.

Working Long Hours
You are the breadwinner, and your new family consumes a lot of bread. So like about half of all new dads, you need to spend more time at work. Or maybe it's just easier to be at work than at home these days. Either way, if you are not there to connect with your child, it is a problem requiring a constructive solution.

Feeling Ambivalent, Inadequate
Let's face it, after a while you can get sick of watching your baby's face scrunch up and hearing those blood curdling screams. Especially if you feel useless when she needs care, while your mate, through natural instinct, seems to be able to calm her just by picking her up. Many guys facing this situation simply withdraw.

Caregiver Fatigue
Doing your best and then some is required and expected, but it's rarely appreciated by mom or your baby in the first months. And that's when it is the toughest. Are you asking yourself why you bother?

Blaming Your Baby
Who else is there to blame for disrupting your life, and for coming between you and your mate? It may have started with the pain mom experienced in giving birth, or earlier with problems in her pregnancy, and just increased as the initial weeks wore on. And when you try to comfort your crying baby, he seems to be screaming right at you. The fun in your marriage is gone; the future looks bleak, and where is all the wondrous joy of becoming a father?

Anger Towards Your Baby
One of the unique values of Boot Camp is that, with everything said in the room staying in the room, the veterans are very frank about the struggles they have encountered. Many say one of the most intense feelings is experiencing their own anger. Driven by frustration and

Don't sweat the small stuff. I can't expect a spotless home anymore. I will have to accept our home as it is today; cluttered with toys and clothes; walls with handprints, crayon on the walls, and so forth.
Veteran Dad

fatigue and exacerbated by job or financial stresses, it is often aimed at their own babies.

It's common but rarely talked about. It is unnerving to find yourself angry with such a small helpless baby; your own child no less. What generally follows are strong feelings of guilt that undermine your confidence and feed your feelings of inadequacy. This in turn builds a barrier between you and your child, which is the essential problem you are dealing with. Do not let this happen.

Although I hadn't been getting much sleep, I found that a little exercise helps me catch my second wind. And it helps me sleep better through the night.
Veteran Dad

Lighten up on yourself; intense feelings happen. Talk about it with someone you trust to get it off your chest. And then take your baby for a walk (babies are very forgiving, and have short memories). If you feel you may harm your baby in any way, talk to his doctor or call a stress hotline for parents (see *Learning More/Getting Help* in the Appendix).

Are You Jealous of Your Baby, or Do You Miss Your Wife?
Missing your wife, or feeling left out of her exclusive relationship with the baby? These are common feelings of a new father during the initial months and are commonly mischaracterized as jealousy. This notion comes from the era when fathers were routinely left on the sidelines, and any complaint was quickly shut down with the "J"-word. It is still the case.

It is hard to imagine a bigger slam on a new father who is struggling to adapt to a new life and connect with his child, than to be accused of being jealous of his own beautiful little baby. If you buy this nonsense, you will feel dumb and perhaps worthless and will have taken a big step away from bonding with your baby.

Don't buy it. Wanting to spend time with your wife and to be part of your own family are good things, in fact, very good things. This is also an effective response to anyone who suggests it is jealously.

How Are You Feeling?

The range of emotions you might experience at six weeks can be mind-boggling. Confusion – at one moment feeling the pride of having created this new life, and at the next moment disappointment in yourself for not being able to control your baby's crying. Shifting emotions – one day you are feeling a surge of love and the next day you wake up wondering where the feelings went.

You might even wake up wondering if it was all a big mistake and feel the "flight or fight" impulse setting in, a little voice encouraging you to "hit the road, Jack." Then there are the fears – minor and major. The big ones have to do with not being able to live up to your own and others' expectations of you as a dad, as a provider, and as a man.

The minor fears can also dig at you constantly – "I'm doing the diaper wrong, holding the baby wrong, she doesn't like me because I can't make her stop crying." The more tired you get, the sharper these demons can loom up in your imagination.

About a third of new fathers actually get depressed. The stress, fed by fatigue, can be enormous.

Orient Yourself

Now is a good time to step back, take a deep breath, and get oriented. The old notion of "know thyself" is essential at this point. Ask yourself some basic questions. There are no right or wrong answers, but be brutally honest.

Your Baby
- How do you feel about your child?
- How much time have you spent with your baby this week?
- Have you been alone caring for your baby for a good part of a day?
- Are you in the front seat, involved in caring for your baby; or have you been relegated to the back seat by mom or grandma?
- If you're in the back, is it because you have no time? Why have you not made time?
- What frustrates you about your baby? What bores you?
- Are you looking forward to raising your child?

Your Wife
- Have your feelings about your partner changed? Does she treat you differently?
- What do you like most about her? Have you told her lately?
- Do you feel like you are in a partnership, or are you out there alone?
- When was the last time you and your mate had a heart-to-heart talk?
- Have you been sitting on your own feelings, afraid to mention things that are bothering you for fear of upsetting your mate?

Mom overreacts to our baby's illnesses; I underreact. Balancing the responsibility of raising our baby. Mom complains about how much I help, even though I help out a lot; it seems no matter what I do its never enough.
Veteran Dad

- How do you feel about her as a mom?
- Do you both feel the same way about how to handle the baby?

You
- Have you changed? Is the guy looking back at you in the mirror at all familiar?
- What things do you like about being a father?
- Are you satisfied with the job you are doing?
- Are you angry? Does your anger get in the way?
- Are you constructive? Can you take a long view?
- What events or issues in the past four weeks stand out the most in your mind?
- Are you having second thoughts about having a baby?
- How does your role compare to that of your father?

Constructive Solutions

Once you are oriented and have done your status check, the next step is to deal with issues proactively. Focus on any obstacles in the way of connecting with your baby. First though, remind yourself again that you are far from alone - these issues are normal.

Standard Solution
The solution is simple: just keep at it. Review *Earning Your Stripes* – Page 140 – and see how you are doing in relation to the bottom line standards for dads (i.e., select one activity – like bathing – that you own, make it just the two of you on a regular basis). Take a fresh look at *Caring for Your New Baby*, *Troubleshooting Crying Babies*, and *Raising Your New Baby*, and check out *Your New Playmate*. There is no end to the things you can do with a baby. Come up with something new to try out.

Time to Say What Needs to be Said
You have focused a great deal on helping her through pregnancy, birth and the initial weeks of motherhood. You have likely held back on your own feelings because you wanted to be strong for her when she needed you, and didn't want to burden her with your own issues.

By six weeks, though, it is time to start unloading what's on your mind, for your benefit and for hers, as well as your baby's. If you have to go around her to get involved with your own baby, it is time to get beyond being patient and understanding. If you are going to form a parenting

It never dawned on me to think about my own health. I was so concerned about keeping mom and the baby healthy that I neglected to take care of myself.
Veteran Dad

My son took over my spot in the bed. So I slept on the couch in front of the TV for a while. My wife didn't understand why at first, but then I explained to her that it wasn't anything personal. I was just afraid I might roll over and hurt the baby. And that I had a hard time adjusting to this whole idea of sharing a bed with another human being.
Veteran Dad

team, it has to be a two way street. Do it as constructively as you can, but just make sure you do it.

Drawing the Line
Up to this point you may have cut yourself or others some slack on core issues impacting your relationship with your child (intrusion by grandma, a demanding boss, your own participation). If so, it is time to draw the line and say enough. Otherwise these problems are likely to get set in stone for a long time to come. Stand your ground to make sure you are not pushed out of your child's life. You may find the toughest person to deal with is yourself.

If You are Overwhelmed

If you find the whole scene seriously getting to you, do something about it:

- Try to get enough sleep. Grab a nap when possible – a little sleep can go a long way.

- Be realistic. The demands of fatherhood can easily push you past your limits, and you can't do everything. Let yourself off the hook once in awhile and de-stress.

- Take things gradually. Give yourself time to warm up to the big changes you are facing.

- Share your feelings with your partner. Let her help you sort them out.

- Laugh. You can always find something funny in any situation if you try. And sometimes the toughest things you go through are also the most amusing in retrospect.

- Do something creative to break out of the doldrums. Get out the camera and get some pictures of your new family developed and framed and put them up around the house.

- Stay involved. When exhaustion and frustration set in, everything in you wants to back off. You need to do the opposite. When you feel most like tuning out, push yourself to take the baby for a walk or give your partner a back rub. Soon you will find that overcoming your own resistance becomes easier and more gratifying.

I found that even a light 15-minute jog twice a week has helped me relieve the tension and stress of work and being a new dad. I jog…usually when the baby's asleep.
Veteran Dad

Stressed out from the pressures at work and exhausted from not getting enough sleep, I started to take my frustrations out on my wife and baby. Not a good thing to do. So I started exercising and taking my frustrations out on the punching bag in the garage, instead of my wife and the baby.
Veteran Dad

Kick Back With Your Friends

In addition to patience and communication, veteran dads highly recommend that new fathers blow off steam with some friends, perhaps over an occasional beer. It works a lot better if they have babies or kids themselves, as a little appreciation of your circumstances and semi-heroic efforts can do wonders for your attitude.

Don't Get Isolated
Standard procedure for new fathers is to give up the few friends we have (a) because they foster anti-social behavior and (b) they are not interested in the color of our baby's poop. The bottom line is that we get isolated and cooped up just when we need to get out and de-stress.

I felt pressured to always be there for my new family and play Superdad, never thinking that I needed time every once in a while to recuperate and refuel my daddy tank.

Veteran Dad

So, as a new father, hunkered down in a bunker with a new mom and a fussy baby, you need to get out with the guys every now and then. Your buddies provide balance in your life, especially when the pressure builds. So if you are feeling it, for the sake of your family, call up your friends and go out and have a beer. Review the sports section first so you have something to talk about besides the baby.

Talk to Other Dads
Take a page out of the new mom's playbook and network with the dads you know and connect with some new ones. Although they are a good bet, don't limit yourself to the mates of new moms your wife met in your childbirth class. Try your own father – you may be surprised by how much you have in common. Take your baby to go see your brother, or ask the guy down the hall at work or the one sitting next to you on the plane about their kids.

Getting together with some other dads can quickly put you back on solid ground with a fresh head of steam. Bring your baby and score some points in the process. The veterans who do this uniformly report it to be both reassuring and motivating. If someone gushes about how wonderful everything has been since his baby's birth, explain the rules: points are only awarded for get-it-off-your-chest gripes and screw ups, and worst case scenarios win.

Never Look Back

Remember some basic rules to live by from those who have been there:

- With children, the long view ahead is essential. This perspective will enable you to blow off the little things and focus on those that are important.

- To kids, every day is a new day, so any past mistakes or shortcomings on your part can be more than made up for. No matter your track record to date, today and tomorrow present you the opportunity to become a great dad.

- It is Okay to not like your child for a while, as he can be irritating and even embarrassing. However, if the feeling persists for more than a week, you are doing something wrong. Since there are at least a million new things to try, you are never at a loss for opportunities.

Finally, fatherhood fundamentally forces all us guys to grow up. Just don't try to do it all at once.

Life is short and childhood is fleeting. I am more apt to do things now rather than later. I don't ever want to look back and say I wish I had spent more time with my family.
Veteran Dad

The best thing to do is to relax. Take it a step at a time and enjoy it. Because it really is a joy to be needed in that way. You have this completely helpless creature who needs you and it's a way to feel like there is something of value that you can offer.
Veteran Dad

17

Reconstructing Your Relationship

There is no better feeling in a marriage than to know you are doing a good job working together to raise your children.

Veteran Dad

Sooner or later your roller coaster life with a newborn settles down. Your baby eventually eases into something resembling a routine, and you start to catch up on a little sleep. Mom too. Maybe you even begin to think you'll be able to handle all this.

It's time for you and mom to refocus on each other. Your baby will still get plenty of attention, but her long- term needs include parents who love each other and work together to make a good life for their family. Since mom is hardwired to focus on the baby, this will be tough for her, so you will likely have to take the initiative.

Your first date with your wife, away from the baby, is essential, as is relearning to talk about something other than you-know-who. So is resuming some of the activities you both enjoyed in your former life.

It will be something you have to work at, but with a lifetime of raising a family and being together ahead of you, it is well worth the effort. Given the natural tendency of a new baby to push mom and dad apart, your circumstances may require it.

Different Perspectives

Talk to you wife about how you feel. That you're feeling neglected. That as much as she needs to know that you love her, you need her to do the same. Make sure that your relationship stays strong. It doesn't always have to be about the baby.

Veteran Dad

For some couples, a new baby is like a keystone in their relationship; the three fit together like peas in a pod and the adjustment to family life is seamless. If this description fits you, consider yourself very fortunate, and then review this chapter to get ideas on strengthening your relationship even further. If not, pay close attention.

New Moms
To recap, new moms are generally different from pre-baby moms in several fundamental ways. Often thrilled with their babies, they also tend to feel:

- Trapped in a new life as a mom; virtually chained to the baby
- Unattractive, flabby, and certainly not sexy
- Likely to cry often, with dad being a major reason

Her baby commands her full attention and she has neither time nor energy to devote to you. So while she needs you more than ever, she may ignore you altogether.

She has largely forgotten why she loved you in the first place, and now her feelings for you are dependent upon your performance as a father and partner. And no matter how well you perform, it will likely not be good enough, as rationality tends to suffer when one is tired and stressed.

So you have your work cut out for you.

New Dads

Life is not necessarily a bed of roses for you either, as your counterparts collectively indicate.

Your feelings towards mom may be mixed. Several months after the birth, you likely love her and respect her as a mom. But your admiration and sympathy for the pain and the sacrifices she has endured may have worn thin. If she is staying home, you may wonder why she cannot get her act together. And why does she have to take all her frustrations out on you? Why is your time at work considered time you have to yourself? And why is a little consideration and attention, or something resembling a love life so much of a burden? Will it ever get better?

Who Will Step Forward?

The real question is, given that both mom and dad are stressed and tired, who is going to come forward and work to make it better? Once again, you need to dig deep to find the strength to step up to the challenge. This is a big one too, that goes way beyond resuming your love life. Your marriage has reached a crossroads, and it can deteriorate, as about half do after the first baby arrives. Or it can get stronger, richer and even more passionate.

I had a tough time convincing my wife that I needed time to exercise. At first she thought I was trying to avoid having to help her...but then she realized that the stress and pressures of being a first-time dad were no different than her being a first-time mom. So we compromised and blocked out time each week...for ourselves. This worked out great, because when my wife had her time alone, I had time alone with the baby.
Veteran Dad

Communication is the Key

Talking is how we sort out and resolve problems, and several months after the birth the stack can be high. Both of you may be struggling with anger over a variety of issues, including your respective contributions (or lack thereof) to your new family and to each other.

To get beyond such problems, they need to be stated in clear terms and discussed. This may involve some venting, which will not be pleasant, but will get the issues out in the open where they can be addressed.

Over millenniums, men have discovered that women:

1. Like to talk about their feelings
2. Like us to listen and talk back
3. Will expect us to read their minds if we don't listen and respond

There is an immense array of additional insights on relationships in the many magazines, books and talk shows on the subject. But you will be well served to remember the bottom line: communication – talking and listening – is the key.

If talking it over is tough due to strong emotions and knee jerk reactions to hot button issues, try writing her a letter. This enables you to take a constructive approach and clearly state your feelings. You might even bring yourself to give her a coupon for a back rub or something that lets her know, despite your issues, that you still love her (backrubs also constitute foreplay).

How to Have a Fight

My wife had to shift priorities and first be a mother, which required some adjustment for me. This is a constant challenge.

Veteran Dad

It will probably happen, even in the most loving and mellow relationships, that you will have a fight. So try to make them as constructive as possible. Being prepared will help you handle the snipes without wimping out or going overboard. Here are the basic rules:

• When it comes to arguing don't preach, don't yell, don't tell her everything's fine. Just listen and try to look at it from her perspective.

• After you've heard her out, it's your turn. Try to get beyond complaining and down to the basic issues. In other words, try to address the problem, not the symptoms.

• Once you have sorted the issues out in your head, refer them to your heart. You might find yourself just putting your arm around her and assuring her that you can work it out.

An angry confrontation between seriously stressed new parents can enable both to vent festering frustrations and clear the air. These are good things, so consider them objectives. Just remember that "winning" is not the point, and it's not even an option. Follow up with a productive way to address the real problem, as she sees it. Otherwise any kiss and make up phase will be short lived.

Romancing a Mom

If you think Big Picture, as in what kind of relationship you will have over the next decade, you will want to be proactive and positive in reconnecting with your partner. You are ready to take the initiative; what do you do? The basics are as follows:

Understand that You are Starting Over
Re-kindling the romance in your relationship is a lot like starting over on a fresh courtship with a new woman in your life. Plan on a crawl-walk-run approach, with little steps and lots of patience. Don't be put off if she does not respond at first; your patience will pay off.

Encourage and Respect Her as a Mom
Nothing, except maybe getting back to a size seven, will be as important to her self-esteem as the job she is doing as a mom. Encourage her when she is down, tell her often what a great job she is doing with your baby, and appreciate her incredible commitment as a mother. Acknowledge the sacrifices she is making. This works in reverse as well; in fact, mutual respect is the cornerstone of great families.

Do Your Part as a Father
Keep in mind she is now viewing you as her baby's father. When she watches you giving him a bath or rocking him to sleep on your chest, she sees a happy baby and a loving dad. Due to the demands and stress she is experiencing, she may set the bar, particularly regarding housework, impossibly high. Hang in there and it will come down.

Give Her Time Alone
Whenever she is around the baby, she is on call for his slightest need or demand. If she is working, the demands upon her are even more intense. Above all, she needs time for herself. Make sure she gets it. She might even return the favor.

I realized that I should sacrifice some of my free time to relieve my wife and encourage her to go and treat herself to lunch with a friend, a manicure or whatever.

Veteran Dad

Help Her Re-Engage Her Mind

Anything that allows her to feel normal again will help give her a break from obsessing about the baby. Encourage her to read a novel, play games, go to a movie or take up a hobby. (When mom's mind is not on the baby, it is available to be thinking about you.)

Refrain From Pushing Her

When it comes to romance, applying too much pressure on your partner to get things back on track, especially regarding sex, will backfire. She needs to know your priority is her, not getting back in the sack. Backing off too much will not work either, because she might think you don't care. So take a steady, patient approach.

Tell Her Your Dreams

And ask about hers. Talking together about your future, remembering your pre-baby past, and sharing your dreams brings you closer. It also makes very clear your commitment to her and your baby, and sets the stage for passion.

Have Fun

Successful marriages include a strong sense of commitment, the ability to resolve conflicts and a regular dose of fun. Laughing together clears the air of lingering tension, and builds trust in each other and confidence in your relationship (making her laugh definitely constitutes foreplay).

Do Things Together

We make a point to have a date night twice a month and have a relative or friend watch the baby.

Veteran Dad

To get her mind on something other than the baby, try the following. If that something turns out to be you, you are on the road back.

Bring Out the List

Remember the list of the things you like to do together that you made before the baby arrived? It is time to bring it out, pick one of the items and do it. Just spending a little time talking about the activities you enjoyed will remind her of the good times that were special to you both. If you didn't make a list, think about it now – maybe it includes things like renting a movie, playing a board game, or just going out and walking around the mall.

Engage in Adult Conversation

For the first few months, the baby is the sole topic of your discussions. As you engage the outside world at work, your mate is probably at

home talking to the baby, or talking about the baby. Help her break her isolation by asking her about anything other than the baby (current events, her pre-baby interests, what's going on with friends, etc).

Get Out on Weekends
Go on a date with your mate and your baby—to a sporting event, the zoo, or just out for a walk. There's a tendency to associate your house with baby-related chores, so just getting out and doing those baby chores elsewhere is fun.

Eat Together
As simple as it sounds, it's a great way to begin reconnecting with your partner. Prepare a gourmet dinner together.

Exercise Together
A mom who gets regular exercise is a happier mom. She loses weight, increases her energy, tones her body, burns off stress, balances hormones, and enhances her attitude. (Same for you.) Getting exercise together by walking (or jogging or bike riding) with your baby is a particularly great idea. It gets you out of the house, your baby enjoys it, and it provides an opportunity to talk.

Go to Bed Together
Try getting to bed at the same time as your partner. Otherwise one of you inevitably will be asleep when the other one hits the hay. Just having that little window of private time goes a long way. You can use it to chat, snuggle, or whatever else feels right.

Cuddle (Only)
She has a lot of physical contact with a demanding baby and may not want any more at first. Take it slow and give her a foot rub, back rub, some hugs, and warm up to spooning. It is critical that you avoid erogenous zones and do not indicate desire for sexual activity. After several nights of feigning eunuch type behavior, you should be able to move up to foreplay.

Schedule Dates
They don't always work due to changing priorities and intrusions, but if nothing is scheduled, you may never get around to it. Expect excuses, particularly "I am too tired," and be flexible, but stick to it and at some point it will become part of your routine. Perhaps the best part.

Keep a sense of humor. Work, family and marriage all adds up to more that 24 hours and there are places you have to give. There is no perfect formula…a constant balance. But if you keep a sense of humor, you can find the fun in just about everything.

Veteran Dad

Remind Her You Love Her

Getting her to focus on your relationship will generally require more than your understanding, patience and initiative to do things together. You also need to reassure her that you love her and will be there for her forever, keeping in mind that actions speak louder than words.

Proven alternatives that build her faith in you include:

- Quick phone call: "Just wanted to hear your voice, see how you were doing, was thinking of you," etc. A regular call from work in the afternoon is highly recommended.

- Email message: "Had some good news and wanted you to be the first to know," or "How is your day going?," etc.

- Love note: Give her a card that says how much you love her, how beautiful she is, or how much you appreciate the effort she's put into taking care of your new baby.

It's the little things that are important, like when you walk into the house after work, always kiss her first and maybe give her some flowers. That will reassure her that she is every bit of a woman that she has ever been even though she is a mother.

Veteran Dad

Little Things Count
Remember all those little things you did to win over your sweetheart? Try them again, or some new ones:

- On a cold night, lie on her side of the bed to warm it up before she gets in.
- Give her a quick neck rub in the morning.
- Go for a walk and hold her hand.
- When you come home from work, give her a kiss.

Tell your partner you love her often. Part of her strength derives from knowing that she's the most important person in the world—to you. She also thrives on just knowing you are thinking of her.

Bigger Things Count Too
Splurge a little once in a while and do something special:

- Buy her flowers: A surefire way to make her feel good in any situation. Large bouquets can get expensive, so consider buying her a single rose, as it gets your message across.

- Buy her a new outfit: Something that lets her know you understand her body has changed and you want her to look good. A gift certificate for one can work even better especially if you go with her and watch the baby while she shops.

- Put up pictures of her and the baby: "*He bought some frames and put pictures of me and the baby up around the house, and updated them periodically. I looked at them often, and every time it reminded me how much he appreciated me and our baby.*" This was a brilliant move on the part of this dad. You should get into the picture too.

- Get her out with her girl friends: They talk about us when they get together and blow off steam. (Us guys should do that more often with our buddies). Chances are, no matter how angry she may be with you, one of her friends will top her story.

Find or Make Time

Re-igniting the romance requires making time for dates - or fun, or anything else that allows you to burn off pent-up stress together. While going out to dinner and a movie is great, your time with mom doesn't have to be logistically challenging. Sometimes, it just takes a few minutes alone away from your baby to feel like you still have a life together.

Getting Mom Out
Since moms are inextricably connected to their babies, they often find it very difficult to get away at first. No baby sitter can be trusted, the baby might get hungry or cry and need her, etc. Even though the best thing she can do is to get a break from the baby, she may not be able to bring herself to do it, even if she really wants to.

Her link to the baby can be like a sea anchor in her otherwise storm tossed life, and even going out for a few hours can make her feel she is cutting her moorings and abandoning her baby. She needs to get out, and you need to figure out how to make it happen. Planned outings that don't work out represent progress, so be patient and persistent. Even if she seems to sandbag the whole process, when moms finally get away, their relief and relaxation is obvious and appreciated.

Pre-Arrange a Date Night
Schedule it well in advance. Ask her what she might want to do and arrange it. Ask a close friend or relative (who is familiar with the baby) to watch him for a few hours so you two can spend time alone together. Don't be disappointed if it does not work out at first, as new

parents report the scheduled date strategy works less then half the time. Keep at it.

Find a Good Babysitter:
You and your partner will be much more comfortable leaving the house without your baby once you find a trustworthy babysitter. Standard recommendations:

- Ask for referrals from friends with babies.
- Interview babysitter candidates—prepare a list of questions beforehand.
- Ask the sitter for references from other clients and check them.
- For infants, use a mature babysitter—that is, an adult.

Date at Home

We had a hard time at first adjusting to each of us getting less attention from each other.
Veteran Dad

While getting out is important, so is relearning to have fun together in your own home. Try a video date, blanket in front of the fire, a puzzle, or music, candles and wine.

Save Water in the Shower
You're both going to take a shower at some point. So why not take one together?

Sleeping Like an Angel
When the baby has just been put to bed, you have an opportunity to do something romantic with your partner. Establishing a little "our time now" on a regular basis is a huge milestone for new parents, and even an hour or so while your little angel sleeps works.

Who Will Bring Home the Bacon?

In years past, societal norms were clear: dads worked and moms stayed home. Today, there are an expanding variety of options as parents explore different work combinations. While options are great, choosing among them can be difficult and even divisive.

You and your mate are unique individuals, with unique experiences, education, hopes and values. Every family situation is different. Every career has its own demands. Your challenge is to mutually make the best choice for your unique family.

For dads who wrestle with the choices, the issues can include:

- I really want her to stay home to take care of our baby but I am not able to earn enough to afford it. She has to work.

- She wants to quit work to stay home with the baby, even though we can't afford it. I will have to work more to try to make it, so what about my time with the baby?

- She wants to go back to her career and I want her to stay home to care for our baby. I make twice what she does, and whatever she makes gets spent on day care and taxes.

- One of us should stay home; I would like to and she makes twice what I do.

Or perhaps variations or a combination of the above. Basic considerations for different arrangements are as follows:

Both Dad and Mom Have to Work

Some couples simply cannot afford to raise a child without two incomes. For them, as soon as paid maternity leave (and any accrued vacation) have been exhausted, it's time to arrange daycare for the baby and for mom to rejoin dad in the workforce.

Before you conclude that you must have two incomes, factor in the costs of the second salary: daycare, transportation to work, baby formula (if mom will need to stop breastfeeding), lunches, parking, and higher taxes. Unless that salary is sizeable, you might do better if one parent stays home, even with a reduced standard of living.

> **Practice Leaving Your Baby at Day Care**
> This can be an emotionally wrenching scene, and can be devastating for moms and some dads who have no experience being separated from their babies. Practice by using babysitters before DC day occurs. Consider it a dry separation run. Also ask the daycare folks for their suggestions.

Mom Wants to Work

Despite the urge to become the fantasy stay-at-home mom with an oven full of cookies and a yard full of kids, some women actually enjoy working. They take pride in their jobs and find work brings them satisfaction, a sense of accomplishment, contact with other adults, mental stimulation, and other intangible rewards that have little to do with money. Such mothers may feel conflicted after baby arrives, torn between the desire to resume a fulfilling career and the urge to fit the ideal of a stay-at-home mother.

If the baby is crying and if you wife is taking care of the baby, the best advice I can give you is to get busy cleaning something! Get a broom in your hand, wash the dishes. Do something because then you're covered. And there is no resentment.

Veteran Dad

Mom Wants to Stay Home

Many couples are able to survive, or even thrive, on dad's salary, and mom stays home. Some moms take to it like a duck to water, but for many others becoming a stay-at-home mom is far removed from the fantasy. Changing endless diapers and wiping up spit-up is not glamorous. Certainly the ever-present reward of being the all-important person in her precious little one's life is incalculable. But babies are lousy conversationalists. And they are not particularly mentally stimulating. Bringing up a baby can be boring and draining at the same time.

Dad Stays Home

The flip side (with a twist) of the above scenario is when dad stays home. Despite a deeply ingrained belief that women should take care of babies and men should bring home the paycheck, men today are increasingly becoming primary caregivers. This is newly charted territory and can feel uncomfortable for both parents. But when families choose this route, old stereotypes get blown away by positive experiences.

My wife still feels she does things better but we're very good at divvying up duties. Our care of the baby is very different - methods are different - results are the same.

Veteran Dad

While stay-at-home moms are often distressed when the reality of full time baby care does not meet the fantasy they've nurtured since playing with dolls, the twist is that dads who do so are often surprised to find that the reality exceeds their own expectations and breaks the perception that men do not belong at home.

But whoever ends up at home, the primary caregiver will probably struggle with a sense of lost freedom and may end up longing for adult contact and challenges that go beyond visits to the pediatrician or inventing a new way to entertain the baby.

Creative and Courageous Choices

Some parents are able to create alternative solutions, such as working from home, or arranging part-time, flexible work. These arrangements allow them to be home much of the time while still maintaining an income and a life beyond the baby. Others make sometimes difficult or even courageous choices, such as moving to a lower cost community, cutting back career aspirations to spend more time at home, or even giving up their dreams of becoming pro athletes, race car drivers or rock stars (serious sacrifices here) to assure stable paychecks for their new families.

No one can tell you what's right for your family, but no matter your choice, it will be the right one if you and mom make it work together.

And remember: There are no perfect families. There are just people trying to do their best.

Working Out the Workload

Parenting responsibilities used to be well defined. Mom did the housework, took care of the baby and had dinner on the table when dad came home with the bacon. Today, no matter your circumstances, all bets are off, and dividing family work responsibilities has become an upsetting, festering issue among way too many parents.

Teamwork Is the Gold Standard

Working together is the key, but with so much arguing and tension out there, teamwork on the home front is elusive. Couples who split up income production, household and baby care responsibilities in a realistic and predictable way are able to get the jobs done efficiently and minimize conflict over who does what, saving energy for things they like to do together.

No 50-50 Solution

The 50-50 workload split is an illusion. Trying to share the household and baby care chores equally is impossible unless both parents essentially spend the same amount of time at home and there are no outside work considerations. Mom's and dad's perceptions of what is fair can differ widely. Your mutual objectives should be to get the jobs done and make your family life all that it can be, rather than splitting hairs over who is doing more vacuuming or diaper changing.

Dads Do More

The best move is to just start doing more when the baby arrives – housework, baby care or cooking. When you take on new tasks, approach them constructively so you ultimately get a sense of satisfaction (you don't have to enjoy mowing the lawn to feel good about it when it is done and done well). Stake out your turf and then learn how to do a good job at it. Keep in mind that a mom's standards regarding domestic duties usually come from her own mother, while yours probably comes from your father.

Work Out a Plan

Make a plan and then live with it. The antidote to the avoidance game of who should do what is to make a list of chores and assign realistic responsibilities that work with the hours you both have available. Make

It's been wonderful. Although it can be very tiring and demanding, I handle all the evening activities, such as bath time, bed time, book and bottle almost every night. And one weekend day take care of the baby to give my wife a break.
Veteran Dad

it specific enough to be meaningful, and make sure you write down everything you can think of, such as paying bills, gardening, car maintenance, grocery shopping. Include both your work hours and commute time.

Remember the Long Term

Parents who work together on the incredibly important challenges presented by a child develop a deep respect for each other. On top of your inherent love, this can make for a beautiful marriage in decades to come.

18

Re-Igniting Romance

Let's be honest. What most men really want to know is: What about sex? When will it resume, and how will it be? There's no simple answer, of course, as every couple is unique, and there are many complicating factors.

A healthy sex live is the cornerstone of a good relationship. But getting it restarted after a baby is born can be tough. Not only has her furnace not been fired up in months, her pilot light has blown out and her components need to be restored. She may get plenty of intimacy from her baby and not be interested, or she may simply be exhausted with all the demands on her. Tired, frustrated moms do not make good playmates.

Resuming romance requires patience and an acute understanding of the changes in your mate. Whether it's doing fun stuff with just the two of you or making love, getting your romantic life back means taking it slow, getting some rest, and remembering that making each other a priority is one of the best things you can do for your baby.

Making Love Again

Making love celebrates your commitment to each other and regenerates your passion. It renews your bond by purging the small irritations that build up, and by reminding you both that you love each other and are much better together than alone. An active, enjoyable sex life is essential to your relationship, the foundation upon which families are built.

Now that you know how babies are made for real, sex can mean more than just getting back in the sack. It needs to mean more because there are major challenges to your post-baby love life, as various surveys have found:

- The vast majority of couples report less sex.
- A third report their formally active love life has redlined.
- Half are quieter in bed and do not experiment as much.
- For about 10% it has gotten hotter.

The initial glow does fade into equal part of love and frustration. But when arguments arise - and they do, from sleepless nights and juggling chores - my wife and I look at our little tyke, pause for a breath, and make up faster than ever. Because we love the little guy, and he's teaching us to love each other better.

Veteran Dad

The widespread notion that fathers are left wanting is only partly true; moms want more as well. Once the baby is sleeping through the night, most women begin to desire a more active love life. In fact, only about a third of moms of young children are happy with the passion in their lives.

It doesn't get much better as children grow. Once sleep deprivation is put to rest, roaming and inquisitive children can make privacy a pre-baby luxury. So while both moms and dads ultimately want more, circumstances will conspire to rain on your parade. To avoid this fate, you will have to work at it based upon a well informed strategy.

While you are likely feeling sex starved and in serious need of conjugal relations at this point, there is a lot more at stake than getting your rocks off. If you want to strengthen your marriage and avoid several decades of sexual frustration, another round of sex education focused on post baby issues is an essential first step. Due to the obstacles new moms face, if it is going to be good for you, it may need to be better than ever for her.

A Note to New Moms from New Dads

If you are reading this, we appreciate your interest in what is going on with us as we become fathers. As you can see from the rest of this book, we try hard to understand what motherhood brings to you and trust that our great respect for mothers is clear. With all the changes going on around us, this mutual understanding is critical to the future of our new families.

While our individual circumstances vary, a concise summary of our collective experience regarding our relationships with the new moms in our lives is as follows:

1. We miss you. It is not that we don't understand the new demands you face as a mom, it is just that we miss you and what we had together when there was just two of us. Since this reflects our love for you, it should be viewed as a good thing.

2. We don't understand all that is going on with you, or even ourselves, and expect the opposite is true as well. We should talk more, which for most men does not come naturally.

3. Again, we miss you. Having fun together and making love is important to us, and should be for you too. While it helps balance our lives and cements our relationship for the long term, somehow it gets relegated to last on the priority list.

Over the 15 years that we have conducted our Boot Camp workshops, we have talked to thousands of new moms. We would like to hear from you as well, and invite you to visit us at www.newdads.com to let us know what is on your mind.

Hit The Ground Crawling

Moms and Dads Place Different Values on Sex

The now celebrated differences between men and women, perhaps best chronicled in *Women are From Venus, Men are From Mars*, have a major impact on how we experience the rewards of sex. These differences are intensified by new family stresses and a woman's changing priorities, which are reflected in her evolving needs under the covers. You will need to refocus your priorities as well to keep up.

While unique to each couple, sex offers two major rewards beyond the obvious one (the baby in your lap). The rewards, and mom's and dad's differing valuations of them, are as follows:

A. Dads value intense pleasure first
    For most men, sex is first about pleasure, and the more the better. We are straightforward in our desire; there is no mystery about it to our mates, for whom sex is often a reward to us for loving them and making them happy. Our sex drive culminates quickly, and when we climax, we're done, or so it appears.

    Actually, as we lie there, perhaps even snoring, in addition to savoring the pleasure of sex, we also enjoy the warm and satisfying feeling that comes from knowing we are wanted by the woman we love. The latter feeling is the one that lingers.

B. Moms value an intense emotional connection first and last
    For most moms to enjoy it, sex needs to be an act of love. Being in the mood is not simply being horny as it is for men; they need to experience a strong sense of affection for us and feel we love them back. Anything that gets in the way may be a mood killer. And with new moms, there are many issues that can get in the way.

    While women ultimately can experience intense pleasure as well, they are likely to value our sensitivity and attention to their emotional needs, both before and after intercourse, just as much. Therefore, when we summit, rolling over and starting to snore, even with a smile on our face, may not be smart. She might want to stay connected, get hugs and kisses, and savor her intense feeling of love and being loved. Otherwise, when we are finished, she might just be getting started.

It helps to think of it as making love rather than just sex, because it needs to be for her to enjoy it.

Sex in Six Weeks to Six Months

Most doctors say six weeks after a normal vaginal delivery and she is good to go. Actually, she will be good to go not only when she is physically ready, but when she feels like it, which means when she is feeling rested, good about her baby, good about her body, and good about you. With all the changes she is experiencing, this could take awhile.

While six weeks may seem like an agonizingly long time to the sex-starved male, this period of post-delivery abstinence is generally a best-case scenario. While she may want to accommodate your eager advances on day one of the seventh week, don't be unduly disappointed if it does not happen.

Factors that conspire to interfere with intercourse include:

Fatigue
This is the big one. With the baby waking her up regularly at night and demanding continual care throughout the day, by the time the next evening rolls around, she is generally exhausted. On top of just being tired, the massive changes in her life leave her stressed out, overwhelmed and without the desire or energy necessary for sex. Even when she is willing and ready for the big night, more often than not, her head hits the pillow and she is out.

Soreness and Pain
While some moms who had a Cesarean delivery may actually be able to enjoy intercourse earlier, many women experience complications such as perineal tearing and episiotomy, which can extend the recovery period. She may be experiencing extra pain and need more time before the stitches heal or she is otherwise physically ready.

Feeling Unattractive
While her bodily transformation reverses course at delivery, it is going to take many months for her to get back to normal, and her body will never be the same. In the meantime, she can feel like a deflated, floppy balloon, and feeling unattractive is a huge turnoff for her. She wonders "will I ever feel desirable again?," oblivious to the fact that you feel she is. Again, it is not your feelings, but hers that count.

Nobody Loves Raymond
In an interview about sex after marriage, Ray Romano, a father of four and the star of "Everybody Loves Raymond," told Newsweek: "After kids, everything changes. We're having sex about every three months. If I have sex, I know my quarterly estimated taxes are due. And if it's oral sex, I know it's time to renew my driver's license."

Fear of Getting Pregnant Again

The last thing she wants to do is repeat her ordeal while it is still fresh in her mind. While contraception is available, complete abstinence provides the best assurance.

Demands of the Baby

Mom's attention is always on the baby: "She might wake up and we won't hear her," or if the baby is in the room, "We might wake the baby." She may find messing around with the baby nearby makes her feel uncomfortable or even ashamed. It's also tough to make love when your ears are fine-tuned to pick up the slightest peep from the baby. One needs to focus on turn-on's, and any distraction is by definition a turn off. Of course, ardor fades rapidly when interrupted by crying.

Side Effects of Breastfeeding

Breastfeeding has great benefits, but there is a downside when it comes to lovemaking. Hormones associated with milk production cause vaginal dryness, a condition that makes sex unattractive, if not painful. It is also common that breasts and nipples are too sore and tender to touch, or are simply off limits to dad as they are "for the baby." While you may be banished from the breasts until further notice, breastfeeding does facilitate mom's pregnancy weight loss.

Lost Libido

After giving birth, mom is awash in a stew of hormones, which do not subside quickly, especially if she breast feeds. Her biology, coupled with everything else going on in her life, may put her sex drive in reverse. The major reason new moms want to delay making love is that they just don't feel like it.

Touched Out

While a mother's wonderful intimacy with her baby is very fulfilling, it can replace her need for a sensual relationship with dad. If she's breastfeeding a baby six or so times a day, she can get to the point that she just does not want anyone else to even touch her.

Frustration

Frustrated women rarely find themselves in the mood, and new moms have a lot to be frustrated about. Feelings of lost careers, an inability to catch up on the housework, a life controlled by feeding schedules can all add up to major frustration. She may be angry with you over a myriad of issues, and even jealous if she feels she has taken the brunt of new baby responsibilities. Lingering resentment is a major issue, and sex is usually the first casualty.

What Does a Red Blooded Male Do?

As you move beyond your initial six-week start time, you may experience a serious case of "blue balls," perhaps thinking that sex would be an appropriate payoff for good behavior. Or maybe you just want to be wanted again. However, acting as though you were raised by wolves and demanding sex is highly counterproductive, and is simply not what a man does.

Your strategy of choice is to remember you have lots of company and be patient, proactive in helping mom overcome the obstacles on the road back to bed, and to continue handling your own needs by yourself.

The sex has decreased because I expected it too. It hasn't been a big deal with me. I've found great comfort in not even thinking about sex for a while. I've been too busy thinking about other things. Besides, it's a small price to pay when you think about all the other things that are more important.

Veteran Dad

Be Patient and Ready with a Rain Check
Getting off on the right foot may mean not getting off with mom at all for awhile. Think big picture about the future of your new relationship with mom, which is of course tough with your brains in your pants. Encourage her, but be patient and ready with a rain check for the inevitable false starts.

Talking About Sex
Talking about it is a good way to approach the sex issue, ranging from casual conversation, like asking what makes her body feel good, to direct questioning about when she thinks she'll be ready. Discuss mutual fears and desires, and do some brainstorming, which sometimes leads directly to love making.

Do Not Pester, Whine or Beg
Badgering her into intercourse might just work – if you enjoy necrophilia. When you catch your breath afterwards, ask yourself would you not have been smarter to engage in some alternative. And begging is just a wimpy form of demanding.

Try Non Coital Alternatives
After the cuddling only phase, you should consider the alternatives before you focus on vaginal sex. They include mutual masturbation and oral sex. About 20 percent of new parents try them out within a month after birth. They can help mom regain her feelings of sexuality without the issues presented by intercourse, and mutual orgasms during the first months can provide both mom and dad a release of pent up tension and renewed sense of hope and energy.

If She is Never in the Mood

Almost half of new moms have little to no desire for making love three months after birth, with some experiencing an actual aversion to sexual activity.

Sexual issues are much more complex for mom, and often leave her puzzled or confused. Combined with the many other issues with which she must contend, her obligation to resume sex may simply be the "straw that breaks the camel's back." She may be angry over real or perceived pressure from you to engage in lovemaking, and at the same time, feel inadequate since she cannot perform for you.

Sex is basically a distant memory.
Veteran Dad

She may also be unhappy, or downright angry, regarding your contributions as a father and husband. Her expectations, driven by the demands she faces and her own considerable needs, may be extreme and impossible to meet. Regardless, the net result is that she withholds the rewards offered by her treasures.

If you had significant conflict in your relationship prior to her pregnancy, your unresolved issues are going to be in play. While the stress added by a new baby will intensify them, your baby will also provide a new and overarching motivation to make a fresh start on resolving them. In this situation, sex deprivation is a symptom of a larger problem, which will be magnified if you focus only on sex.

If your love life crashed and burned early in the pregnancy, you will generally have a tougher time getting back on track.

No matter the cause, a patient, proactive approach focused on strengthening your relationship, rather than satisfying your own immediate urges, is the strategy of choice. Suggestions include serious communication coupled with assurance of your commitment to her and your baby, physical closeness in the form of hugs without even perceived pressure for sex, and all of the other ideas contained in this chapter.

Sometimes it is a matter of breaking the ice; just getting back on the horse so to speak. Make sure there are opportunities for time alone together, and a fresh approach that exceeds her expectations of you and creates a new path to intimacy.

In other cases, deep, divisive issues that present a danger to your marriage need to be handled. Get some professional help in the form of counseling. Give it time, and don't give up.

If You are Never in the Mood

It is supposed to be mom who is too tired or simply doesn't feel like it. In reality, it is often dad who is hesitant about resuming sex after mom is good to go. Common hurdles include:

A. New dads have a lot on their minds
    You have a new focus in life or are pre-occupied with problems you face (financing a new family for example). This leaves you with little interest in sex.

B. Moms do not make good sex objects
    The naughty imagery that drives sex can clash sharply with the picture of your mate breastfeeding or changing a diaper. It can be especially hard to feel lusty when she suddenly reminds you of your own mom.

C. Her new body is unattractive to you
    Extra weight, flabby tummy, stretch marks, and a lack of time to take care of herself does not fit the average guy's notion of a sex goddess. It is hard for her to feel sexy as well, which can leave little inspiration all the way around.

A variety of other serious turnoffs can apply: nervousness about intercourse during pregnancy lingers, graphic birth images stick in your mind, etc. The result is you are having a hard time becoming re-attracted to your mate as your lover.

An active love life is important, of course. You have lost your sex kitten, and your lack of interest may leave your partner feeling rejected, unattractive, unfulfilled and unloved at a time she needs you more than ever. Believing you no longer find her appealing can be devastating to her. You are not going to be feeling great either.

Suggestions from Those Who Have Been There
It happens, and you need to deal with it proactively. Ideas from guys who have been down this road include:

1. Talk about it with her and reassure her that you love her.
2. Exercise or try some new activity together.
3. Try cuddling, massage and other non-sexual intimacy.
4. Turn out the lights and let her seduce you, or try mutual manual sex.
5. Get away overnight without the baby, where she has the opportunity to take her time, dress up and look her best.
6. Engage in a mild fantasy that shakes up your normal images of each other.

Again, give it time, but don't give up. Talk to a counselor if it gets serious. This is one issue you definitely want to take care of for both of you.

The First Time

The first time making love after having a baby is generally awkward, often uncomfortable. If you do it right, it's very special. It might also be funny, but hot sex it is usually not. Give her the opportunity, but don't expect her to achieve orgasm.

Major precautions regarding copulation include the following:

Green Light from the Doctor
Again, six weeks for vaginal sex is the doctor's standard rule of thumb. Your mate's doctor may have a different take depending upon her unique circumstances, and will want to make sure her uterus and cervix are healed along with any episiotomy, C-section incision, etc. Basically, having a baby wrecks havoc on her sexual organs, which take time to heal. A key concern will be the risk of infection, and the doctor's green light after a physical exam is the first hurdle to resuming vaginal sex.

Careful Around Her Breasts
Several sizes larger on top, your breastfeeding mate may look great to you, but she may be feeling like a dual spigot fountain. Be sensitive to her feelings, especially because her nipples will be tender from the baby's vigorous sucking, and her breasts may leak on you, perhaps embarrassing her. This is due to the "letdown syndrome" caused by an increase in the hormone oxytocin. If you catch a stream of milk in the eye, just laugh it off. Feeding the baby first helps – along with a sense of humor. Nuzzling her breasts may lead to oral contact with her milk; inadvertent tasting is interesting, and no big deal.

Lubrication Often Necessary

Her vagina may lack much of its natural lubrication, especially if she breastfeeds, so invest in a tube of vaginal lubricant - like Astroglide - and use it liberally.

Keep Her Comfortable

Even after her doctor pronounces her functional, she may still feel tender and even sore, and perhaps like her insides have been rearranged. Precautions include:

- Go slow and be cautious.
- Use positions that let her control the action (mom on top, side-to-side, spooning).
- Do not switch positions on the fly.

If it becomes painful, of course, stop. This may be difficult for a deprived dad in the heat of passion, but you will regret causing her pain, and it may interrupt your love life for another month or so.

Too Soon for Another Baby

You'll need to consider contraception before jumping back in the sack, because the very notion of another baby so soon can quickly extinguish a new mother's dawning desire. Also, while nursing moms are not as fertile, risks of pregnancy increase over time and knowing just when fertility returns is not possible. Be prepared to provide contraception in the form of a well-lubricated condom. Get a good supply (unless you choose a vasectomy after one baby) to give her plenty of time to arrange an alternative. While she has a wide variety of alternatives, they all represent more work for her.

Make It a Special Event

Make the first time back a special milestone for your new relationship as parents by doing it up right. Make sure she feels ready, rested, and relaxed, and make her feel attractive and treasured by telling her she is a beautiful mother, admiring her new curves, and perhaps buying her a pretty nightgown or her favorite perfume. Start with a gentle massage, kissing and hugging, and sweet nothings in her ear. Take your time and be very gentle.

Set the Stage

Make sure the baby is handled, and if possible, place your little bundle of distraction in the nursery versus your own room. Soft music, a candle and perhaps a little wine all help to put her in a romantic mood, and help her focus on the issue at hand.

It was painful for her. I was almost embarrassed for asking.

Veteran Dad

Talk It Through

Every step of the way. Let her know that you care, do not want her in pain, and want to know what she thinks will work best. If you don't talk, she may feel pushed into something she is not ready for, may try to tough out pain, or just feel that between you and the baby, she no longer has control over her own body. The first time will help set the course for your future love life, so make sure there are no unspoken issues you may regret.

Keep Expectations Low and Be Flexible

With all that is involved, your objective should be basic lovemaking and nothing more. Even then, her focus on the moment may be transcended by real or imagined whimpers from the baby or thoughts of household duties, fatigue or worries about other issues. If lovemaking doesn't happen, reassure her that you understand and love her; absolutely no pouting.

And keep talking. It is amazing how many couples do not talk about what they prefer in lovemaking. It may be uncomfortable to talk about at first, but not talking constrains our sex lives. Use the unique circumstances of resuming lovemaking to ask specific and explicit questions, such as what she liked, didn't like or might like.

If Moms Were Rational Like Guys (a note from one of the guys)
Most men's sexual dynamics are simple: the more the better. We are highly motivated and will go to great lengths to score. We make it obvious how important sex is to us; there can be no doubt in her mind that there is nothing we would rather be doing (on regular occasions).

If our mates were rational, instead of rationing us and making us guess what they want, they would specify exactly what they want and would offer hot sex as an exquisite, renewable reward for our good behavior. If they kept us happy in bed, we would smash through brick walls to make them happy. Everybody is happy.
(Anonymous & Still Frustrated)

Bringing Out the Hottie in Her

As new moms rediscover their sexuality after birth, an opportunity for you to take your sexual relationship to the next level presents itself. In addition, working together in the parenting trenches fosters a more intense relationship, and as couples discover new reasons to love each other, making love can also be a continual process of discovery and increasingly intense intimacy.

Avoid the Obligatory Sex Alternative
The alternative is essential to understand and avoid. Many new moms engage in sex because they feel obligated to meet their mates' basic sexual needs. She might be doing it because she loves you or to reward you for good "daddy" behavior, but it is not because she enjoys it. Her motivation will be reflected in her performance.

Celebrate Your Emotional Connection
Sex can be a richer experience to parents, as your baby reflects the real purpose and potential of making love. Moms find dads who care for them and their babies to be very appealing. Watching a father lovingly give the baby a bath or walk a baby with colic all night can trigger strong feelings of love and respect for this man who shares her new love. Inhibitions and distractions go by the wayside and the woman you love, who knows exactly what and how you like it, is open to sex becoming more erotically intense. You just may live happily ever after.

Discover New Sensual Opportunities
Her new body presents new sensual opportunities for an educated dad. Nursing moms can find the increased sensitivity of their breasts enjoyable. While tired moms find orgasms take longer to attain, they report that they can be more intense and exciting. It may turn out that increased blood flow in her pelvic region during pregnancy does not fully dissipate, leaving her more sensitive on a long-term basis. Her new sensitivity enables new levels of erotic intimacy for her, and it is only natural that she comes back for more, which is why a significant portion of women report that their sex lives become better after having a baby.

Have More Fun as Adults
Children push us past our self-centered focus, which in turn opens the door to a better sex life. When two people in love focus on each other's needs, the sky, in terms of erotic intensity, is the limit. Experienced lovers know one another's hot buttons, and the trite issues that restrain our pushing on them tend to fade. Inhibitions fall by the wayside when two consenting adults are fully committed to each other, so don't be surprised if she asserts herself sexually.

Every moment with Audra is a reward. Linda is a wonderful mother and a wonderful wife. We are not forgetting that in addition to having a family, we have a great marriage.

Veteran Dad

Ideas For Getting Ahead of Her Curves

It is All About Her
Being generally deprived, your initial thoughts, emanating from your pants, are all about a hot time in the sack doing (and receiving) what you like. The less frequently we get it, our pent up demand has us coming on like a bull in heat. Which of course is not what she is looking for.

She wants a warm, gentle, laid back approach from a guy who makes her feel like a hottie, no matter what she sees in the mirror. A little anticipation stokes her embers, where too much creates unwanted pressure. (Keep your comments and props to a minimum, as gentle actions like a body rub speak much more effectively). Make sure she gets hers; generally first.

Learn What She Likes
Let her know her pleasure is your top priority. As a new mom, her likes and dislikes might have changed. Your focus on learning what really turns her on will be appreciated and eventually answered with guidance on pushing her buttons. Avoid treating your inquiry as a clinical diagnosis by constantly asking, "Does that feel good?" or, "Are you there yet?". Concentrate on what she suggests and how her body responds.

Help Her Feel Sexy
Being sexy is mostly about attitude, and she will be if you treat her so. With her flabby tummy, stretch marks and lack of time to take care of her looks, she will likely feel she no longer appeals to you, and so you are out-of-luck. Make her feel wanted, appealing, even a sex goddess by letting her know you think she is, and it will become a self fulfilling prophecy. Tell her she is beautiful, hot, and soft, and pat her on the butt, kiss her on the neck, etc.

Help Her Lose Her Pregnancy Weight
Take a constructive approach like telling her how good she looks, and she is more likely to respond, negative comments that indicate you feel she is fat will invariably backfire. Encourage her to take a class while you cover at home; yoga, spinning, belly dancing, etc. all get her on the road to feeling and looking good and give her some essential time to herself. You might even suggest sex as the great aerobic exercise it is (we have actually never found this approach to be effective, but hope springs eternal, and you may be the first to succeed).

She was feeling dowdy, so starting with her hair and down to her toes, I told her why I loved everything about her. I said her stretch marks reminded me of what she went through to give us our baby. I could tell it meant a lot to her.
> *Veteran Dad*

Let Her Take Control

To really light her jets, she needs to relax and focus on what turns her on. At the same time, she has a lot of distractions (demanding baby, horny husband) that compete for her attention. Her body, upon which the baby has staked an irrefutable claim, is also more sensitive, and she is anxious about what you want to do to her. Back off and let her take control, and you will get farther.

Learn Bedroom Finesse –Perhaps for the First Time

Most guys aren't exactly Don Juan in bed. If you want her to enjoy herself as much as possible, you may need to learn how to really turn her on. Men's magazines are full of advice and ads for better sex videos, so some of us must be buying them and using what we learned. A variety of books and alternatives exist; keep in mind that a little education might go a long way.

Get Away

An overnight trip + a romantic location not too far from home + a trusted babysitter = sexual nirvana. Her constant focus on the baby can subside, allowing her to enjoy herself and you. Be flexible, enable regular communication with the baby sitter, and if she is breastfeeding, don't forget the breast pump.

Bring The Pump! We finally got our weekend away, and put a few miles between us and our new reality. It was great! Until we realized we forgot the breast pump. Her breasts got engorged and hurt, and our options were not conducive to romance.

Boot Camp Formula for Success

One dad who survived for seven months past the arrival of his child without any lovemaking was desperate for advice. He explained that he had tried everything he could think of to jump start his love life with his exhausted wife. After hiring a babysitter, taking his wife to dinner and retiring to a hotel room, his carefully orchestrated rendezvous fall flat when his weary spouse fell asleep as soon as she hit the mattress.

The other men in the room nodded their heads in rueful understanding; they'd all been there, or were still experiencing similar frustration. Then a dad named Rick chimed in: "That happened to me, but I figured out how to get it handled." All eyes were riveted on him as he continued. "Like most important things, it takes time. In this case, two days. On Saturday you've got to take the baby all day and make sure your wife gets out, gets her hair done, goes shopping, visits her friends - whatever. Make sure she gets a long nap to catch up on her sleep, too. The next day," he continued, "get the baby sitter, then take your wife to dinner, and then maybe to a hotel. Go early. Then go slow and easy."

This simple strategy seemed to work like magic, and the following month one dad spoke for the group when he declared "Rick, you're the man!"

Seek Sexual Spirituality

A baby enhances the innate spirituality shared by a couple, which can bring new meaning and more profound passion to your lovemaking. While spirituality may seem the polar opposite of the feelings of naughtiness that drive sexual desire, it can add serious icing to the cake when sex is viewed as a celebration of mom's and dad's love and commitment.

Foreplay is Your Ticket to Heaven

When asked "how can your spouse help you get in the mood" in a BabyCenter.com survey, 60% of moms said foreplay (hugging, stroking, kissing), and another 23% said massage, another form of foreplay. If 83% of new moms say foreplay is what gets them in the mood for making love, what do you think might work for you?

For the record, when men were asked the same question, 98.5% said that what helps them get in the mood is any indication that she might be in the mood. 1.5% said "cook my favorite meal."

While men are raring to go at the drop of a skirt, women stay in neutral for a while. Extensive, sensitive foreplay demonstrates our love and enables new moms to shed lingering tensions and insecurities about their bodies. This allows them to focus on the passion, which is when our sex kittens come out to play. Only after they have become aroused and are enjoying the feeling do they shift gears and catch up with our craving for action under the covers.

Basic principles regarding foreplay:

Broaden Your Definition of Foreplay

On the day of the event, foreplay could include letting her sleep in, go out by herself, get a nap in the afternoon (highly recommended for sex that night). It could also include buying or making her something, or frankly anything that makes her happy.

Verbal Foreplay

Try a little wine and conversation in front of a fire once the baby is asleep. Talk about your lives before junior arrived. Remind her of the fun and good times you had together; talk about your dreams for the future.

Don't Ask, Just Rub

New moms may be skittish about sex, and instinctively reject any indication or suggestion they might have such feelings. Asking is like throwing rocks in a pond just before you want to go fishing. You have to move slowly and get them interested. Try the progressive massage that starts with her feet.

Quadruple the Warm-Up Period

A general rule of thumb. Go with what her body responds to, not your well-defined but ill-fated plan to do what you like and assume she will respond. The longer you take in caressing and kissing, the more she will warm up. And the hotter she gets, the more she will enjoy it.

Making Love Strengthens Your Marriage for the Long Run

A baby presents the opportunity to improve a marriage, and new couples who take advantage of the opportunity talk more, love each other more, fight less, and take pride in their marriage and family. Their initial anxiety is replaced by a new sense of confidence that together they will be just fine. A feeling of permanence and commitment sets in. Making love both celebrates and rejuvenates this critical relationship.

Sex is Good for Moms

Passion serves as a much needed diversion from her unrelenting focus on the baby. She realizes that she is more than a mother. Bringing some balance to her life will help her be a better mom.

Sex is Good for Dads

Frequent sex greatly improves a father's attitude and lowers his stress levels. It can also sharply reduce a man's risk of heart attacks or strokes, according to a ten-year study of men in a Welsh village who had sex three-four times weekly. The researchers (likely all men) concluded that sex should be redefined as vigorous activity.

Happy Parents Produce Happy Kids

The research is clear; kids thrive in homes with low levels of conflict and stress, and they learn to have healthy relationships when they see mom's and dad's affection for each other. A healthy, active love life provides the glue that will help hold you and mom and your family together.

Sex is Good for Your Health

Although it is but one aspect of the larger spectrum of romantic activities, your sex life should be renewed at some point. Sexual activity is good for your well being, as reported in a 1997 article in *Men's Health* magazine:

- Better Than Jumping Jacks: Making love is physical exercise. Can you think of a more fun way to burn some calories?

- Lung Capacity: Sex increases the oxygen intake of your body's cells, which assists in the functioning of your organs.

- Muscle Man: Sex boosts testosterone production. Testosterone helps maintain the strength of muscles and bones. You do the math.

- Cholesterol: Sexual activity has been found to slightly lower overall cholesterol levels, while converting bad cholesterol into good.

- Bad-Back Relief: The mix of hormones emitted into your blood stream during and around orgasm can increase your tolerance for pain.

- Prostate Protection: Regular ejaculations clean the pipes out (so to speak) and this decreases your risk of getting prostate cancer. The benefit is lessened, though, if you have sex in spurts - a whole bunch of times this month, none next month, for instance.

- Relax, Get To It: Sex increases your body's overall-relaxed state.

- Oxy What? During sex, your body experiences heightened levels of the hormone oxytocin, and this leads to a heightened sense of love or bonding.

I think the rearranging of your life style is the most stressing on a relationship. It's hard to learn how to adjust. But you need to stress the learning aspect. It's a curse in life that pays forever. Never take your spouse for granted. It works both ways.

Veteran Dad

19

We Are All in This Together

One of the cool things about Boot Camp workshops is that we get men from all walks of life. You'll see a young truck driver orient a corporate lawyer on the fine points of burping a baby, or an African American veteran showing an Asian rookie how to change a diaper. And when those babies start crying, we all react the same way. At Boot Camp, men from different cultures, ages, and incomes quickly find mutual respect when working together to learn how to care for their babies. It is clear that we fathers are all in this together.

We are Brothers

I have six brothers, and I can tell you that it feels very good to have other men respect and understand you and give you a hand when you need it. Over the past fifteen years, Boot Camp has worked the same way: we look out for each other and extend a hand through our advice and by just listening. We are all brothers in a sense.

We were sitting around the fire at an Indian Princess campout and we started talking about our girls. It lasted for over an hour, and it struck me how important our daughters were to us. I was relieved that my worries were minor compared to some of the guys, and inspired that no matter what they were dealing with, there was nothing they would not do for their daughters.
Veteran Dad

Lets Reach Out to Each Other

When you see another new dad, ask him how old his baby is and whether he is getting any sleep. Then with a nod to his baby, tell him "nice job". He will light up; you will have made his day. A quick glance of understanding to the father struggling with a crying child, will strengthen his patience. Ask the guy on the plane or in the next office about his kids and you will make a friend. You will also find that what goes around comes around.

Give the Next Guy Along a Hand

When you connect with new fathers you know or meet, don't be shy about telling them what you have learned as a dad. You can also pass on what you have learned to other rookie dads by taking your baby to a Boot Camp workshop or posting your comments on www.newdads.com. Ask your questions as well, and hear what the experience of other fathers has taught them.

Let's Make the World a Better Place for All Our Children

You do your job, and your brothers, cousins and friends (and eventually your own sons) will notice and follow. If we all do our jobs, we will be leaving the world that our kids inherit in better shape than we found it. Not a bad legacy.

Fatherhood presents each of us a tremendous opportunity. Let's help each other make the most of it.

APPENDIX

Appendix I

Learning More/Getting Help

Whatever problems you may experience as a new father, always remember you are not alone, and as a result, there are many resources available to you and your new family. To help you learn more about your circumstances, and if necessary, to get help, we have compiled this New Father Resource Catalog.

We have included a representation of organizations, web resources, articles and books that address the variety of issues encountered by dads and information that will equip you to help your partner. Check out www.newdads.com for updates and additions, or to recommend new resources that may help other fathers.

BABY CARE

American Academy of Pediatrics
141 Northwest Point Boulevard
Elk Grove Village, IL 60007-1098
Phone: (847) 434-4000; Fax: (847) 434-8000
www.aap.org

Sponsored by the National Institutes of Health, Medline Plus has baby care and health related information from a variety of sources including the Mayo Clinic and The American Academy of Pediatrics.
www.nlm.nih.gov/medlineplus/infantandnewborncare.html

www.babycenter.com
Good baby care advice from experts and other parents. This site includes solid information on infant development including a weekly calendar that shows your baby's development from conception to three years.

www.fathersdirect.com
Website from the UK with baby care information just for dad.

www.babyzone.com
Your online destination for highly personalized and localized parenting content and tools.

Books
Baby Basics: A Guide for New Parents (Anne K. Blocker, 1997)

The Baby Book: Everything You Need to Know About Your Baby from Birth to Age Two (William & Martha Sears, 2003)

Baby Bargains: Secrets to Saving 20% to 50% on Baby Furniture, Equipment, Clothes, Maternity Wear, and Much, Much More! (Alan & Denise Fields, 2003)

Caring for Your Baby and Young Child: Birth to Age 5 (American Academy of Pediatrics, 1998)

Preemies: The Essential Guide for Parents of Premature Infants (Dana Wechsler Linden, et al, 2000)

BABY PROOFING

American Association of Poison Control Centers
Phone: (800) 222-1222; 212-POISONS
www.aapcc.org

International Association for Child Safety
P.O. Box 801, Summit, NJ 07902
Phone: (888) 677-IACS
www.iafcs.com

www.babyproofingplus.com
Site offers baby proofing equipment for sale. Cabinet latches, plug protectors, safe toys, etc.

www.poolfence.com/intro.htm
This site has lots of information about making your house safe and it is organized in a convenient room-by-room format.

www.nsc.org/library/facts/babyprf.htm
Hosted by the National Safety Council, you will find a good overview of the most common infant safety issues

www.schmidty.com/diane/articles/babyproof.asp
This web page takes baby proofing outdoors and has good information for safety around the yard. It also contains a guide to the types of plants that are poisonous.

Books
Baby Proofing Basics: How to Keep Your Child Safe, 2nd Ed. (V. Lansky, 2002)

CHILD ABUSE

Prevent Child Abuse America
200 S. Michigan Avenue, 17th Floor
Chicago, IL 60604-2404
Phone: 312-663-3520; Fax: 312-939-8962
mailbox@preventchildabuse.org
www.preventchildabuse.org
"Remember, a child is helpless – you are not."

Department of Health and Human Services Administration for Children and Families
DHHS maintains a list of statewide contacts to call for information and assistance
www.acf.dhhs.gov

National Child Abuse Hotline
1-800-4-A-CHILD
For parents seeking information or help with feelings of frustration and violence
www.childhelpusa.org/report_hotline.htm

National Institute for Neurological Disorders and Stroke, Shaken Baby Information Page
www.ninds.nih.gov/health_and_medical/disorders/shakenbaby.htm

www.saferchild.org/families.htm
Links to resources and information on abusive behavior, signs of infant abuse.

Books
Violent No More: Helping Men End Domestic Abuse
by Michael Paymar, Hunter House, Inc. 2000
The author guides readers through the process of recognizing abusive behaviors, taking responsibility for them, and learning to express anger without violence.

CHILD PASSENGER SAFETY

National Center for Injury Prevention and Control
Mailstop K65, 4770 Buford Highway N
Atlanta, GA 30341-3724
Phone: (770) 488-1506; Fax: (770) 488-1667
Email: ohcinfo@cdc.gov
www.cdc.gov/ncipc/factsheets/childpas.htm

National Safety Council National Safety Belt Coalition
1025 Connecticut Ave., NW, Suite 1200
Washington, DC 20036
Phone: (202) 296-6263; Fax: (202) 293-0032
Email: guzzettc@nsc.org
www.nsc.org/traf/sbc/sbcchild1.htm

National Highway Transportation Safety Administration
The NHTSA hosts this site and offers a look-up finder for local child safety seat inspections.
www.nhtsa.dot.gov/people/injury/childps

www.aap.org/family/cps.htm
Car seat use guidelines

www.hsrc.unc.edu/pubinfo/child_main.htm
Basics of installation

www.safeusa.org/move/childpassenger.htm
Child passenger safety information

CHILDBIRTH PREPARATION

National Association of Childbearing Centers
3123 Gottschall Road, Perkiomenville
Pennsylvania 18074
Phone: (215) 234-8068; Fax: (215) 234-8829
Email: ReachNACC@BirthCenters.org
www.birthcenters.org

International Cesarean Awareness Network, Inc.
Email: info@ican-online.org
www.ican-online.org

Lamaze International
2025 M Street, Suite 800, Washington DC 20036-3309
Phone: (202) 367-1128; Toll-Free: (800) 368-4404
Fax: (202) 367-2128
www.lamaze-childbirth.com

International Childbirth Education Association, inc.
P. O. Box 20048, Minneapolis, MN 55420
Phone: (952) 854-8660; Fax: (952) 854-8772
www.icea.org

www.midwifeinfo.com
All about midwives with links to birthing and alternative birthing information. Search for a midwife near you. Find out about breastfeeding, birth centers, birthing balls, doulas, childbirth ed, epidurals, episiotomy, exercise, herbs, newborns, pain relief in labor, TENS, and waterbirths

www.birthprep.com
Information and products geared to Spanish speaking populations.

www.kasamba.com
This site allows you to email questions about childbirth to various experts

pregnancy.about.com/od/pregnancyphotos
All around information about pregnancy, labor and birth

www.childbirth.org
Has information on everything from choosing a midwife to a free online birth class

Books
Pregnancy, Childbirth, and the Newborn: The Complete Guide (Penny Simkin et al., 2001)

The Birth Partner: Everything You Need to Know to Help a Woman Through Childbirth, 2nd Ed. (Penny Simkin, 2001)

The Thinking Woman's Guide to a Better Birth (Henci Goer, 1999)

Birthing from Within: An Extra-Ordinary Guide to Childbirth Preparation (Pam England, 1998)

Natural Childbirth the Bradley Way (Susan McCutcheon et al., 1996)

An Easier Childbirth: A Mother's Guide for Birthing Normally (G. Peterson, 1999)

COLIC/EXCESSIVE CRYING

www.colicnet.com
Colic Net is an online support group for parents of colicky babies.

www.colichelp.com
Good resource for tips on helping a baby experiencing colic. Includes stories from parents who have dealt with colic.

www.drgreene.com
Information about colic and a parent bulletin board with postings about colic.

Books
Crying Baby, Sleepless Nights: Why Your Baby Is Crying and What You Can Do About It (Sandy Jones, 1992)

The Happiest Baby on the Block: The New Way to Calm Crying and Help Your Baby Sleep Longer (Harvey Karp, 2002)

CONFLICT/ANGER MANAGEMENT

The Conflict Center
4140 Tejon Street, Denver, Colorado 80211
Phone: (303) 433-4983; Fax: (303) 433-6166
Email: info@conflict-center.org
www.conflictcenter.org

www.12promises.com
The Self Awareness Institute offers workshops in anger management, including a certificate recognized by most courts.

www.relationships911.org
Information about conflict in a variety of different relationship scenarios. A resource for articles and books on the subject.

www.pacskills.com
Resources for dealing with conflict in married relationship.

www.chacocanyon.com/pointlookout/030205.shtml
Articles dealing with the topic of anger/conflict management

www.dontshake.com
Information about the importance of controlling anger when caring for baby.

Books
Beyond Anger: A Guide for Men (Thomas J. Harbin, 2000)

Overcoming Anger and Irritability (William Davies, 2001)

The Anger Habit (Carl Semmelroth and Donald E.P. Smith, 2000)

Love and Anger: Managing Family Conflict (Mary Tjosvold, Jenny Tjosvold, Dean R. Tjosvold, 1991)

COOL BABY GEAR

www.bizrate.com
This site offers a way to compare online prices on popular baby equipment

www.consumerreports.org
Offers ratings on some baby equipment tested by consumer reports

www.babyage.com
Online shopping site and discounted prices

www.babycenter.com
Baby Center - offers 15% off

www.expectantmothersguide.com/library/newjersey/bringing.htm
A checklist of supplies for new babies

DAD DIVERSITY (GAY, SINGLE-PARENT, OLDER, TEEN)

www.teendads.org.nz/teendads/teendads.html
Information for teen dads. Also, offers an email newsletter for teen dads

www.fatherandchild.org.nz/Resources/res_teendads.htm
Helpful advice and information for teens. Archive of articles.

www.menweb.org/throop/single-dad.html
Offers a wide range of information for single dads including custody and legal advice.

singleparents.about.com/od/singledads
Advice and articles about single fathering

www.fathers.com
Articles addressing the challenges of parenting as an older dad

www.fathersdirect.com/fatherfacts/?page=sub&sub=53
A few articles about older fathering

content.gay.com/channels/home
Articles and links for gay fathers

Books
Rich Dad Poor Dad for Teens: Money - What You Don't Learn in School (Robert T. Kiyosaki, Sharon L. Lechter, 2004)

Teen Dads: Rights, Responsibilities and Joys (Jeanne Warren Lindsay, David Crawford, 1999)

Daddy's Little Matchmaker: Single Father (Superromance) (Roz Denny Fox, 2000)

Gay Fathers: Encouraging the Hearts of Gay Dads and Their Families (by Robert L. Barret, Bryan E. Robinson Publisher: Jossey-Bass, 2000)
Written from a therapeutic and academic perspective and filled with the insights of gay fathers themselves, as well as the authors (Bryan Robinson is a professor of child and family development, Robert Barret a professor and psychologist), Gay Fathers draws on new research to explain the difficulties that gay men face in parenting

DAY CARE

NACCRRA-Child Care Resource and Referral
1319 F. Street, NW, Suite 500, Washington, DC 20004-1106
Phone: (202) 393-5501; Fax: (202) 393-1109
www.naccrra.net

www.babysitters.com
Childcare referral company focused on helping parents find the type of babysitters that matches best with the needs of their children. Includes babysitting guide and information for parents.

www.childcare-tips.com
Offers hundreds of approved tips and links related to childcare providers and the issues that arise with childcare. Also includes links to other childcare-related resources.

www.localdaycare.com
Childcare referral company focused on helping parents find local childcare that matches best with the needs of their children. Includes extensive directory of childcare providers, articles and resources

www.kidsource.com/kidsource/content/infant_care.html
Research based articles on various child care related topics

www.questia.com/popularSearches/child_day_care.asp
Online articles about children in day care

DOULAS

Doulas of North America
PO Box 626, Jasper, IN 47547
Phone: (888) 788-DONA; Fax: (812) 634-1491
Email: dona@doula.com
www.dona.com

www.doulaworld.com
Learn what a Doula does, and search for local Doula by services

www.doulanetwork.com
Information and referral resource

www.childbirth.org/doula123.html
Doula information

Books
The Doula Book: How a Trained Labor Companion Can Help You Have a Shorter, Easier, and Healthier Birth (Marshall H., M.D. Klaus, John H., M.D. Kennell, Phyllis H. Klaus, Marshall H. Klaus, John H. Kennell, 2002)

The Birth Partner, Second Edition (Penny Simkin, 2001)

Special Women: The Role of the Professional Labor Assistant (P. Perez, 1994)

DRUG AND ALCOHOL ASSISTANCE

Alcoholics Anonymous
Grand Central Station, P.O. Box 459, New York, N.Y. 10163
www.alcoholics-anonymous.org

Fetal Alcohol Syndrome Prevention Section
Division of Birth Defects and Developmental Disabilities
National Center for Environmental Health, MS F-15
Centers for Disease Control and Prevention
4770 Buford Highway NE
Atlanta, GA 30341-3724
Phone: (770) 488-7370; Email: ncehinfo@cdc.gov
www.cdc.gov/mmwr/preview/mmwrhtml/rr5114a2.htm

www.drug-abuse-treatment.org/resources.htm
Information and referral

www.a1b2c3.com/drugs
Information on all kinds of drugs, from caffeine to opiates.

Books
Cool Water: Alcoholism, Mindfulness, and Ordinary Recovery (William Alexander, 1997)

Alcoholics Anonymous: The Story of How Many Thousands of Men and Women Have Recovered from Alcoholism (Author, 2002)

Many Roads, One Journey: Moving Beyond the 12 Steps (Charlotte Davis Kasl, PhD, 1992)

Addiction & Grace (Gerald G. May, MD, 1991)

The Road Less Traveled, 25th Anniversary Ed. (M. Scott Peck, MD, 2003)

GENERAL FATHERHOOD

National Latino Fatherhood and Family Institute
5252 East Beverly Blvd, Los Angeles, CA, 90022
Phone: (323) 728-7770; Fax: (323) 728-8666
www.nlffi.org
NLFFI's "Con Los Padres" is a nationally recognized mentoring program designed to foster the early development of responsible, nurturing parents by teaching young fathers about their child's development and their legal rights and responsibilities as fathers.

The National Center for Fathering
P.O. Box 413888, Kansas City, MO 64141
Phone: (913) 384-4661or (800) 593-DADS
Fax: (913) 384-4665; Email: dads@fathers.com
www.fathers.com
NCF's goal is to help men be better fathers by offering practical tips and suggestions on how to improve their fathering

National Fatherhood Initiative™
101 Lake Forest Boulevard Suite 360
Gaithersburg, Maryland 20877
Phone: (301) 948-0599; Fax: (301) 948-4325
www.fatherhood.org
NFI's mission is to improve the well-being of children by increasing the proportion of children growing up with involved, responsible, and committed fathers.

Boot Camp For New Dads
230 Commerce, Suite 210, Irvine, CA 92602
Phone: (714) 838-9392; Fax: (714) 838-9675
Email: debbie@newdads.com
www.newdads.com
www.bcnd.org

www.suite101.com/article.cfm/humor/11654
Articles and information about fatherhood

www.parenting-advice.net/links/singlefathers.html
Advice for single dads

www.interactivedad.com
Online magazine for fathers.

www.geocities.com/WestHollywood/1001
Advice for gay fathers

www.parentstages.com/content/newdads.asp
Information and additional links for new dads

Books
Fathering the Next Generation (William J. Jarema, 1995)

Tackling Single Parenting: From a Man's Point of View (Steve Horner, 1996)

The Expectant Father: Facts, Tips, and Advice for Dads-to-Be (Armin A. Brott and Jennifer Ash, 2001)

The Father Factor: What You Need To Know To Make a Difference (Henry B. Biller and Robert J. Trotter, 1994)

Fathering: Strengthening Connection with Your Children No Matter Where You Are (Will Glennon, 1995)

The Gift of Fatherhood (Aaron Hass, Ph.D., 1994)

The Heart of A Father: How Dads Can Shape the Destiny of America (Ken Canfield, Ph.D., 1996)

Uncommon Fathers: Reflections On Raising A Child With A Disability (Donald J. Meyer, 1995)

Working Fathers (James A. Levine, 1998)

GRIEF/LOSS

Grief Recovery Online for All Bereaved (GROWW)
Many great links to organizations and online resources to help deal with the loss of an infant and recovering from grief in general.
www.groww.org/resource.htm

Center for Loss in Multiple Birth, Inc (CLIMB)
www.climb-support.org

www.ivf.com/misc.html
Article with information about losing a baby

Books
*After the Darkest Hour the Sun Will Shine Again: A Parent's
Guide to Coping with the Loss of a Child* (Elizabeth Mehren,
1997)

Anna: A Daughter's Life (William Loizeaux, 1993)

*Always Precious in Our Memory; Reflections After
Miscarriage, Stillbirth or Neonatal Death* (Christine O.
Lafser, 2003)

*Empty Cradle, Broken Heart: Surviving the Death of Your
Baby* (Deborah L. Davis, 1996)

Give Sorrow Words: A Father's Passage through Grief (Tom
Crider, 1996)

IMMUNIZATIONS

National Network for Immunization Information
66 Canal Center Plaza, Suite 600, Alexandria, VA 22314
Phone: (877) 341-6644; Fax: (703) 299-0204
Email: nnii@idsociety.org
www.immunizationinfo.org

Center for Disease Control and Prevention (CDC)
1600 Clifton Rd
Atlanta, GA 30333, U.S.A
Phone: (404) 639-3311 / Public Inquiries: (404) 639-3534
Toll-Free: (800) 311-3435
www.cdc.gov
Immunization Hotlines: English: (800) 232-2522
Spanish: (800) 232-0233
Immunization Information Pages
www.cdc.gov/nip/menus/groups.htm#child

American Academy of Pediatrics
Immunization Information Website
www.cispimmunize.org

www.immunize.org
Information and immunization schedule

www.partnersforimmunization.org
Immunization information

www.immunofacts.com
Facts about immunization safety

www.aap.org/new/immpublic.htm
Tips from the American Academy of Pediatrics on evaluating
immunization information

INFANT/CHILD DEVELOPMENT

www.zerotothree.org
Information for parents about child development in the first
three years with an emphasis on brain development.

www.nlm.nih.gov/medlineplus/infantandtoddlerdevelopment.html
Information and links cover developmental mile stones to
age twelve.

www.lhj.com/home/Stages-of-Child-Development.html
Early child development and growth information. Printable
child growth chart.

Books
*Touchpoints: Your Child's Emotional and Behavioral
Development: Birth-3: The Essential Reference for the Early
Years* (T. Berry Brazelton, 1992)

*Infants, Children, and Adolescents (International Edition) 5th
Edition* (Laura Berk, 2004)

*What's Going on in There?: How the Brain and Mind
Development in the First Five Years of Life Guide* (Lise
Eliot, 2001)

INFANT HEALTH

American Academy of Pediatrics
141 Northwest Point Boulevard
Elk Grove Village, IL 60007-1098
Phone: (847) 434-4000; Fax: (847) 434-8000
www.aap.org

www.envisagedesign.com/ohbaby/healthy.html
Information and articles about keeping baby healthy along
with links to infant and baby health resources

www.infantmassage.com
Infant Massage: a holisitic approach to infant health

Babycenter
Set up a birth calendar and track your baby's development
week by week – from conception to three years old.
www.babycenter.com

Books
Healthy Sleep Habits, Happy Child (Marc Weissbluth, 1999)

Motor Assessment of the Developing Infant (Martha C.
Piper, Johanna Darrah, 1994)

Baby's First Year (Jeanne Murphy, Cathie Lowmiller, 2000)

A Good Start in Life: Understanding Your Child's Brain and Behavior (Norbert Herschkowitz, et al, 2002)

Having Twins And More: A Parent's Guide to Multiple Pregnancy, Birth, and Early Childhood (Elizabeth Noble, 2003)

See How I Grow (Angela Wilkes, 2001)

INFANT CPR

American Red Cross Headquarters
431 18th Street, NW, Washington, DC 20006
Phone: (202) 303-4498
Information on infant CPR classes
www.redcross.org/services/hss/courses/infchild.html

University of Washington
Instruction sheet on infant CPR to print out
www.depts.washington.edu/learncpr/infantcpr.html

Books
The Pocket Guide to CPR for Infants and Children (Gloria Blatti, 1998)

A Parent's Guide to Medical Emergencies: First Aid for Your Child (Janet Zand, et al., 1997)

Pediatric First Aid and CPR (National Safety Council, 2001)

Infant and Child CPR (National Safety Council, 1997)

The American Red Cross First Aid and Safety Handbook (American Red Cross, et al., 1992)

LACTATION

La Leche League International (LLLI)
1400 N. Meacham Rd, Schaumburg, IL 60173
Phone: (847) 519-7730
www.lalecheleague.org

www.bflrc.com
Articles and information, including a primer on how to get started with breastfeeding.

www.breastmilk.com/more_great_links.htm
Breastfeeding supplies and links to other resources.

www.parentsplace.com/expert/lactation
An I-village online community for parents. Ask questions of a lactation consultant, post messages on a bulletin board for support, read articles, etc.

www.breastfeeding.com/helpme/helpme_video.html
Videos and information on breastfeeding.

Books
Breastfeeding and Human Lactation (Jan Riordan, 1999)

The Ultimate Breastfeeding Book of Answers: The Most Comprehensive Problem-Solution Guide to Breastfeeding from the Foremost Expert in North America (Jack Newman, Teresa Pitman, 2000)

MARRIAGE COUNSELING/ROMANCE

www.couples-place.com
Site offers books, quizzes, and surveys

www.marriage.about.com/cs/support
Online support. Links and resources

www.12promises.com
The Self Awareness Institute offers information and weekend workshops on relationships.

www.saferchild.org/families.htm
Safer Child's "Families in Crisis" pages offer resources and links for all types of relationship conflicts

Books
Becoming One: Emotionally, Spiritually, Sexually (Joe Beam, 1999)

His Needs, Her Needs: Building an Affair-Proof Marriage (Willard F. Harley Jr., 2001)

Pillow Talk: The Intimate Marriage from A to Z (Karen Scalf Linamen, Karen S. Inamen, 1998)

Two Hearts Are Better Than One (Barbara Rainey, et al, 1999)

Forever Love: 119 Ways to Keep Your Love Alive (Gary Smalley, 1996)

Rocking the Roles: Building a Win-Win Marriage (Robert Lewis, William Hendricks, 1999)

Building Your Mate's Self-esteem (Dennis Rainey, 2000)

MEN'S HEALTH

www.vix.com/men
Men's issues data base of articles and links

www.healthfinder.gov
Database of health information

Books
Lore of Running (Timothy Noakes, 2003)

8 Minutes in the Morning: a Simple Way to Shed up to 2 Pounds a Week (Jorge Cruise, 2002)

The Complete Book of Men's Health: The Definitive, Illustrated Guide to Healthy Living, Exercise, and Sex (Men's Health Books, 2000)

Death Defiers : Beat the Men-Killers and Live Life to the Max (Selene Yeager, Kelly Garrett, 1998)

Fight Fat: A Total Lifestyle Program for Men to Stay Slim and Healthy (Stephen C. George, Jeff Bredenberg, 1996)

Guy Knowledge: Skills, Tricks, and Techniques That Your Father Meant to Teach You—But Probably Didn't (Larry Keller, 1999)

Men's Health Real Life Survival Guide (Larry Keller, 2001)

NEW MOMS

www.myria.com
Information and support

sheknows.com
A network of information and resources, including recipes, information on going back to work and health issues.

www.workoptions.com/newmoms.htm
Information for new working moms

www.momscape.com
Ideas, projects and information for parenting with spiritual support.

www.momsnetwork.com
Advice and online community to help moms succeed at mothering and in life.

Books
The New Mom's Companion: Care for Yourself While You Care for Your Newborn (Debra Gilbert Rosenberg, Mary Sue Miller, 2003)

Secrets of the Baby Whisperer: How to Calm, Connect, and Communicate with Your Baby (Tracy Hogg, Melinda Blau, 2002)

The What to Expect When You're Expecting Pregnancy Organizer (Arlene Eisenberg, et al., 1995)

PRODUCT SAFETY

U.S. Consumer Product Safety Commission
Washington, D.C. 20207-0001
Phone: (301) 504-6816; Fax: (301) 504-0124 or 504-0025
Email: info@cpsc.gov
www.cpsc.gov

Safer Child Inc.
P.O. Box 48151, Spokane, WA 99228-1151
www.saferchild.org

www.cpsc.gov/cpscpub/prerel/category/child.html
Information on baby product recalls – great for checking on second hand equipment.

www.kidsource.com/CPSC/safety_tips.html
Safety articles and advice

www.kidshealth.org/parent/firstaid_safe/home/products.html
Advice for choosing safe products

Books
Guide to Baby Products, 7th Ed. (Sandy Jones, 2001)

POSTPARTUM DEPRESSION

**National Women's Health Information Center
Department of Health and Human Services**
www.4woman.gov/faq/postpartum.htm
Information and links

Postpartum Dads
www.postpartumdads.org
Support and information for fathers whose partners are suffering from postpartum depression or "baby blues"

www.psycom.net/depression.central.post-partum.html
Heavily oriented towards treatment with drugs, information on postpartum depression and depression in general.

www.postpartum.net
Articles and links to other resources

Books
This Isn't What I Expected (Karen Kleiman, Valerie Davis Raskin, 1994)

Overcoming Postpartum Depression & Anxiety (Linda Sebastian, 1998)

The Postpartum Husband (Karen R. Kleiman, Karen Kleiman, 2001)

Depression after Childbirth: How to Recognize, Treat, and Prevent Postnatal Depression (Katharina Dalton, Wendy M. Holton, 1996)

Sleepless Days: 1 Woman's Journey Through Postpartum Depression (Susan Kushner Resnick, 2001)

SPECIAL-NEEDS BABIES

Technical Assistance Alliance
8161 Normandale Blvd
Minneapolis, MN 55437-1044
Voice: (952) 838-9000; TTY: (952) 838-0190
Fax: (952) 838-0199; Toll-Free: (888) 248-0822
Email: alliance@taalliance.org
One national center and six regional centers to assist parents of children with disabilities connect to a network of parent training, information and resources.
www.taalliance.org

The Arc of the United States
1010 Wayne Avenue, Suite 650
Silver Spring, MD 20910
Phone: (301) 565-3842; Fax: (301) 565-3843
The Arc is the national organization of and for people with mental retardation and related developmental disabilities and their families.
www.thearc.org

La Leche League
Information about breastfeeding a baby with special needs
www.lalecheleague.org/FAQ/disabled.html

Special needs family fun
Family fun and family health resources for families with special needs.
www.specialneedsfamilyfun.com

Exceptional Parent Magazine
Information, support, ideas, encouragement & outreach for parents and families of children with disabilities, and the professionals who work with them
www.eparent.com

Books
Babies With Down Syndrome: A New Parent's Guide (The Special-Needs Collection) (Karen Stray-Gundersen, 2003)

The New Language of Toys Teaching Communication Skills to Children with Special Needs: A Guide for Parents and Teachers, Third Edition (Sue Schwartz, Ph.D., 2004)

STAY-AT-HOME-DAD

www.slowlane.com
Links to local groups, resources and articles

www.fatherhood.about.com/cs/stayhomedads
Articles and information on stay-at-home and work-at-home dads

www.work-at-home-stay-at-home-dad.com
Website created by a disabled father who works and parents from home.

www.dadstayshome.com
Up front and personal website for stay-at-home dads, with resources, stories, insights and a bulletin board.

Books
Stay-at-Home-Parent's Survival Guide : Real-Life Advice from Moms, Dads, and Other Experts A to Z (Christina Baglivi Tinglof, Christina Baglivi Tinglov, 2000)

Staying Home (Darcie Sanders, Martha M. Bullen, 2001)

Stay-At-Home Dads: The Essential Guide to Creating the New Family (Libby Gill, 2001)

SUDDEN INFANT DEATH SYNDROME

American SIDS Institute
509 Augusta Drive
Marietta, GA 30067
1-800-232-SIDS (7437)
www.sids.org

sids-network.org/source.htm
Information and location finder for resources in your area

www.sidsalliance.org
Information about SIDS and support for parents who have experienced a still birth or SIDS.

TOBACCO CESSATION

American Lung Association
800-586-4872
Information about lung cancer, asthma and other types of lung ailments. Links to local chapters, opportunities for involvement in smoking cessation programs..
www.lungusa.org/tobacco

www.tobacco.org/Resources/tobsites.html
Quitting resources and anti-tobacco activism

www.mayo.edu/staff/ndc/FAQ.html
Mayo Clinic site includes articles, research and tips on quitting smoking.

www.quitsmoking.about.com/mbody.htm
Cessation support website with articles and links

www.quitnet.org
Cessation information and a free stop smoking program.

Books
Cure Your Cravings (Yefim Shubentsov and Barbara Gordon, 1999)

1440 Reasons to Quit Smoking (Bill Dodds, 2000)

Quittin' Time (Jenny N. Duffey, 1993)

How to Quit Smoking Without Gaining Weight (Martin Katahn, 2004)

TWINS/MULTIPLES

The Center for Study of Multiple Birth (CSMB)
Suite 464, 333 East Superior Street
Chicago, IL 60611
Phone: (312) 266-9093; Fax:(312) 280-8500
Geared mainly to medical professionals, website contains research and articles about giving birth to and raising multiples.
www.multiplebirth.com

ITA International Twins Association
c/o Lynn Long or Lori Stewart, 6898 Channel Road,
Minneapolis, MN 55432
Phone: (612) 571-3022 or 571-2910
An organization started in 1934 dedicated to twins.
www.intltwins.org

www.twinslist.org
Information and links to twins organizations and resources

www.tripletsandus.com/triplets/msub2.htm
A directory of organizations for twins and multiples and their parents.

www.twinsmagazine.com
Article archive and subscription

Books
The Art of Parenting Twins: The Unique Joys and Challenges of Raising Twins and Other Multiples (Patricia Maxwell Malmstrom, Janet Poland, 1999)

Raising Twins (Eileen M. Pearlman, 2000)

When You're Expecting Twins, Triplets, or Quads: A Complete Resource (Barbara Luke, 1999)

Twins! : Expert Advice from two practicing physicians on pregnancy, birth and the first year (Connie Agnew, 1997)

WORK FAMILY BALANCE/TIME MANAGEMENT

www.fathersdirect.com/workspace/?page=sub&sub=45
From Fathers Direct in the UK, ideas and a quiz on balancing work and family.

www.mygoals.com
Award-winning website helps with setting goals of all kinds – from financial to health to organization and relationship issues.

www.businessweek.com/smallbiz/content/mar2000/wf000327.htm
Article about the benefits to small companies of offering flextime to dads.

www.kidsource.com/kidsource/content2/news2/fathers.time.3.html
Article by Roger Merrill, vice president of Covey Leadership Center and a well-known authority on time management

www.explorefaith.org/lifelines_managing.html
Articles and advice-Christian perspective

Books
The Way We Really Are (Stepanie Coontz, 1998)

The Time Bind (Arlie Russell, 2001)

How to Choose Your Next Employer (Roger Herman, 2000)

Working Fathers (James A. Levine, 1998)

Appendix II

Babies With Special Needs

There are many books and resources that address the issues surrounding babies with special needs. Our purpose here is to touch on a few of the key points that have specific implications for fathers.

There are over 300 categories of birth defects and developmental disabilities listed in the National Birth Defect Registry. Most types are rare; for example, hypoplastic left heart syndrome affects about 3 of every 10,000 babies, and cleft lip with or without cleft palate affects about 1 of every 1,000 babies.

From autism to scoliosis, however, one in 33 babies in the U.S. is born with some sort of birth defect. While it is inconceivable to most people that their baby might have a disorder, it does happen. Sometimes parents find out about a disability, such as Down syndrome, during pregnancy. At other times, there's a dramatic surprise, a cleft palate or heart problem, which surfaces at birth or later on.

It goes without saying that babies born with disabilities will require extra care. However, the extra care required is not usually as demanding as the psychological process we must confront as parents of a baby with special needs.

Receiving the News

Whether during the pregnancy or after the birth, the news of a birth defect shatters our fantasy of what it will be like to be a dad and leaves us facing a vast unknown. Dads who have confronted this challenge agree - your baby needs you now more than ever. Your baby must have everyone in her corner, advocating for her and seeking to understand how best to care for her.

Be prepared for the fact that, especially at first, even your closest friends and relatives may not know how to help you deal with your new situation. They may ask hurtful questions, offer bad advice, or generally just shy away until they figure out how to handle their own emotional responses.

It is critical that you and mom stick together. Talk to her early and often so you both know what is going on with each other.

Give It Time

It is likely that your vision of fatherhood includes an image of you and a child that runs, plays, and laughs. You may see yourself in the future passing on your wisdom to this child that represents the continuing generations of your family. If your child has a disability, this vision may require realignment.

Coming to grips with your child's new realities does not happen quickly. The initial shock of finding out usually gives way to a long period of denial. Somewhere within these two stages the flight-or-fight response is triggered, sending some dads running from their family, trying to escape this daunting challenge.

Running, of course, is not an option for you. In fact, by hanging in there and giving it time, you will be building a bond with your child that is deeper than anything you imagined prior to his birth.

Circle the Wagons

The most effective way to focus your worries and concerns on something productive is to start assembling your resource team. This will include friends, family, medical experts, and some form of emotional counsel. The best place to begin is the hospital where your baby was born. Often the staff that is treating your baby will be your first resource for basic medical advice about your baby's particular condition and how to care for your baby properly. The hospital's social worker will know of resources in your community that can be helpful in supporting you.

The Blame Game

As with any situation that feels out of our control, a baby born with a disability or illness can trigger in us a need to blame something or someone. Often mothers take on the guilt for not having produced a perfect child, even if the cause of the disability runs in the genetics of the father's side of the family. The point here is that no matter what, blaming another for the situation you are in will only delay the necessary process of getting to know and love your child and at the same time could cause a fracture in your marriage.

Make Your Relationship Stronger

You might hear that a child who is ill or disabled will make you and your partner feel closer, but this is not necessarily true – especially at first. The added demands impact every area of your life. Work, friends, family relationships, finances, and self-concept are just a few of the areas that take a hit. So the question becomes: what can you do to help your relationship weather the storm? The answer is, a lot.

- **Don't isolate**. A baby who is different makes for parents who are different from other parents. It is easy to feel cut off from the support that you need as a couple if you can't share common challenges with parents who understand where you're coming from. Search your community for parent groups that are geared to parents of children with special needs.

- **Seek professional help**. One of the keys to pulling together with your partner is sharing your perspective with someone who is experienced with the situation you are going through. This kind of support can create a safe environment to explore the issues and emotions associated with caring for your baby as well as your relationship.

- **Validate your partner**. Every mother needs to know she is a good mom. This concept is tantamount as it applies to the mother of a child with special needs. You can strengthen your connection with your partner by giving her positive feedback about her skill as a mom. Spend time on a regular basis pointing out all your child can do, see, and hear instead of only what they can't.

- **Practice self-care**. You will be the most help to your family if you take care of yourself. Take a bit of time each day to do something you enjoy. Even 30 minutes will strengthen your ability to cope with stress and help you keep a positive perspective.

A Deeper Kind of Love

If you hang in there and stay focused on what is important, the chaos surrounding your unexpected circumstances will give way to loving your child for who they are. Parents who successfully navigate these turbulent waters find that they come to a place where they are able to celebrate their child's smallest victories and accomplishments. This is where you're headed and when you get there you will know it because your heart will be filled with pride, humility, and love. Start by spending as much hands-on time as possible with your baby and learn how to care for him.

The Loss of a Baby

The only outcome more unthinkable than a child born with a disability is one that is still-born or dies shortly after birth. Although you don't want to dwell on this possibility, it is important to remember that most hospitals have loss and grief support for parents dealing with this circumstance. The process usually includes on-going individual counseling for both parents as well as groups for parents who have lost a baby.

This form of support typically has two goals. One goal is to help the family work through the myriad of emotions associated with the death of a baby and the other is to help the family incrementally evaluate their readiness to have another child. For some couples this is a relatively quick process and for others it can take a while. In the end most couples who have lost a child at or shortly after birth go on to have another pregnancy that results in a successful outcome.

Appendix III

Protecting Your Baby and Family

Little is worse than your child being seriously hurt, particularly if you could have prevented the injury. For your child, little is worse than something bad happening to dad.

The rationale for baby safety is obvious. Why dad safety? First, male pre-baby behavior tends towards risk-taking macho. Second, you are the only dad she has, and she will need you for a long time. You want to be around to do the job.

New fathers tend to avoid safety issues until a problem arises. Try to adjust your thinking. Strive to always think ahead when it comes to your baby's safety. A newborn is barely able to move her body, but it's amazing how fast she can fall off a changing table, how easily she can tip over her baby seat, or how quickly she can wiggle out of your grasp during a bath.

And while it may be tempting, and no matter how much they like it, tossing your baby in the air is a very bad idea. There may come a day when your growing child reacts differently while in the air, and you flub the catch.

Buckling Up for the First Ride Home

The car ride from the hospital to home is your first opportunity to demonstrate your forward thinking. Make sure the car seat is ready when you take your first steps from the safety of the hospital.

To avoid problems, get the infant seat installed ahead of time. Consider using a baby doll to practice adjusting the straps. Some car seats are tricky. Ask your car dealer for help; many sponsor programs to help you learn about installing and using your baby's car seat safely. You can also ask the highway patrol or your fire department for help. It's worth the effort.

The National Highway Traffic and Safety Administration (NHTSA) provides specific recommendations about car-ride safety for your baby. They include:

- Use a rear-facing convertible or infant-only seat the first year.
- Tightly install child seat in rear seat, facing the rear (base should not move more than 1 inch).
- Never use in a front seat where an air bag is present.
- Child seat should recline at approximately a 45 degree angle.
- Harness strap slots should be at or below shoulder level (use lower set of slots for most convertible child safety seats). Keep harness straps snug.
- Place chest clip at infant's armpit level to keep harness straps in place.
- If necessary, place rolled towel around baby's head and neck for support.

Because there are so many car-seat manufacturers and models, it's difficult to provide specific instructions about the safe installation of any one of them. In addition, it's nearly impossible to stay on top of which ones are safe to begin with. Luckily, there are a number of valuable resources at your disposal.

Visit the NHTSA website at www.nhtsa.dot.gov/people/injury/childps to obtain the following information:

- Child Safety Seat Ease of Use Ratings (check before you buy)
- Infant Child Seat Use and Installation Tips
- Child Safety Seat Inspection Station Locator (have a certified technician show you how)

The Fit for a Kid (www.fitforakid.com) website is loaded with information on car-seat safety, including instructional videos for free download.

Car Safety

Auto crashes are a major cause of children's deaths, so with your child in the car, "defensive" driving takes on new meaning. Of course, auto crashes kill fathers as well, so even when you are driving alone, be safe out there.

Do Not Leave Your Child Unattended in a Car
Leaving a child alone in a car, even for a few minutes, is another very bad idea, as well as illegal in most states. Cars quickly heat up even in moderate weather to levels that are fatal for a child. This can happen even if you park in the shade or leave a window down.

Do Not Forget to Take Your Child Out of the Car
Every year babies die because their parents accidentally leave them in the back seat of the car. In their very busy lives, they simply forget they were there. They may fail to remember to drop them off at day care, and go on to work and park, or some similar scenario. Instead of being safe and sound, they are left in a hot car, which often results in an unimaginable tragedy.

Here are some tips to make sure this does not happen to you:

- Always put your briefcase in the back next to the baby.
- Put the diaper bag in the front seat where it signals that there is a baby in the back.
- Arrange for your day care provider to call you if the baby is not dropped off by a designated time.

SIDS: Putting Your Baby to Bed

During the first year, your baby should sleep on her back. Why? Because putting babies to sleep on their backs has significantly cut the number of babies suffering Sudden Infant Death Syndrome. SIDS claims the lives of more babies in the first year than any other cause, though numbers have been declining since 1992, not in small part to the efforts of the Back to Sleep Campaign sponsored by the National Institute of Child Health and Human Development (NICHD).

> **Back to Sleep Campaign: SIDS Facts**
> - SIDS is the leading cause of death in babies after 1 month of age.
> - Most SIDS deaths happen in babies who are between 2 and 4 months old.
> - Most SIDS deaths happen in colder months.

The Centers for Disease Control (CDC) defines SIDS as "the sudden death of an infant under one year of age that cannot be explained after a thorough case investigation, including a complete autopsy, examination of the death scene, and review of the clinical history."

Factors other than sleeping on the back seem to increase the risk of SIDS in babies. With this in mind, here are some recommendations:

- Avoid putting quilts, blankets, or other soft beddings in the crib, or having any of these items close to baby as she sleeps.
- Never let your baby sleep on a waterbed or sofa cushion.
- Do not smoke.

Baby-Proofing Your Child's Environment

When it comes to baby safety, nothing is more true than the old adage: *anything that can happen, probably will happen.* A dressing table mat that is not tied down can somehow slide off the table with your baby on it. The adorable stuffed monkey that guards his crib can fall across your baby's face.

Adopting a "Baby's-Eye" View
You won't need to do a thorough baby-proofing of your home until your baby begins to move around and grab things. But even during his first months there are dangers, and you should assess the safety of your baby's environment continually. One way is to get down to his level and look around. Is the surface he is lying on secure? Are there small objects around him that could get into his mouth? Sharp objects he can grab?

Things to Look Out For
Some things to look out for during the first few months:

- Things that could entangle your baby – curtains or curtain strings blowing too close to his crib or swing, for example.

- Things that could obstruct his breathing - fluffy bedclothes or pillows, a mattress or sleeping mat that is too small, blankets used for support that have loosened, crib padding that is not tightly tied to the bars.

- Smoke. Unlike you, your baby can't move out of harm's way. When you smoke around him, he gets even more of a hit than you do. Fanning the smoke does little to lighten this load.

- Toxins. Paints, lacquers (even nail polish and remover), insecticides. Do not use them indoors or in the vicinity of your baby. A newborn's immune system is not yet developed, and these substances can be extremely harmful, even in small doses.

- Sharp objects. Pencils, pens, cell phone antennas. Take them out of your pockets when handling your baby. Be extremely careful about using them with your baby in your arms.

Employ the Slide-and-Hide Technique

Used toilet-paper tubes are useful for more than just arts and crafts. They also make superb measuring devices. If an object can slide down the tube, it can also slide down your baby's breathing passage. Don't let your baby fall prey to asphyxiation or choking. Be sure to put those items out of your baby's reach!

Some problem items: Coins, buttons, beads, latex balloons, marbles, small balls, batteries, broken crayons, tacks, pen caps, paperclips, nails, screws, jewelry, hair clips, and bottle caps.

Baby-Equipment Safety

When using baby equipment – cribs, changing tables, bassinets, swings, and infant seats – don't assume your baby is safe. With few exceptions, supervision is necessary.

Your best bet is to always use safety-certified equipment. The Juvenile Products Manufacturers Association (JPMA) sponsors a safety-certification program. Check for their seal.

- *Swings:* Use only if equipped with a crotch restraint. Check that the swing base is sturdy. Many hand-me-down and foreign-made swings are unequipped with crotch restraints and have bent supports. Never leave your baby unattended in a swing.

- *Infant Seats:* Avoid setting an infant seat down on high surfaces, such as the top of a dresser or table, unless you are standing there with one hand on it. Never use an infant seat in place of an infant car-seat. Always use the safety straps that come with the seat, and never leave your baby unattended.

- *Bassinets:* Make sure the bassinet has a sturdy bottom and is equipped with a snug mattress.

- *Changing Tables:* Just because your baby is strapped to the changing table, don't be fooled into thinking she's safe. Never walk away. Falling from any height can cause serious injury.

Tangling Hazards

Newborn babies do not grab at things yet, but there is still a risk of strangulation when a baby becomes tangled in a cord or piece of clothing. Fortunately, this hazard is avoidable, especially if you use some forethought in baby-proofing your home. Once your baby can reach or grab for things, be wary of anything with a string or cord that he could get tangled in.

Here are some important ones and what you can do to look out for your baby's safety:

- Keep the crib away from any cords.
- Never use a lanyard (a looped cord) to hang your baby's pacifier around her neck.
- Never hang toys on the crib with a string.
- Use the crotch strap in strollers, high chairs, and baby seats; this keeps your baby from sliding down and strangling herself.
- Baby clothes with drawstrings are illegal today, but in the past they were not. Be careful when accepting hand-me-down clothing.

Poisons and Other Toxic Substances

During your pre-baby life, you may have had a haphazard approach to the use, storage, and disposal of medicines, paints, and household-cleaning agents. Now that you share a house with your new baby, you'll have to use more caution. Here's a list of common items that could potentially harm your baby if ingested, inhaled, or rubbed in her eyes:

- Prescription and over-the-counter medications
- Cleaning products
- Poison and insecticides
- Hobby paints, glues, and other products
- Alcohol
- Cigarettes and cigarette butts
- Lead, mercury, and carbon monoxide
- Cosmetics

As with a number of safety issues, poisoning becomes a real problem when your baby begins to explore her environment, grabbing and putting everything within reach in her mouth. To protect against this, you should never leave a toxic or poison substance within reach, including on the counters or under the sink. Lock them up in a high cabinet. Always use original packaging – which should be childproof – and dispose of old, unused medications and cleaners.

Just in case, keep the phone number of your local poison-control center handy.

Carbon Monoxide

Carbon monoxide is a colorless, odorless gas that can poison your new baby. Poisoning is immediate and can lead to death. Consider investing in a carbon monoxide monitor for your home. To insure your house is poison-free:

- Make sure household appliances are installed properly.
- Never use or service fuel or gasoline-burning equipment in your home.
- Never leave your baby unattended in a running vehicle, or leave a vehicle running in an enclosed garage.

Lead

Lead is an elemental metal which can cause severe problems in the development of your child's nervous system. It may be in your family's home, including in some older paints, the soil, and some imported mini blinds. Remove any lead paint and repaint with a lead-free variety (this is typically not a problem for houses built after 1978). Also monitor painted baby items for paint chips that she might swallow.

Pesticides

Commonly used ant and roach sprays, flea foggers and other pesticides contain highly hazardous toxic substances. They are especially harmful to babies, whose immune systems and nervous systems are very vulnerable to toxic exposures. Never spray any sort of pesticide near your baby, or on carpets, furniture or equipment which your baby uses. Research now shows that there is no acceptable level of pesticide exposure in infants.

Lacquers and Paints

Household water-based wall paint is much safer than lead-based paints once were, but it can still contain harmful vapors. Do not paint or use lacquers with a baby in the room.

Toxic-Substance Resources
For more information about toxins, including monitoring their intake and what to do if poisoned, consult these websites:
- US Center for Disease Control and Prevention (www.cdc.gov)
- US Agency for Toxic Substance and Disease Registry (www.atsdr.gov)

Pools, Buckets, and Other Drowning Hazards

You can prevent drowning by paying close attention to your baby when she is near water and to potential water-based hazards at all times. According to the US Center for Disease Control and Prevention, drowning is the second-leading cause of accidental death in children – over 1,000 deaths per year and many more trips to the hospital.

Putting a baby-proof fence around your swimming pool is a productive first step toward drowning prevention. Additional measures you can take include:

- Eliminating deck clutter, which causes a tripping hazard.
- Keep the pool covered when not in use; use a rigid cover.
- Always have rescue equipment handy; never use it as a pool toy.
- Always attend to your baby in the pool; drowning deaths happen quickly and without a sound.

A report from *Pediatrics* (2001) found that children under one year old drown most commonly in bathtubs, buckets, and toilets. From ages one to four, residential swimming pools were the most common culprits in drowning deaths.

Your baby can drown in as little as two inches of water. For this reason, almost anything that holds water and your baby fits into is a drowning hazard.

- *Bathing:* Never stray more than an arm's length from your baby while she's bathing. In addition, baby bath-seats seem like a safe accessory, but they can trap your baby underwater if she slips or slides down into them.

- *Toilets:* Consider putting safety latches on your toilet seats. Curious babies can climb into toilets.

- *Buckets and other Containers:* Empty all coolers and car-wash buckets after use. Be aware that even your dog's water bowl, if big enough, is a hazard.

- *Wading Pools:* Always drain and store wading pools safely after use.

Falling, Crushing, and Other Accidents

Baby-proofing your home ensures that your baby can move around in a safe environment. Start by covering unused electrical outlets with safety covers, but understand that this is just the beginning. With care and forethought, you can minimize the risks of a number of household hazards, including falling, crushing, guns and weapons, and fire-related hazards.

Falling
Make no mistake, your baby starts life with an underdeveloped sense of height and the injuries caused by falling. Here are some precautions you can take:

- Close and lock (with as high a latch as possible) all doors at the top and bottom of staircases. If you have no staircase doors, install hardware-mounted safety gates at the top and bottom of the stairs; spring-mounted gates are not advised. If your stair rails are less than 3" apart, install mesh or plexiglass to block the openings.
- Never put baby seats on high surfaces; set them on the ground.
- Put stick-on padding on the corners of tables.
- Use baby equipment – high chairs, etc. – with wide, sturdy bases.
- Secure or remove loose rugs.
- Install baby-proof latches on windows.

Crushing

Look for things around your house that might fall and crush your baby. From a "baby's-eye" view, you'll find that everything's a skyscraper. Dressers and bookshelves that stand at chest height for you tower over your baby. A tall potted-plant is a tree when looked at from down there.

Here are some precautions you can take:

- If furniture can be tipped over, bolt it to the wall.
- Babies love to yank tablecloths; use placemats instead.
- Secure drawers with safety locks.
- Use safety gates to block children from going into unsafe areas.
- Make sure the baby cannot bring a TV down by pulling on the cord.

Other Accidents Waiting to Happen

- Lock up your gun cabinets.
- Keep all knives and scissors in locked cabinets.
- Make sure your smoke detectors are working.
- Plan and practice fire escape with your baby.
- Set your water heater to 120°F.

Smoking, Drinking and Drugs

Much of the advice for parents regarding smoking, drinking, and drugs is aimed toward mothers and the birth-defect consequence of engaging in these behaviors. While you should provide support for your mate in abstaining from these destructive habits, you should also think about your own behavior and its effect on your family.

If you smoke:

- Your wife and baby are adversely affected by second-hand smoke, while pregnant and after your baby is born.
- Cigarettes and cigarette butts can kill your baby, if he eats them.
- Smoking contributes to the risk of SIDS.

If you drink or use drugs:

- Your child is at higher risk for child abuse.
- Your ability to safely operate a vehicle is impaired.
- You may not make sound decisions.
- If ingested, alcohol or drugs can kill your baby.

Abuse/Violence

Your baby is crying; you're having a hard time meeting your financial responsibilities; things aren't going well with your wife. All these things cause stress and stress can cause anger and lead to abuse.

Face the facts: violence and abuse towards children is much too common – around one-quarter of all children suffer abuse. Abuse comes in a variety of forms, including:

* Physical abuse
* Emotional abuse, also known as verbal or psychological abuse
* Sexual abuse, also known as pedophilia or incest
* Neglect

For more information or help with violence or abuse:
National Committee to Prevent Child Abuse (www.childabuse.org)
Survivors and Victims Empowered (http://child.cornell.edu/save/home.html)

All forms of abuse are severely damaging to your child. Don't turn your back on your family. Understand that if you have abused your child, or are tempted to, you can go to jail. Be aware that your child is at risk for being abused by others – your spouse and relatives, babysitters and other caregivers. If you think or know your baby is being abused by anyone, it is of course your basic duty as a father to protect her. Contact a child abuse hotline, and act.

If you are abusing your child or even entertaining thoughts of abuse, you must also act. Immediately call Child Help USA at (800) 424-2246, the nation's largest anonymous child abuse hotline. Their trained counselors will provide you expert guidance on what you need to do to protect your child.

Pet Safety

Like anything involving your baby you must use common sense and patience. Do your homework by contacting your pediatrician and your local kennel club. Find out as much information as you can about the type of pet that you have and ask your pediatrician for helpful tips.

Dogs
We hear a lot of horror stories when it comes to new babies and dogs, and the statistics are sobering: Each year dogs bite an estimated 4.5 million people, and children are by far the most common victims. Seventy percent of fatal dog attacks involve children. There are currently more than 60 million pet dogs and nearly 70 million pet cats in the US. If you think such an attack could never happen in the safety of your home, you should be aware that the majority of dog attacks happen in the victim's home or in a familiar place nearby. More than three-quarters of the dogs doing the biting belong to the victim's family, or to a friend.

Dogs have a tendency to become territorial and jealous. From the family dog's perspective, a newborn may appear to threaten the dog's position in the family hierarchy. Many dogs willingly accept a new addition to the family and may even become protective of this new "pup". But other dogs may resent the intrusion of another individual vying for the attention of the masters. Others may simply be confused and unaware of what's expected of them in this new situation.

Some pet owners choose to shower the family pet with additional attention in anticipation of the baby's arrival, knowing that they will likely be unable to devote as much time to caring for and interacting with the pet once the baby arrives. But experts advise the opposite approach. In the weeks before the baby's arrival, gradually reduce the amount of time and attention the pet receives. The reasoning goes that the pet will be less likely to negatively associate the baby's eventual presence with being ignored.

If your pet has any undesirable behavior problems, it's best to resolve them before baby's arrival. Such problems will tend to be magnified once the baby arrives in the home. If your pet has been obedience trained, review and reinforce commands before the baby's arrival. Remember to reward good behavior with gentle praise, caresses and treats, rather than focusing on punishing poor behavior. If your pet has not been neutered, consider rectifying this situation as soon as possible. Male dogs are about six times more likely to bite than female dogs, and male dogs that have not been "fixed" are three times more likely to bite than neutered males.

Introducing a Newborn to Your Dog
The number one piece of advice given to dog owners is to have a proper introduction between your baby and dog.

Before the baby arrives, familiarize your pet with the scents that will be associated with the baby. Let your pet smell and inspect a blanket that has been used to swaddle your baby in the hospital. Make a positive association with the baby's scent by talking gently to the animal and giving treats. You may even wish to allow your pet to sleep with the item.

It may also be helpful to make a tape recording of your baby's cries in the hospital. Or record a friend's infant. Bring the tape home and play it for your pet, while gently playing or otherwise positively interacting with your pet. As your pet grows accustomed to these new sounds, gradually increase the volume.

Several tips you should consider:

- It's important to carry out the usual welcome-home ritual. It might be a good idea to have someone else carry your baby into the house so you can greet your pet as you usually do.

- Don't lock the dog in a room or remove him from the house when you bring the baby home for the first time. The dog may interpret this as punishment and become aggressive.

- Allow the dog to see the baby from a safe distance initially. Place a leash on the dog for easier control. The dog will most likely be interested in sniffing the baby. Remember that he is forming an opinion; be positive and cautious at the same time. Talking calmly, offer petting and praise. <u>Do not force the dog toward the baby</u>.

- When the baby cries, make sure the dog understands that this is okay. You don't want the dog to think you're hurting the baby.

- Animals can also be jealous of newborns. Try to give your pet as much attention as you did before the baby arrived.

Doing What You Need to Do
If the dog shows aggression, or if you don't fully trust him, remember your priority is to protect your baby. This means the dog must go. With a brand new baby you barely know, and a dog that has been by your side for years, this may be a difficult concept to grasp. But think it through, and do what you need to do.

Breeds of Concern
Certain breeds are believed to be more aggressive than others. But the American Veterinary Medical Association cautions against relying on such beliefs. Aggressiveness in dogs is related to a variety of factors. Experts advise vigilance to prevent the opportunity for an attack, rather than avoidance of any specific breed. That said, it could also be argued that several breeds of dogs are statistically more likely to attack. According to a report published in the Journal of the American Medical Association, dangerous breeds include pit bulls — which are three times more likely to attack than German shepherds — the next most commonly reported aggressive breed. Other experts note that animals that have been bred for protective traits, such as chows and rottweilers, may not be the best choice for families with children. In contrast, sporting breeds such as labradors and golden retrievers may make excellent pets for children.

Cats
Cats are less likely to interfere with an infant than dogs, but they still present potential problems. Scratches are obviously a danger. Cats are also better able to jump up to get at an infant, so extra vigilance is in order. Never leave your baby unattended where a cat may reach him. While it's a myth that cats will attempt to "suck the breath" out of a sleeping infant, it's not unheard of for a cat to attempt to curl up and sleep on a warm baby. Obviously this poses a risk of suffocation and should be prevented.

Cats also startle easily at loud noises, such as sudden crying from an infant. They are likely to scratch when startled, so never leave a baby alone with a cat.

Exotics
We're talking birds, reptiles, and amphibians. If you own a large carnivorous reptile you probably don't need reminding that they can be dangerous. Anything that considers your infant to be a potential snack should be either removed from the home or monitored with extreme care. They don't call these wild animals for nothing. Enough said.

Smaller reptiles and amphibians can harbor dangerous bacterial diseases. Remember to wash thoroughly after handling them and before touching anything else, especially your baby.

Birds may harbor parasites, and many people are allergic to feathers. Birds that are allowed to roam freely about the home pose obvious risks. Any pet may harbor parasites and diseases, some of which may infect humans. Be sure that all pets are healthy and well cared for. Consider a veterinary check-up for pets before the arrival of your newborn.

Resources

American Pet Association- Web site www.apapets.com Phone: 800-APA-PETS (800-272-7387)
Centers for Disease Control and Prevention- Web site www.cdc.gov   Phone: 1-800-311-3435
American Veterinarian Medical Association- Web site www.avma.org   Phone: 847-925-8070

Appendix IV

Recording Your New Family

If you are unfamiliar with cameras, the good news is that you don't have to be an expert and you don't need expensive gear to get great pictures today. Mostly, you just need to keep a camera, or a video camera or even a tape recorder handy, and use it to record the images and sounds of your new baby and your new life.

Number one rule: start right away. You can never recapture those wonderful first hours after your baby is born and the constant stream of precious times during your baby's first years. You are creating a portrait of your new family, a catalog of visual memories that captures its development. The smiles that your pictures will elicit throughout your life will be plenty of payback for your efforts.

When, What and Where to Shoot

Photographing a Pregnant Woman
Pregnancy has become fashionable, and pregnant women are finally allowing themselves to look and feel beautiful. Pregnant celebrities adorn the pages of glamour magazines, and clothing for pregnant women is far from the boxy old shirts that were meant to hide her "condition" from the world a generation ago.

A great way to let your mate know that you think she's still beautiful, and sexy, is to tell her you'd like to take some pictures of her while she's pregnant. Many couples go to a photography studio to have special pictures taken, but you can get great shots on your own. Consider shooting your pregnant wife in black and white for a mood-provoking approach to photographing the pregnant form. If your camera has the capability, set it for automatic shooting and jump into the frame with her.

Photographing a pregnant woman means helping her to not feel embarrassed about the shape of her body. You can get some great shots with a little experimentation. Suggest a few different types of pictures: Photos of her wearing something sensual, or colorful; shoot her in an outdoor setting and capture her smile and joy. Take a picture of her in silhouette sitting in the window of the soon-to-be-occupied nursery. Don't be afraid to focus on her belly, or on her whole body. These photographs will form an everlasting source of good memories for the rest of her life.

Filming the Birth: Cameraman or Father?
Filming or taking pictures of the actual childbirth is a choice some couples embrace and others distain. If done well, with sensitivity and a bit of artfulness, it will provide a meaningful memory for you and your partner.

There are a number of issues involved in this process, but perhaps the most important for you is juggling the role of cameraman and father. As cameraman, you'll want to focus on getting good pictures. As father, you'll want to focus on making sure your wife is comfortable (see Chapter 9, *Your Baby's Birth*).

So that your attention can be focused toward your wife rather than taking pictures, consider having another person at the birth taking the pictures or shooting the video.

Another important issue is permission. Before bringing out the camera, you'll need to get permission from hospital staff. Some hospitals have specific regulations and instructions for taking pictures or video of the birth.

Also, try to absorb some of the advice from the Getting Good Pictures section of this chapter. Your mate will be exhausted and washed out due to the pain and hard work involved with labor. Try to capture her—and your new baby—in the best light possible.

If you film the birth, don't expect your friends to want to watch it with you. The only two people who will enjoy the footage are you and your partner.

Tips for Taking Pictures or Filming the Birth
In the frenzy and excitement of labor and birth, it's easy to end up with a bunch of disappointing and unflattering pictures, or hours of boring footage of the back of people's heads, bright lights and strange angles of various body parts.

To increase your chances of getting great pictures of this once in a lifetime event, follow these tips:

1. Call the hospital in advance and make sure they allow photographing or videotaping. Some hospitals do not, and others have rules about what can and cannot be photographed. Some hospitals have restrictions about plugging in equipment or lights. Others do not allow filming of certain medical procedures.

2. If you make the wise decision to appoint someone other than yourself to be the photographer, go with him or her to the hospital and ask to take a tour of the birthing area. It's also a good idea to watch a film of an actual birth in advance.

3. Make a decision, along with your partner, about how "graphic" you want the filming to be. Do you want close-ups of the baby being born? If not, ask the photographer to take shots from the side, or to avoid extreme close-ups.

4. Take pictures of facial expressions, candid shots of dad and mom working together, mom's face as she rests between contractions. Capture details – close-ups of dad holding mom's hand, or bending down to give her an encouraging kiss.

5. Avoid using a flash or bright lights, as this can be distracting and annoying to mom and the hospital staff. Definitely do not use a flash to shoot the baby as he's being born – it might hurt his eyes.

6. The photographer needs to understand that there are real priorities during labor and birth. Staying out of the way of nurses and doctors is priority number one.

7. Don't let enthusiasm get in the way of sensitivity – it's probably not a good idea to stick a camera in the face of a woman during a contraction.

8. Catch pictures of family and friends who might be present, or who are in the waiting area. A photo of your partner's mom rubbing her back, or an embrace by her best friend will be treasured for years to come.

9. When the baby arrives, capture her face. Ask the attending nurse where to stand for the best view.

10. Make sure you have a picture of yourself bending down to kiss your baby for the first time.

11. Get lots of close-ups of the baby's fingers and toes and other details.

12. If there is to be a surgical birth, ask the doctor or head nurse if you can take pictures. It's probably not a good idea to shoot photos of the surgery itself, but have the camera ready at hand to capture those first shots of your newborn baby.

Photographing Your Baby

Document Her Development
Take a series of pictures once a week that represents your baby's growth and developmental stages. By using the same location each time, the pictures will evolve into a story without words.

Unplanned (Candid) Shots are Best
When models are doing a photo shoot, they typically just do what they do and the photographer tries to capture it. Rarely do they contrive poses for pictures. Aim for the same with your baby pictures. Just try to get him doing his thing.

Good Mood Baby
The best baby pictures are taken when she's rested, warm, and comfortable. While grumpy-baby pictures are cute, happy-baby pictures are cuter.

Warm Up to Him Before Snapping
Spontaneous pictures are good. Loud, abrupt noises are bad. Warm up to your baby before getting acrobatic with your camera. You want to take some pictures, not settle down a crying baby.

Careful With The Flash
Try to shoot the picture in a place where there is natural light, outdoors or next to a window, so you don't need to use a flash. If you use a flash, take the picture from a distance, so the light doesn't flash directly into his eyes. This could not only scare him, but might be harmful. Your baby's eyes are sensitive, so don't get flash-happy on her.

Getting Good Pictures

One of the best kept secrets of professional photographers is they take lots of pictures. The more you shoot, the better your chances are of getting a really good picture. This is especially true with digital cameras, which allow you to shoot many pictures without the cost of film and developing.

This doesn't mean you just shoot away and hope for the best. There are some things you should think about before pointing and shooting.

Use Natural, Soft Light
With natural light, your baby's face will glow. Camera flashes and indoor lamps tend to make your baby's skin appear mottled. Using natural light is best, and most cameras will tell you when you don't have enough light to make a good shot. Try opening the drapes or window shades, or moving to an area with more light.

Use a Tripod
When shooting in low light conditions, use a tripod to steady the camera. If there's no tripod available, set the camera on any steady surface – a stepladder, or ledge will do the job.

Shoot Outdoors When You Can
The colors and vibrancy of outdoors can give you great backgrounds for your photos. Try to stay out of the direct sunlight, and never shoot into the sun.

Get Snapshots from Every Angle
Photograph your baby from above as she's looking up at you from her bed or infant seat, or even stretched out on your lap, with her head at your knees. Most people never think of shooting photos of the backs of their babies, but these can be great shots and a charming way to capture body language.

Silhouettes
Set up a shot where your baby is facing sideways in front of a sunny window. The picture will cause her to be blacked out, or silhouetted, evoking an interesting and beautiful mood. Play around with the angles of your silhouettes, and you'll end up with something you'll want to frame.

Baby's-Eye View
Don't be afraid to get down and dirty when taking baby pictures. Photos taken on their level are charming, to say the least.

Try Black and White Film
Black and white pictures accentuate the details of your baby's face and body, plus it gives them a nostalgic feel.

Getting Good Video

Video is a unique medium for recording your family, because it allows you to capture dynamic, action-filled images. A video can engender deep emotions and enjoyment, a feeling of reliving an experience. Or it can be boring, confusing and dizzying.

Many people buy expensive video cameras and end up rarely using them, or using them and doing nothing with the pile of tapes that are generated. The problem is that video cameras are very easy to use; the tapes are long and so is the battery life. You end up with hours and hours of video footage and few people who want to sit through watching them.

Be selective about what you are shooting. Before you flip on the "record" switch, think about what you plan to shoot and how you can best capture it. After you get what you want, pause the tape and wait for your next opportunity.

When shooting video, always "pan" slowly across a room. Avoid jerky movements and pause the recording when going from one person to another. Try not to stay on one thing for too long.

Focus on details. If your baby is staring at a mobile, point the camera at it for a moment. You can capture things like breastfeeding in an artful way by zooming close in on his face as he's nursing, or shooting over Mom's shoulder from behind.

If you're shooting with a digital video camera, you can edit movie clips from the footage you shoot, and then you'll have something memorable and easy to share with friends and family. These cameras come with their own software for editing, or you can purchase various movie-making packages.

Making Movies on Your Computer
All of these software packages require digital video capabilities. So, if all you have access to is the old VHS, you won't be able to use them:

Apple iMovie ($79): This affordable package for Mac users allows you to edit DVD-format movies. You can even add a scene-selection screen, just like in your favorite DVDs.

QuickTime Pro ($29.99): A powerful video editing program at a good price for Mac and PC users.

Microsoft Movie Maker (Free with Windows XP): Allow you to edit film, and add text and special effects. Not as feature-rich as the more expensive products, but it gives you the basics.

Screenblast Movie Studio ($69): Their website (www.screenblast.com) allows you to share your movies over the internet.

Storing Your Pictures/Video

Storing and organizing your pictures is a key step in the process of recording your family. Sure, it's easiest to leave them in the envelope the developer sent you home with, but it leaves the loop open.

Take some care in putting together a viewable collection of pictures. This ranges from mounting them in albums or creating a virtual Museum of My Baby on your computer (see the section below).

Video is a little trickier, but the cost of making digital movies is getting lower every year. At the very minimum, you should make sure to clearly label your videos with the date and a descriptive title. This way, you can reference them easily in the future. If you want go all out, enhance your movies with video-editing software.

Here are some additional storage tips:

- Put your prints in acid-free storage boxes.
- Add the date on the back with an acid-free pen.
- Never store photos in the garage or any place with variable temperatures.
- Use acid-free albums.

Pictures and Your Computer

The Computer Age brought with it a paradigm shift in how we take, store, and distribute our pictures.

Taking Digital Pictures
Consider investing in a digital camera. Instead of recording the images on film it records them digitally—in memory, or on a disk or some sort of other removable media.

With a digital camera, you can take as many pictures as your camera holds (which can be anywhere from 10 to 100s of pictures). You can view a picture you just shot and re-shoot if it is not what you wanted. You can browse through the pictures in your camera and choose those you'd like to keep, or download them to your computer and print them, share them online or store them in your pictures folders. For a very good tutorial on digital photography, go to www.vividlight.com/articles/3116.htm.

Understanding Megapixels
The first thing you'll notice when attempting to purchase a digital camera is that they come in a variety of "megapixel" sizes. Basically, the larger the number of megapixels (millions of pixels per inch), the higher the resolution of your pictures. The higher the resolution, the better your prints will look. But don't be lured into spending over $1,000 on a 5.0 or 6.0 megapixel camera unless you plan to become a serious photographer. You can get great 5" X 7" or even 8" X 10" prints with a 3.2 megapixel camera without breaking the bank.

Most digital video cameras also allow for shooting still pictures, which is a nice feature, but the quality is much lower than what you get with a digital still camera. Conversely, new digital still cameras will shoot 15 second to 3 minute movies, many with sound.

Storing Digital Pictures

Storing digital is easy. Once they're uploaded to your computer, you can store them in folders. Create a subfolder in My Pictures for your baby pictures. That way, they won't get mixed with your other pictures.

If you don't have a digital camera, you can still produce digital photos. When you get a roll of film developed, ask for the pictures to be put onto a CD-ROM. You can do this in addition to prints, or instead of getting prints made. You can also scan prints into your computer with a scanner.

Distributing Digital Pictures

With traditional shoot-and-develop pictures you typically get 1 or 2 copies of each picture. With digital photography, you can distribute pictures to as many people as have access to a computer.

Online photo sharing websites are very popular. Kodak's Ofoto (www.ofoto.com) is one of the best, but there are plenty of others. These websites allow you to upload your images, create albums and notify people by email to take a look at your pictures – all at no charge. They are extremely easy to use. The websites make money by offering special deals on printing your pictures or creating actual photo albums with your pictures.

You can also email photos, but this is sometimes more trouble than it's worth. Many spam filters are suspicious of attachments and might put your email in the recipient's spam box. If you are attaching photos to an email, make sure that each photo is no bigger than 1 megabyte. Even at that size, it could take a long time for someone to download. Don't add more than two or three pictures to an email.

Another way to distribute your photos is to put them on a CD-ROM, duplicate it a bunch of times, and send it by regular mail. Many photo outlets have automated CD-ROM creators that allow you to pick the photos you want on the CD and create as many CD's as you want at a nominal charge. If you have a CD burner on your computer, you can also create your own.

File Formats for Dummies

The most common format for computerized pictures is the JPEG (filename followed by .jpeg or .jpg), because it's universally readable and is capable of holding enough color information to reproduce photos pretty well. Bitmaps (filename followed by .bmp) are another format, but only usable on MS Windows formats, and thus less sharable. Another common format is the GIF (filename followed by .gif), but this is inappropriate for color pictures. It doesn't hold enough information about colors.

Appendix V

New Family Finance

From the moment you have the life-changing revelation that your new baby is on the way, chances are you'll spend a lot of time worrying about how to make ends meet and how to assure the financial well being of your new family. This section will help you get a handle on these important issues.

A Well-Intentioned Plan

For new parents trying to pave the best road for their family, budgeting is essential—plain and simple. But, it's important to understand that no matter how carefully you craft your budget, you'll probably stray from it during pregnancy and the first year. That's okay, most new parents do.

If you do nothing else, make sure to write out a month-by-month list of expenses to help you get a handle on where your money is going. If your budgeting and other financial planning includes complex calculations, consider computer software programs such as Microsoft Money (www.microsoft.com) and Quicken (www.quicken.com).

Book Resources
Check out these books...but understand that changes in laws and other factors of family finance occur:

How to Raise Kids without Going Broke: The Complete Financial Guide for Parents (A Smart Money Book) by, Peter Finch, Delia Marshall (Avon Books, 1999)

Family Finance: The Essential Guide for Parents, by Ann Douglas and Elizabeth Lewin (Dearborn Trade, 2001)

However well intentioned your budget, chances are it'll take some creative thinking (and spending) to make it work. Don't let your budget rule your life, but do consult it before making impulsive purchases. Stay positive, and don't be afraid to ask for a hand from your family during those initial months after your baby arrives.

Budgeting the First-Nine Months

As mom grows, your bank account will shrink. Luckily, many of your extra expenses during pregnancy are medical—and, thus, usually covered by insurance. But there are also significant costs associated with getting your house ready to accommodate your new baby.

Medical Costs
From the first trimester to the birth of your baby, you'll incur so many doctors' fees that your head may spin.

According to the Health Insurance Association of America, the average bill for doctor fees and hospital charges runs around $6,400 for a normal delivery and roughly $10,600 for a surgical birth. This does not count prenatal doctor visits or tests. This is why insurance is very important, so do your best to get covered.

To plan your budget accurately, you'll want to contact your insurance provider as soon as possible. Ask how much you'll need to pay out of pocket (called your co-payment) and if you face any restrictions on your choice of health-care facilities for the following expenses:

- Routine doctor visits
- Tests and screenings
- Hospital stay for labor and problem-free vaginal delivery
- Caesarean section, if necessary
- Nursery costs in the hospital
- Extra nights in the hospital, if necessary
- Special care or treatments for your baby, if necessary
- Vaccinations for your baby

If you want to work with a midwife or doula, or have an underwater birth (or some other arrangement), find out the extent to which your insurance provider will cover the cost. In some states it is required by law that insurance providers cover these arrangements to the same extent they cover regular hospital births.

Uninsured?

If you're one of the 82 million people in the United States who were uninsured during 2002 and 2003, you'll have to cover these expenses out of pocket, or get insurance—fast! If paying the premium will make it hard to make ends meet, turn to one of the many programs that assist expectant families with financial need, such as Medicaid.

The Woes of the Working Poor
Medicaid is typically reserved for financially disadvantaged people, leaving a gaping hole in coverage for the "working poor"—primarily middle-class people with incomes too high to qualify for many social programs, but too low to pay for adequate insurance.

If you have no insurance, you might be able to save thousands of dollars by purchasing a PPO maternity card, which provides you access to much lower hospital rates negotiated by insurance companies. Consult an insurance agent, as each state has different regulations. (Be wary of "maternity cards" that are advertised in magazines and on the Internet; some of these cards require you to pay a $1,000 membership fee.)

As an alternative, you can negotiate lower rates yourself. Hospitals, and many doctors, will usually offer you a lower price if you are uninsured; perhaps even a lower one if you prepay your expected expenses. Sometimes they will let you pay it off during the pregnancy. Call your hospital and speak to the billing department to get the ball rolling.

Nesting Costs

Nesting has many meanings, but in the months or weeks or days before the birth of your baby, it will mean only one thing—creating a suitable environment for raising your child. Some of the things you'll spend money on are:

* Stocking your shelves with food, baby supplies and other necessities
* Buying baby clothes
* Buying a crib, dresser and changing table
* Buying an infant car-seat and other equipment

Raising Your Child

The government estimates that the average middle-income family will spend roughly $10,000 on child-related expenses in the first two years of life ($8,000 for a second child), and some experts suggest that figure may be too low. You can count on spending at a minimum of $25 a week ($1,250 per year) on diapers, formula, and baby food alone.

Interested in finding out the total costs of raising a child? The BabyCenter's website (www.babycenter.com/costofchild/) features the 'Cost of Raising a Baby Calculator' that itemizes all the costs, including (can you imagine?) college costs. Keep in mind that this exercise is fun, but can be misleading. The calculations are for the average parent, not the money-wise dad like you.

Budgeting the First Year After Birth

You'll happily spend your extra money on your new baby during the first year after her birth.
Diapers and food are just the beginning. Any necessities you didn't buy during your partner's pregnancy, you'll have to buy now.
During the first few months, your partner will probably take a leave of absence from work. This strikes another blow to your budget. Fewer paychecks can deplete your savings quickly. After both of you have exhausted your work-leave entitlement, you'll face decisions about whether to return to work. If you do both work, you'll have the added financial burden of daycare costs.

> **Internet Resources**
> The MetLife website (www.metlife.com) is loaded with informational articles for parents on making ends meet, and other parenting issues.

Suggestions for making ends meet in these lean times:

* **Do your best to get the most for your eating dollar:** Don't buy the most expensive food items. Boot Camp veterans say it helps to never shop on an empty stomach. Try to eat out less. Men make great chefs – this is a golden opportunity to hone your culinary skills. In other words, learn how to cook.

- **Cut down baby costs:** Buy used stuff (more on this later), buy wholesale, or do without. Over the next year, you're going to need a lot of diapers; why not buy them in bulk? Try www.diapersite.com.

- **Avoid impulsive purchases:** Don't buy something until you've thought through whether or not you really need it.

The Money-Wise Dad: Car, Home, and Utilities

Here's a sampling of what the Consumer Federation of America (www.consumerfed.org) recommends in their report 66 Ways to Save Money.

Your Car
Save fuel money by comparing prices at local gas stations, keeping your car tuned up and your tires inflated correctly. Have your repairs done by a certified mechanic that you trust. Ask friends for recommendations.

When buying a new car, consider all the factors that contribute to how much the car will cost you: purchase price, financing, insurance, gasoline, and maintenance costs. When shopping for a new car, get quotes from a handful of dealers before making a purchase - and, do so only after you have negotiated with the dealer.

If you're considering leasing a car, consult the Federal Trade Commission's report, "Keys to Vehicle Leasing: a Consumer Guide, " (www.ftc.gov).

Your Utilities
Make sure your gas and electric appliances are operating efficiently, or consider buying new ones. Clunky appliances cost consumers millions of dollars in utility bills every year. Many utility companies will do efficiency audits for free or a nominal fee. Contact your local provider for more information.

Review your phone bill and find a calling plan that fits your needs. The long-distance companies are fiercely competitive and will help you identify a well suited plan - if you ask them to. If you're paying for any extra services that you rarely or never use, eliminate them.

If you have wireless service with free long distance at night and unlimited off-peak minutes, use your cell phone to call your family during these off-peak times.

Your Home
If you're getting work done on your house, get quotes from several licensed contractors for the job. If you're considering buying a house, you can often arrive at a lower price by hiring a buying broker, who advocates your needs, not the seller's. Always have the house inspected before purchasing.

If you rent, expand your search beyond the classifieds. Contact the building manager of places you'd like to live and ask about availability. In tight housing markets - like San Francisco, New York City, or Seattle - you should consider using a renter's service. With these services, costing about $50 for three months, you get access to a large database of properties for rent along with phone numbers.

If you sign a lease, chances are you'll be obligated to make monthly payments for the duration of the term. But state laws vary. Contact your local housing advocate for information on prematurely terminating a lease.

Buying Cheap, Borrowing or Doing Without

Your baby's new, but her stuff doesn't need to be. Many of the items you'll need for your baby can be bought for a significant secondhand-discount. Or better yet, you can often borrow items from friends or family.

Clothes, for instance, are a great hand-me-down item. Just wash them thoroughly in warm water and they're ready to go.

Baby equipment - strollers and cribs, for example - are also great hand-me-down items. Just make sure they're compliant with today's understanding of infant safety, and that they haven't been recalled. See the Safety chapter for more information on baby-equipment and toy recalls.

Used Baby Equipment: The Flip Side
Sure, used baby equipment can help your budgetary bottom line, but there are some items that you just shouldn't buy used. Infant car seats are one example. If it's been in an accident, whether it was damaged directly or not, the baby seat is considered unsafe. If you don't know an item's history, it's best to steer clear.

Another thing to consider is that you won't have an opportunity to register your used equipment. That means that if the product is recalled, you won't be notified.

You should also consider doing without some items. Clearly, there are some things it would be tough to do without,.and some make your life so much easier that they're worth the cost. Others, however, are nothing but the latest and greatest gizmo or gadget. Ask yourself: Do I really need this?

Getting Organized

If you're like many dads, your system is nothing more than a stack of papers. With a baby on the way, it's a good idea to put together a well organized system for filing important documents. One way to do it is to create a hanging file for each broad category and fill it with manila folders for more specific topics. With the system in place, you'll have quick access to whatever you need, whenever you need it.

Examples of typical family files:

Birth Certificates & Social Security Numbers
Medical Records
       Baby medical records
       Mom's medical records
       Dad's medical records
Medical Expenses
Utilities (Phone, electricity, cable, etc)
Car Expenses
Furniture and Equipment
Credit Cards
Mortgage or Rental contracts/Payments
Insurance papers
Taxes
Wills or Family Trust Documents

Make sure to carefully label every file. Otherwise, you'll end up with the same pile of stuff you had before—just stacked horizontally instead of vertically.

Better yet, buy a family/home organizing system that comes in a notebook or file box with pre-printed files for important contacts, wills, bank documents, etc.

Now, where did you put that birth certificate?

Protecting Those Important Files: You should consider getting a fireproof file for your most important papers. We've even heard of one dad who bought an old refrigerator to use for this purpose—fireproof and cheap, but ugly.

A Diatribe on Debt

Debt,the polar opposite of savings, mires many new families in the financial bog. Begin chipping away at those credit-card and other balances now. To do so, you'll have to make more than the minimum required payment the minimum was specially designed by a team of crack mathematicians figuring out how to keep you in debt to their companies for the rest of your life. Consider negotiating with your creditors. In many cases, they'll settle for a lump payment (or payments) that total far less than the actual amount owed.

Credit counselors are a dime a dozen these days (and many are being investigated by the feds for fraud-see the Federal Trade Commission's website at www.ftc.gov) but the National Foundation for Credit Counseling (www.nfcc.org) stands out because of their ethical positioning and online discussion boards where you can interact with others in the same position.

Interestingly, a 2003 Redbook survey found that differences in attitudes over debt and spending causes more marital disagreement than any other financial issue.

Getting Insured

These days, health and life insurance plans are expensive - even if your employer pays part of the cost. But, for most new families, it's an expense that must be calculated into the budget.

Health Insurance

Getting health insurance for your family is super-important for expectant parents. Yes, the costs of getting coverage have risen substantially in the recent past. But it's a drop in the bucket compared to what you'll shell out without it—especially with your partner's doctor visits, tests, screenings, hospital stay, and possible unplanned costs, such as a surgical birth or special care if complications arise.

And, what if your baby has special medical needs? It's not a pleasant thing to think about when planning your new family, but it's an issue for more than just an episode of ER - it happens to real people with real lives.

Even if you're currently covered, the policy may be insufficient to cover everything.

Think deeply about the coverage you have and consult some insurance resources about getting a more comprehensive plan. It may seem expensive, but you'll have to do the math. What's more expensive: the monthly premium or the actual costs of the pregnancy and first few years of raising your child?

Life Insurance

Life insurance for the family's breadwinners is important. Many expectant and soon-to-be parents overlook this type of coverage, even though it's most important, and least expensive, in the early stages of parenthood.

Why? As your child gets older, you have a smaller overall financial burden. In other words, if your child is 10-years old and you plan to support her until age 18, you have only 8 more years of financial responsibility. Upon the birth of your child, you have 18 years of financial responsibility.

Life insurance policies come in numerous varieties. Term insurance, which typically pays off in the event of death, is the least expensive. Other forms of insurance serve as an investment vehicle and cost more. To learn more, visit www.consumerfed.org.

Life Insurance on the Internet
These websites provide quick-and-easy ways to get life-insurance quotes, and each has received the highest rating from the Consumer Advocacy of America:

www.insweb.com
www.accuquote.com
www.quotesmith.com

Living Will/Trust

Although your living will and trust are primarily legal documents about financial matters, they're also of great importance to a parent.

Do you want the State to decide who raises your child if you and your spouse die unexpectedly, heaven forbid? This is a tough topic to ponder, but it's important. You should designate someone you trust, who understands the responsibility involved and who would be able to provide for your baby - and who would be willing to provide support, even during the college years.

Considering the credentials of the likely candidates - your friends, siblings, or other relatives - is difficult, but it's part of your responsibility.

Understand that the person you've entrusted to handle your child may not be the best person to handle your estate. The complexities of drafting a legally binding living will require outside consultation to do it right.

Living Will Resources
FindLaw Legal Resources (www.findlaw.com)
Nolo Books – Estate Planning Resources (www.nolobooks.com)

INDEX